MW01121287

Europe as an Economic Powerhouse

Europe as an Economic Powerhouse

How the old continent is gaining new strength

Heino Faßbender

KOGAN PAGE

London and Philadelphia

Publisher's note

Every possible effort has been made to ensure that the information contained in this book is accurate at the time of going to press, and the publishers and author cannot accept responsibility for any errors or omissions, however caused. No responsibility for loss or damage occasioned to any person acting, or refraining from action, as a result of the material in this publication can be accepted by the editor, the publisher or any of the authors.

First published in Great Britain and the United States in 2007 by Kogan Page Limited

120 Pentonville Road
London N1 9JN
United Kingdom
www.kogan-page.co.uk

525 South 4th Street, #241
Philadelphia PA 19147
USA

© Heino Faßbender, 2007

The right of Heino Faßbender to be identified as the author of this work has been asserted by him in accordance with the Copyright, Designs and Patents Act 1988.

This work is an adaptation and derivative of the book *Wirtschaftsmacht Europa* by Heino Faßbender and Jürgen Kluge, originally published in 2003 by Redline Wirtschaft, Redline GmbH, Heidelberg, Germany, a division of Süddeutscher Verlag I Mediengruppe.

ISBN-10 0 7494 4556 4
ISBN-13 978 0 7494 4556 0

British Library Cataloguing-in-Publication Data

A CIP record for this book is available from the British Library.

Library of Congress Cataloging-in-Publication Data

Faßbender, Heino.
 Europe as an economic powerhouse : how the old continent is gaining new strength / Heino Fassbender.
 p. cm.
 ISBN-13: 978–0-7494-4556–0
 ISBN-10: 0–7494-4556–4
 1. Europe–Economic conditions–1945- I. Title.
 HC240.F385 2007
 330.94–dc22
 2006036751

Typeset by Saxon Graphics Ltd, Derby
Printed and bound in Great Britain by MPG Books Ltd, Bodmin, Cornwall

Contents

Preface

This book has two ancestors. In 2003 I published, together with my colleague Jürgen Kluge, the first edition in German entitled *Wirtschaftsmacht Europa*. It was followed in 2005 by a Portuguese edition, *Conquistar o futuro da Europa*, co-authored by our colleagues in Lisbon, Raul Galamba de Oliveira and João Castello Branco.

When we first conceived the idea of writing a book on Europe, we asked ourselves what economic agenda the European Union should set itself in order to stay in the global economy's first league. What does Europe need to do to realize its full economic potential? How can the European Union provide its inhabitants with the highest possible prosperity and quality of life? What will it take to sustain Europe as a true 'economic powerhouse' and prevent it from sliding back into 'eurosclerosis'?

Today these questions are more relevant than ever. Relative to its potential, the European Union's economic situation is disappointing, current and prospective growth rates are low, and pressures from within the enlarged union as well as from globalization are rising. Since the halt of the ratification of the European Constitution in the summer of 2005, many avenues for change have seemed blocked by decision-making gridlock.

Despite the obstacles, we continue to believe in the European Union's potential to bring about the changes necessary to return to success. In taking a primarily economic perspective, we have applied our specific lens as management consultants to preparing a thorough analysis of the state of the European Union. The extensive fact base at our disposal has been continually updated, and through critical evaluation and discussion with our international colleagues, we have distilled our recommendations into a four-point plan. While Europe's economic problems are significant, we suggest that if they are tackled systematically, the European Union can surpass the United States in quality of life and achieve an equal footing with it in gross domestic product.

This could well be a realistic aspiration when we take a closer look at the combined effects of the four initiatives we see as priorities: completing the single market, adopting 'smart' regulation, pursuing category definition (not only in products, but also in processes and at the industry-wide level), and transforming the state system to free up funds, particularly for investment in education and research.

Our primary audience is policy makers and executives, the active leaders of Europe today, as well as other readers interested in a positive transformation of European economic performance. Our objective is to contribute to the ongoing public debate with an integrated perspective on the roles of the state and the economy, and thus with realistic suggestions for addressing the main economic challenges of the early 21st century. Among the most important issues are globalization and its consequences for employment, the demographic trend and its impact on the size of the working population, and the absolutely vital role of higher productivity growth in creating the surplus needed to sustain and expand European prosperity in line with European values and to help shape Europe's agenda as an economic powerhouse for years to come.

Although the book would not have been possible without the tremendous efforts from McKinsey's Research Department and the valuable input from my colleagues, especially Jürgen Kluge – who was the first to have the idea of writing a book from the special angle between practice and science, and who contributed major concepts to our vision of a strong Europe – it reflects personal opinions and not those of McKinsey.

I should like here to thank all those who have contributed to it. My particular gratitude goes to Joachim Voth, Universitat Pompeu Fabra, Barcelona, for his invaluable help during the whole process from conceptualizing to writing.

Introduction

In an address to the Universal Peace Conference in Paris in 1849, Victor Hugo evoked a vision of a new and wonderful Europe:

> A day will come when you France, you Russia, you Italy, you England, you Germany, you all, nations of the continent, without losing your distinct qualities and your glorious individuality, will be merged closely within a superior unit. A day will come when the only fields of battle will be markets opening up to trade and minds opening up to ideas ... when the bullets and the bombs will be replaced by votes, by the universal suffrage of the peoples, by the venerable arbitration of a great sovereign senate which will be to Europe what parliament is to England ...
>
> (Mayer, 1966)

Barely a century later, in 1945, most Europeans would probably have responded to Victor Hugo's political vision with derision or cynical laughter. By then, two wars begun in Europe had sparked off a worldwide conflagration. Europe's great cities lay in ash and rubble. At the end of the Second World War, the continent survived only with aid from abroad.

Yet only 60 years on, most of Victor Hugo's dream has come true. Apart from former Yugoslavia, war and internecine strife are now the stuff of history books for Europe's current generation. Today, close cooperation between former adversaries has become a pillar of a new era of peaceful cohabitation. The starving, freezing Europe of 1945 has become a continent that seems to be struggling with abundance – too much coal, too much steel, too much milk, too much wheat, rye and wine. Europe is no longer a continent of emigration. Millions flock to its shores, and many millions more would happily come if they were admitted. In large parts of Europe, crossing a border is now as simple as driving past road-works. Finally, in most of continental Europe, it is now possible to pay for goods and services with a single currency, the euro.

From the European Union's earliest beginnings in the 1950s, the realization of Victor Hugo's vision of political union proceeded slowly and incrementally. Economic success, by contrast, was vigor-ous and materialized relatively quickly. Year on year, Europe's national economies became more integrated, trans-European trade flows grew, and customs and trade barriers were overcome. The European Coal and Steel Community gave way to the European Economic Community (EEC), then the European Community (EC) and finally the European Union (EU).

Although the political aspect of Hugo's ideal was echoed in the Treaty of Rome in 1957, which called for 'an ever closer union', it still had a long way to go during most of the latter half of the 20th century. Furthermore, the path forward was to be far from straight.

True, by the early 1990s, it seemed as if European nations were on the way to becoming a confederation in every sense of the word. At that point, much was already on the drawing board that previously would have been unthinkable for each participating nation-state, from a fully integrated single market to a common currency and shared foreign and defence policies. While the European Union still defies political scientists' classical definitions – being neither a feder-ation, a confederation or simply a free-trade zone – it appears to have crossed the threshold to becoming a state in its own right. In some cases, EU law already supersedes national law. There is also a common budget, albeit a small one when compared with the budgets of Europe's nation states. While the public sector's share of the economy in Europe hovers around 47 per cent, the European Union itself is only permitted to spend 1.045 per cent of its member countries' gross national product in the period from 2007 to 2013 (EU Presidency, 2005).

Although the European Union's revenues are restricted, spending on agriculture and on structural operations (a much smaller share of the budget) is all fully planned. While millions of civil servants in all European countries keep the state machine going, the EU Commission in Brussels has only 23,000 permanent employees (European Commission, 2004a).

Free trade and increasingly similar standards are obviously also possible among independent nations. To this end, and as a supplement to the Single European Act of 1986, Europe's heads of state set themselves the goal in 1992 of dramatically accelerating the process of political integration. In particular, in foreign affairs and defence, the European Community was to speak with one voice.

Perhaps most importantly, Europe decided to put an end to its multiple national currencies. A single, yet-to-be-named currency was set as a goal to be achieved within the next decade. The Dutch city of Maastricht, where the treaty was signed, became a symbol for this leap forward and, it was hoped, Europe's liberation from the political stagnation of the 1970s and 1980s. If Europe ever experienced a 'federal' turning point in the Anglo-Saxon sense – in which federal means the centralization of power as opposed to the continental European notion of simply dividing power among states – Maastricht was it.

Most of this sounds impressive, especially considering the starting point. But despite the enormous progress made in the past 50 years, Europe today can be considered a continent in crisis. Maastricht raised high expectations. Enthusiasts for Europe hoped that member states would soon have a common foreign policy. However, the first opportunities for coordinated European action, in the former Yugoslavia and Iraq, have revealed a wide gulf in national attitudes and policies, and the standpoints of the national states prevailed. In 2005 the process of introducing a European constitution with provision for a foreign minister came to a standstill.

Europe's political weakness weighs all the more heavily because the continent as a whole also looks like having lost a great deal of its economic dynamism. In the decades following the founding of the Coal and Steel Community, Europe defined itself primarily as an economic success story. But since 1990 not much has remained of that tradition.

The continent's long list of economic woes is well known. For at least a decade and a half, European growth rates have been disappointing, and nothing seems able to reduce Europe's high unemployment. Neither the euro nor the integrated single market has managed to turn Europe into an engine of the world economy – a role still commonly ascribed to it in the 1970s.

Despite the high hopes invested in 'Europe 1992', the programme has not resulted in a rapid increase in trade between member states. On the contrary, trade figures are now increasing much faster for trade between EU members and economies outside Europe. In real economic terms, it appears that globalization is advancing faster than European integration.

Importantly, these developments cannot be attributed to any iron-clad laws of economics: analysis shows that Europe's relative loss of significance in economic matters could well be home grown and can thus be resolved. Until now, EU plans for increased competition among products and services, higher rates of innovation, faster capital market integration and more mobility have largely remained wishful thinking. Although the European Union is falling further and further behind these old plans, new and even more ambitious ones were agreed upon in Lisbon in 2000. At the halfway point in 2005, no one in Brussels harboured any further illusions about the European Union becoming the world's most dynamic economy by 2010. So far, the European Union has proved able to tap only a fraction of the economic potential that a fully integrated single market should offer.

The European Union urgently needs to make good on its decades-old promises. With 'Europe 1992', it sought to regain its traditional strength as an engine of economic development. And until this step succeeds, it probably cannot take the next step towards greater political integration. In particular, Europe needs to re-examine long-held principles, such as subsidiarity, which delegates decision making away from Brussels. The incomplete implementation of 'Europe 1992' is one outcome that speaks for the need to reallocate decision-making authority in the European Union; the fate of the Lisbon agenda so far is another.

In this book, we want to address the question of how Europe can achieve the status of an economic power as the basis for further progress on the political front. Hence, our central focus is on Europe's economic agenda.

While the economic situation today is far from healthy, the outlook for the future seems even worse. In the next 30 years, populations throughout Europe will age dramatically, putting an unprecedented burden on its constituent economies and social security systems, which already account for 50 to 60 per cent of public spending. Furthermore, Europe does not look particularly attractive either to the world's top talent or to global capital. Other economic centres appear to have more to offer: more room for entrepreneurship, more freedom for ideas, greater rewards for talented people and more potential for earning an attractive return on investment.

The European tax system is also far less generous as a social welfare tool than is commonly believed. Progressive income tax rates do serve to level social differences. Yet at the end of the day, the United States (until the Bush reforms) actually taxed its rich more than Europe. Europe's high consumption (sales) taxes ultimately impose an outsized burden on low- to medium-income groups. High non-wage labour costs, especially in continental Western Europe, diminish the chances for higher employment. Social dynamism – movement across social strata – is also low.

We want to highlight Europe's options and opportunities for regaining the dynamism it has lost. To achieve this, in our opinion, Europe cannot afford to set its sights low. It must aim for the stars. We believe Europe has what it takes to become a world leader in productivity and quality of life, provided it uses its natural strengths and does not allow itself to be obstructed by poor institutions. Governments at all levels of the European Union must contribute by adopting reforms that will play a role in taking the region to the top.

This book seeks to combine a diagnosis of Europe's present state with a proposal for a cure. In Part I, we discuss Europe's strengths and weaknesses and explain why we think Europe needs to find its own, European, way to the top, rather than simply borrowing recipes for success from the United States. By 'top', we mean more than just a maximized gross national or domestic product. Instead, we offer a quality of life index that considers other criteria in addition to economic output as a more accurate way to measure prosperity and growth.

Part II presents our suggestions for overcoming the ills dogging Europe: a course of treatment to return it to economic health and vitality. Stations along the way, in our view, include the long-overdue completion of the European single market, the adoption of smart regulation in place of myriad individual rules and strictures, successfully defining categories that set the standard for product and service performance in growth industries, and finally, the reform of the state to unleash the potential of the people. If this therapy succeeds, Europe will not have to scrape by. It will be able to invest abundantly in a prosperous, satisfying, and inherently European future.

Part 1

Analysis of the state of Europe

1

Europe's lost decade – '1992' and all that

In the late 1980s and early 1990s, Europe seemed in the ascendant. Growth was outpacing that of the United States. Germany was a powerhouse of economic dynamism, not least because of the open-handed deficit spending that followed reunification. Once-backward countries like Spain and Portugal had begun to make massive advances. The United States, on the other hand, was stuck in one of the worst recessions of the post-war period. Unemployment was rising, the education system was in a desperate state, and the dollar fell to new lows.[1] The *Economist* magazine asked without hyperbole 'Can American business compete?' Its assessment was not all negative, but the fact that it asked the question at all reflected the widespread scepticism about the economic power of the United States. Americans were thoroughly unhappy with their political leadership. George Bush (Senior) was voted out of office. Bill Clinton won with the campaign slogan 'It's the economy, stupid!' Meanwhile, MIT economist Lester Thurow predicted that the United States would trail Europe and Japan for many years to come.

Europe, on the other hand, seemed to be going from strength to strength. After decades of growing faster than the United States, it was launching an ambitious programme to complete the single market. Plans for a common currency were beginning to take shape. Instability in the Balkans called for the European Union to act as peacekeeper. Many observers predicted that this would be Europe's decade, the one in which it would come of age as a political and economic power in its own right.

What a difference a decade can make. Today, with hindsight, we know how far off the mark these predictions were. The United States is still the world's only superpower. It dominates the world scene politically, culturally and militarily. In January 2003, US Defense Secretary Donald Rumsfeld made comments about 'old Europe' that played on the common perception of gradual decline. While the United States has prospered, Europe's high hopes have been dashed.

What happened? How could such a reversal of fortunes occur so quickly? To explain it, we shall first look at the American malaise, its causes and its cure in the early 1990s. We then discuss how Europe's plans and hopes, not without foundation, ultimately failed on implementation but could still have future potential.

THE WORLD CHAMPION CHALLENGED!

We normally associate the United States with optimism and self-confidence by the bucketful. In early 1992, the country seemed to have precious little left. The *Economist* wrote, under the headline 'Sam, Sam, the paranoid man':

> When Americans look at their economy these days, they are horrified ... a 'double-dip' recession, with the second dip possibly worse than the first; crumbling international competitiveness in industries crucial for long-term growth; an economy hobbled by a naïve commitment to 'free trade', while competitors play by rules of their own. Sapped of strength at home and conspired against abroad, America is failing. This amounts to a national emergency, no less.

> > (*Economist*, 1992a: 13–14)

Perhaps, the *Economist* argued, things were not quite as bad as all that. It predicted, however, that any expansion would probably be weaker than earlier ones. Yet the budget deficit was coming under control, and share prices and export orders for capital goods were on the up. At the same time, the journalists argued that the United States was saddled with low investment, an outlandishly wasteful and expensive healthcare industry, a legal system that acted as a heavy tax on business and an education system that left too many young adults unequipped for work. With a tough reform agenda, even Uncle Sam could possibly return to moderate levels of growth.

Where did this wave of pessimism come from? Since the beginning of the recession in 1990, 1.5 million jobs had been lost. The unemployment rate had soared to 7.5 per cent. At the end of 1991, General Motors announced that it would let 70,000 workers go over the following four years – the equivalent to today's total workforce of Merck & Co. The front cover of the 13 January 1992 issue of the news magazine *US News and World Report* asked, 'Is your job safe?' The cover story opened with Jerry Brown, a 41-year-old unemployed meat packer in Detroit, Michigan. Like people during the Great Depression after 1929, Jerry stood for hours at a downtown street corner with a hand-lettered sign saying: 'Will work for food.' Hungry, he wondered how he would survive the winter.

Except for the Great Depression, no economic crisis had ever lasted so long in the United States. It was also the first time that America's middle class – the majority of the population – had faced large-scale economic uncertainty. Even during the recessions of 1973–74 and 1981–82, the economy generated an average of 800,000 white-collar jobs. In the early 1990s slump, however, 200,000 such jobs disappeared. Surplus capacity squeezed margins, and new investments all but dried up (see Figure 1.1). Capacity utilization seemed to fall with each new economic cycle; the nation's rate of fixed capital formation was at its lowest point since 1945. In US cities, more commercial buildings stood vacant than at any other time since the Second World War. Even those who kept their jobs did not feel secure as both incomes and asset values melted before their eyes. The income of a typical family with two or more children below 18 years age was lower in 1992 than it had been five years

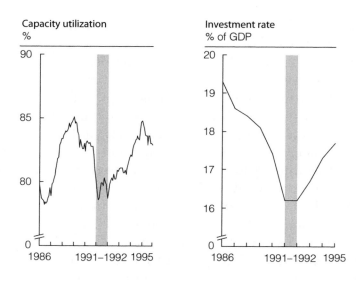

Sources: Federal Reserve, 2002; OECD National Accounts database.

Figure 1.1   Economic crisis in the United States, 1991

previously. For example, the average family earned US $45,600 in 1987 (median income after transfers and based on purchasing power in 2001), but by 1992 could expect to earn only US $44,600 – a drop of 2.2 per cent (US Census Bureau).

In short, 1991 was the *annus horribilis* of the US economy. Consumer spending was flat and economic output fell by around 0.5 per cent. In stark contrast, the official statistics published for the reunified Germany showed an increase in economic output of 5.1 per cent. This surge could not be attributed solely to reunification, as the previous years had also seen annual growth of between 3.7 and 5.7 per cent. In 1992, unemployment in West Germany was actually lower than in the United States, a situation unimaginable today (Figure 1.2).

Political observers and voters overwhelmingly blamed President Bush (Senior). The White House had concentrated on foreign policy and done little to boost the economy. It had failed to reduce the enormous budget deficits inherited from the Reagan era. The Federal Reserve could do little to loosen monetary policy in the face of macroeconomic imbalances.

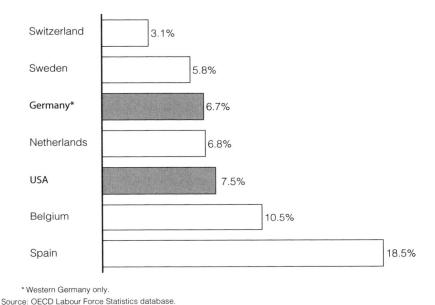

Switzerland 3.1%

Sweden 5.8%

Germany* 6.7%

Netherlands 6.8%

USA 7.5%

Belgium 10.5%

Spain 18.5%

* Western Germany only.
Source: OECD Labour Force Statistics database.

Figure 1.2   Unemployment rates of selected countries, 1992

What was really keeping Americans awake at night was the collision of cyclical and structural influences. Upturns and downturns are normal in any economy, but the particularly painful consequences of the crash in the early 1990s revealed big cracks in the US economy. As Paul O'Neill, then CEO of Alcoa (and treasury secretary under President George W Bush until 2002), remarked, 'Every time I come back to the United States and drive from LaGuardia or Kennedy [airports] into New York City, it's like I'm arriving in a Third World country' (*Fortune*, 1992: 91).

US workers even lacked basic skills. So dramatic was the shortfall that presidential candidate Bill Clinton promised an immediate aid programme of US $220 billion over four years to finance training programmes and university fees. Companies would be forced to invest at least 1.5 per cent of their revenue in training. Clinton's labour secretary, Robert Reich, preached that the United States had much to learn from Germany. He particularly admired management for the long term, a financial system based on bank lending rather than capital markets, and long apprenticeships followed by gradual promotion. It was not only professional training and continuing education that seemed to be in crisis – even the elite universities were struggling with problems, seemingly due to high costs.

The economic crisis and the seemingly unstoppable decline in competitiveness also threatened to undermine the United States' influence on world politics. The Yale historian Paul Kennedy described a basic rule of history in his book *The Rise and Fall of the Great Powers* (1987): a nation's ascent to world power, driven by economic success and ambitious politics, normally leads to 'imperial overstretch'. Excessive spending on defence and foreign policy undermines the nation's influence, and in the end, a decline is inevitable. He saw the United States as being in exactly this position at the end of the 1980s. President Reagan's defence programmes led Kennedy to caution that 'a very heavy investment in arms ... may so erode the commercial competitiveness of the American economy that the nation will be less secure in the long term'. The typical dilemma of great powers, Kennedy said, was that overseas obligations continued while their economic power was already in decline.

Today, we know that many of the bleak forecasts were vastly exaggerated. The United States has emerged as the only superpower of the early 21st century; output and employment have grown quickly. Its monetary and fiscal policies during the 1990s were widely admired. The elite universities are once again models of scholarship around the world, and talk of adopting Germany's model of vocational training has faded.

At the time, such a radical turnaround seemed inconceivable. One can only hazard a guess at what might have happened had a major change of course in US economic policy not coincided with massive technological change. And yet the startling reversal of fortunes happened. The United States began to enjoy the fruits of the deregulation policy that it had started under Reagan, and of its extensive investment in information technology. A lending boom facilitated consumer spending and increased capital investment. Falling public deficits made it easier to repay the mountain of debt. Interest rates fell. In the mid-1990s a step up in productivity kicked in as a result of high competitive intensity. Whereas everyone had expected a vicious cycle of higher deficits, high interest rates, low investment and low growth, there was suddenly cornucopia. This almost irresistible combination became known as 'Rubinomics' (after former treasury secretary Robert Rubin) – one of the major prerequisites of the later 'Real New Economy'.

EUROPE'S PLANS: HIGH HOPES, GREAT EXPECTATIONS

In the late 1980s and early 1990s, Europe seemed to offer the US economic story in reverse. To be sure, Europe's economy also experienced a recession at the beginning of the 1990s, two years after the United States. Growth rates declined in many countries, with only the recently reunified Germany avoiding the downturn thanks to large-scale borrowing, a consumption boom and a high level of investment in former East Germany. However, Europe's crisis proved to be relatively mild. Figure 1.3 compares the annual growth rates of per capita gross domestic product (GDP) in the United States and the EU-14

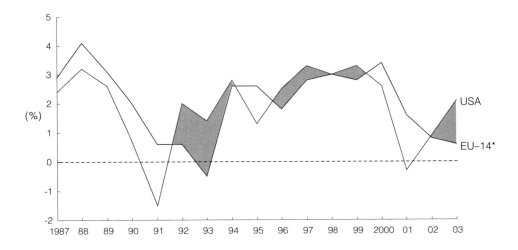

* European Union excluding Germany to avoid bias because of reunification.
Sources: OECD National Accounts database; OECD in Figures 2005.

Figure 1.3 Annual growth rates of real GDP per capita, United States versus EU-14*, 1987–2003

(excluding Germany to avoid bias because of the reunification). Europe's recession turned out to be less harmful. From 1990 to 1991, US economic output dropped by some 1.5 per cent. Two years later, the EU-14 also slipped into recession, but economic output declined by only 0.7 per cent. Despite the worry of unemployment, Europe's constant bugbear, the outlook was not bad at all for the old continent. Whereas 7.5 per cent of the working population in the United States were registered as unemployed in 1992, the jobless figures in Germany, Sweden, the Netherlands, and Switzerland were much lower.

It was not just the economic data that raised hopes of a European decade, however. After the collapse of the Soviet bloc, an ambitious political agenda was drawn up. A gigantic single market, starting with over 300 million people and complemented with a single currency and a common constitution, was to make Europe an economic and political superpower. Enlargement in the East would further strengthen its position. Within a few short years, goals seemed within reach that an earlier generation of Europeans would not have dared to dream of.

The single European market

The first step towards a single European market was taken in the mid-1980s under the then European Commission president, Jacques Delors. Europeans decided to turn the concept of a single market without trade barriers into reality – from the Baltic to the Algarve and from Scotland to the Peloponnesian peninsula. The idea itself was not particularly new: in Rome in 1957, the member states of what was then the European Economic Community had already resolved to remove trade barriers and create a single customs-free economic area.

The European Commission identified seven major non-tariff trade barriers:

- tax legislation, particularly a lack of harmonization of excise duties;
- border controls, especially for the transport of food products and animals;

- production standards, in particular local-content regulations requiring the production of a certain minimum percentage of goods in the given country;
- industry standards, especially for consumer goods;
- national purchasing guidelines – including special preference for national producers;
- transport infrastructure, particularly the incompatibilities between different railway standards and the poor highway links between member states;
- restriction on capital transactions within the European Community.

However, the abolition of non-tariff barriers as well as the removal of protectionist levies on imported goods was a gargantuan task. Without an adapter, continental hairdryers do not work in the United Kingdom. Stacks of forms had to be filled in before food products could be transported across borders, not to mention the paperwork required for inspections. It has been estimated that Germany had around 20,000 national standards for products and production processes, while even the less bureaucratic United Kingdom still had 12,000. Various national laws did nothing to help. For example, the French police could buy only French cars, and the Italian government only Italian ones.

Many countries only permitted the sale of products that had a minimum of 30 per cent locally produced content. Cross-border sales were even more difficult if the sales tax regulations were handled differently or the rates differed significantly from country to country. The lack of integration, and the artificially small domestic markets that this caused, kept companies in many countries below the minimum size necessary to be fully competitive in the international arena. In order to give the European project a fresh impetus, Brussels decided to abolish these incompatibilities.

The Single European Act (SEA) was intended to solve these problems for good. Signed in 1986, it went into effect the following year, and all measures were scheduled to be implemented in national legislation by 1992, creating one market in which all products and services as well as labour and capital could 'flow' freely. Great things were expected from this tour de force. The Cecchini Report, published in 1988 and written to establish the economic case for the single European market, calculated a one-time increase in the European Union's GDP of 4.3 to 6.4 per cent if all of the SEA's measures were implemented (see Figure 1.4).

Only a relatively small portion of the improvement discussed in the Cecchini Report was to come from eliminating border controls or national purchasing guidelines, which are relatively easy to influence. A unified European capital market and the idea of boosting European competitiveness off the back of greater economies of scale were far more important (*Economist*, 1991: 54). Some observers nevertheless accused Eurocrats of being too cautious. The economist Richard Baldwin, then at New York's Columbia University (and today in Geneva), argued that higher capital productivity alone could enhance the expected effect. In addition, he asserted that the single market would not only deliver a one-time increase in

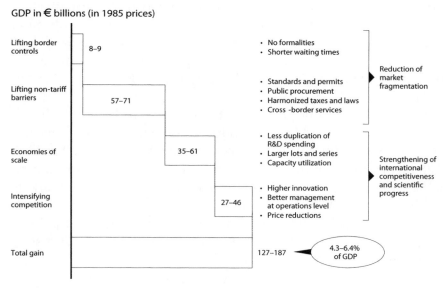

GDP in € billions (in 1985 prices)

Lifting border controls	8–9	• No formalities • Shorter waiting times	
Lifting non-tariff barriers	57–71	• Standards and permits • Public procurement • Harmonized taxes and laws • Cross -border services	Reduction of market fragmentation
Economies of scale	35–61	• Less duplication of R&D spending • Larger lots and series • Capacity utilization	Strengthening of international competitiveness and scientific progress
Intensifying competition	27–46	• Higher innovation • Better management at operations level • Price reductions	
Total gain		127–187	4.3–6.4% of GDP

* Calculations for 7 EU countries: Belgium, Germany, France, UK, Italy, Luxembourg, Netherlands.
Source: European Commission (ed), 1988.

Figure 1.4 Estimated potential macroeconomic benefit of the single market, 1992 (for EU-7)

economic output, but would also drive growth rates upwards by as much as half a percentage point year-on-year (Baldwin, 1989).

It soon became clear that harvesting such tantalizing fruits would not be easy. Implementation by the member states of the 282 measures to remove non-tariff barriers was sluggish. Still, one positive result was the reduction of the numbers of documents required for cross-border goods transport from around 70 to just 1: from 1992 onwards the Single Administrative Document was all that was needed. Similarly, for financial services, a standard European 'passport' was designed to enable employees of financial services providers to conduct business anywhere in the European Community, provided that they fulfilled the regulatory requirements of one member state.

Fifteen years later, the enthusiasm that accompanied the anticipated completion of the single market is very difficult to describe. Even Eurosceptic periodicals in the United Kingdom assumed that 'this is the decade the European Community was invented for' (Economist, 1992b: 5).

Maastricht and monetary union

A common currency was meant to enhance competitiveness yet further and make the single market work much better. After the breakdown of the Bretton Woods system between 1971 and 1973, experiments with fixing Europe's currencies took a variety of forms – and met with varying degrees of success. What began as the 'currency snake' (which permitted fluctuations in exchange rates of the six countries involved only within a band of 2.25 per cent) developed into the European Monetary System (EMS). Target bands were set for exchange rates, and the central banks of the member countries pledged to intervene if rates deviated too far from the agreed parity. Periodic adjustments to the targets balanced the effects of varying inflation rates.

Only in one core group of European countries did the exchange rate system significantly reduce fluctuation, however – the 'DM block' around Germany consisting of Austria, the Netherlands, Belgium (which has a currency union with Luxembourg) and

Denmark. These countries synchronized their interest rates along German lines, and also pursued a fiscal policy that was consistent with low inflation rates. Other countries, notably France and Italy, conducted their interest rate and fiscal policy largely to achieve domestic targets, and were then forced periodically to devalue their currencies against the Deutschmark. Although this gained them some exchange rate stability in the short term, it came at the price of unpredictably large and irregular adjustments. In the late 1980s new members joined the EMS, including the United Kingdom and Spain. Existing members such as Italy and Ireland, which had set particularly wide target bands (6 per cent), followed in the footsteps of other countries, limiting their scope for fluctuation to the usual 2.25 per cent on either side of parity.

This system seemed to work fairly well. Exchange rates were more or less stable, and devaluations largely took the sting out of conflicts arising from different domestic and external interests. Member states voted enthusiastically to adopt the Delors Plan to create a common currency, and it was passed in 1992 in the Dutch city of Maastricht as part of the Treaty on European Union – an extensive programme for the creation of a political union and a more integrated economy.

The driving forces behind Maastricht were not just the comparatively good economic times, the optimism of 1992 and the positive experience with the EMS. German reunification had shifted the economic and political weight in Europe substantially. Many saw the plans for monetary union as a way to check Germany's looming dominance and provide a broader basis for controlling Frankfurt's interest rate policy, which was becoming more and more of a problem for the rest of Europe. 'Maastricht' also raised the hackles of some Eurosceptics in England, because its realization entailed promising deeper European integration as compensation for relinquishing monetary independence.

Tremendous economic hopes were pinned on monetary union. The original architects of the Delors Plan expected the common European currency not only to eliminate transaction costs for cross-border payments, but also to strengthen economic integration within Europe. Their primary hope was that stability would spread – the idea being that the new monetary policy would fight inflation just as the policies of the Bundesbank had done. This would put an end to the damaging price increases in those countries with weaker currencies: Italy, Spain, Portugal, the United Kingdom and (at times) France.

In addition, foreign direct investment would be easier and risk-free, companies could design uniform product/market strategies for Europe, and customers could compare prices quickly and reliably. The higher degree of price transparency that the EMU would create was expected to promote greater competitiveness. The entire euro zone would be able to benefit from the lower real interest rates that prevailed in Germany thanks to the Bundesbank's trustworthy policy. On top of this, the development of an integrated European capital market, which would also ensure lower financing costs for companies, was regarded as nearly synonymous with the creation of a common currency.

Everyone involved in this process in the early 1990s agreed that the goal was still a long way off. In order to achieve monetary union on time in 1999, the participating countries would have to fulfil a large number of prerequisites before 1997. This subjected many member states to a large number of exacting requirements in the form of strict financial discipline, debt reduction, low inflation rates and a convergence of interest rates. But if this all-out effort proved successful, as all hoped, Europe would be able to reap the benefits of substantial growth.

The Lisbon agenda: more cheerleading

After the creation of a European single market and the monetary union, the EU heads of state agreed at a summit in Lisbon in March 2000 that the next goal would be nothing less than to make the European Union by 2010 'the most competitive and dynamic knowledge-based economy capable of sustainable economic growth with more and better jobs and greater social cohesion' (European Council, 2000).

Better policies on R&D were to help, complemented by completing the internal market. Second, Europe would invest more in people and combating social exclusion. Third, macroeconomic policy should aid these measures by maintaining stability. The Lisbon summit was supposed to mark a turning point for EU enterprise and innovation policy. Above all, it painted a picture of the high-level integration of social and economic policy, supported by practical initiatives to strengthen the European Union's research capacity, promote entrepreneurship and facilitate take-up of information technology.

Crucially for the Lisbon agenda, investment in R&D was intended to grow to 3 per cent of GDP. A second lever was the reduction of red tape to promote entrepreneurship. A multitude of measures were defined in order to improve performance. The agenda set forth 28 main and 120 sub-goals as well as 117 indicators of success. The measures were defined at both the European and the member-state levels, yet the majority of reforms and investments were to be the responsibility of the member states. Peer pressure was the only 'agent of change' – a concept very different from 'Europe 1992', when decision-making authority was shifted towards Brussels.

From Nice to a European Constitution?

Along with a single market, single currency and the vision set forth in Lisbon, the European Union was working in parallel on improving its governance structure. The two milestones here are the 2001 Treaty of Nice and the 2004 Constitutional Treaty. Soon after the Lisbon declarations, institutional reform was increasingly pressing, since EU-15 membership was set to widen to 25; in May 2004, 10 new member states with a population of around 100 million joined the Union. Less than a year later, the European Union signed accession treaties with Bulgaria and Romania, and six months after that, it opened negotiations with Turkey and Croatia. Further enlargement is already under discussion.

The Treaty of Nice, approved in February 2001 and in force since February 2003, was a long-overdue step towards institutional reform, above all to cope with the 2004 enlargement. Since the 1950s when the composition and operation of the European institutions and bodies had been agreed by the Union's six founding members (Belgium, France, Germany, Italy, Luxembourg and the Netherlands), the Union had undergone four enlargements. When Nice was ratified, the European Union had 15 member states (the six founding members plus Austria, Denmark, Finland, Greece, Ireland, Portugal, Spain, Sweden and the United Kingdom). Yet apart from the introduction of direct elections to the European Parliament in 1979, and the Treaty of Amsterdam, which extended the scope of qualified majority voting to the Council in 1999, there had been no major institutional reform since the founding of the European Economic Community. Under the Treaty of Amsterdam's provisions, the unanimity rule still applied in 73 areas. Still greater size and diversity made unanimity increasingly difficult to achieve, and with 25 member countries as of 2004 and 27 as of 2007, it would become very unlikely. To make decisions easier, the Treaty of Nice introduced qualified majority voting in a number of key areas. It also enhanced the role of the European Parliament.

After Nice, the Constitutional Treaty was intended to take institutional reform one step further by consolidating the four treaties that governed the European Union. The three original treaties establishing European Communities harked back to the 1950s: the European Coal and Steel Community (1951), the European Economic Community (1957) and the Atomic Energy Community (1957). The fourth founding treaty was the Treaty of Maastricht (1992), which turned the European Community into the European Union. These treaties had been amended in part on several occasions: by the Merger Treaty (1965), the Single European Act (1986), the Treaty of Amsterdam (1997) and the Treaty of Nice (2001). To cut through the clutter, the 'Treaty establishing a Constitution for Europe' (Constitutional Treaty) was devised as a single text to replace all the existing treaties (with the exception of the Euratom Treaty) and to give the European Union a single legal identity under domestic and international law.

The Constitutional Treaty provides for seven important changes to the European Union's institutional structure. First, an exit clause would allow member states to leave the Union. It would define a qualified majority as 55 per cent (but at least 15) of the member states representing at least 65 per cent of the EU's population. A blocking minority could be formed by a combination of four large member states. The European Council would become an institution chaired by a president appointed for two and a half years, renewable once. A new position would be created, the EU Minister of Foreign Affairs, merging the tasks of the High Representative for the Common Foreign and Security Policy and the External Relations

Commissioner. In the Council of Ministers, the presidency of the different Council formations would continue to rotate (with the exception of the External Relations Council) on an equal basis. The constitution would also increase the maximum number of seats in the European Parliament to 750, with the minimum number of seats per country being 6 and the maximum 96. Its powers would be enlarged: 95 per cent of European laws would be adopted under the co-decision procedure. Finally, the principle of one commissioner per member state would be maintained until 2014. Thereafter, the number of commissioners would be reduced to two-thirds of the number of member states, with commissioners to be chosen on the basis of equal rotation among the member states.

In June 2004, heads of EU member states adopted the Constitutional Treaty, giving member states two years to ratify it.

2006: REALITY COMES CALLING

Half a decade after the Lisbon agenda was proclaimed, there is little left of the 'Europhoria'. The euro has failed to unleash economic dynamism, the '1992' programme to complete the internal market appears stalled or is ineffective, and the Lisbon initiatives seem little more than words on paper. Growth has been disappointing, or so most analysts would argue – and not just compared with the turbocharged performance of the US economy, but also with Europe's own lofty aspirations. Unemployment remains high in many countries, and governments are struggling to balance their books. The constitution was roundly rejected by the Dutch and the French in referenda held in 2005. Reaching a compromise over the budget seems as difficult as ever, if not more so. How could things fall apart so quickly and thoroughly?

The single market and red tape

As noted by countless observers, including members of the European Commission, the single European market has fallen far short of its ambitious goals. Hundreds of regulations in the SEA have been translated into national legislation, but the anticipated effects have largely failed to materialize (see Chapter 5). In early 2003, the European Commission conceded that, even under optimistic assumptions, the cumulative gain in economic output since 1992 attributable to the single market appeared to have been only 1.8 per cent. In other words, actual growth totalled barely a third of the expected rate; it also took much longer to arrive.

Europe's inability to fulfil its ambitious goals can be attributed to a number of factors, chiefly relating to implementation. What national governments buy does not depend on legal formalities alone: cultural affinity, lobbying by domestic industry and sheer force of habit still play key roles. The same applies to consumers' decisions. Markets remained fragmented, and many key initiatives, such as a European directive for company takeovers, were abandoned or simply never got off the ground.

Furthermore, some EU states seem to be reluctant to play by Brussels' rules. For example, there was to be no problem with EU citizens taking their cars with them when moving to Spain. However, if the car is less than six months old, then the owner has to pay an 'inspection fee' amounting to 6–12 per cent of the car's value.

People moving to Italy or Spain or elsewhere in the EU still need a residence permit, which may well mean waiting in line for days in overflowing offices and being fingerprinted by the police, although applications from EU citizens cannot be refused. A uniform, integrated market for services and labour is little more than a distant dream.

In crucial areas such as the single European capital market the rate of progress is virtually nil. Europe has more stock exchanges than countries, and cross-border capital flows are still small and expensive. Sending money abroad is now cheaper, but portfolio flows – buying stocks and bonds in other EU countries – remain as expensive as ever. For EU citizens, purchasing shares in a foreign EU company is as difficult as trying to invest in a company listed on the exchanges in the United States or in Hong Kong. Investors thus miss out on the benefits of diversification because their investment portfolios are not sufficiently enriched with foreign securities. Those who want to buy foreign securities must either accept enormous charges in the form of wide price spreads on their domestic exchanges or pay the high fees charged for trading on a foreign exchange.

The single European passport for financial service providers is more theoretical than real; national regulators still require banks and brokers who do business in Lisbon, Copenhagen or Dublin to be supervised by the national authorities. Single Europe or no Single Europe, financial service providers and the related infrastructure remain symbols of national pride.

There has been no effective progress on the harmonization of merger and acquisition rules. The European takeover directive has been so watered down that there will not be an integrated market for corporate control. Mergers and acquisitions across European borders in the order of magnitude of the Unicredito-HVB Group are still the exceptions.

Here, parish-pump politics are to blame. There are other reasons for slow progress elsewhere. In financial markets in particular, the Commission completed a mammoth programme to enact regulations that deserves respect. The problem is that – beyond national pride – national structures in the finance sector are difficult to deconstruct because the definition and use of financial products is closely inter-twined with national legal systems, which have grown organically over many centuries.

Monetary union: an economic dead-end?

Monetary union does not appear to have stimulated growth or created employment – quite the reverse. Nor is there much hope for improvement in the future. Nevertheless, Europe has to live with these economic consequences, painful as they are, and over the long term, will hopefully be able to harvest the psychological advantages from millions of Europeans feeling more bound together. The disso-lution of the EMU would be technically problematic and politically divisive, and cause even greater economic problems than the status quo (not to mention psychological confusion).

That monetary union came about at all must be regarded in retro-spect as a small miracle. The ink had barely dried on the Maastricht

Treaty of December 1991 when volatility on foreign exchange markets ran riot. The tranquillity of the late 1980s proved to be deceptive. Exchange rate adjustments, once a matter of course, had become rare. Despite considerable differences in inflation rates, exchange rates had remained fixed for a long time. Currencies had moved a long way from the rates of exchange required for purchasing power parity.

Moreover, the recession of the early 1990s was dogging EMU candidates: most found reducing their budget deficits and indebtedness an uphill battle. The shaky economy led to shortfalls in tax revenues. At the same time, rising unemployment put upward pressure on government spending. The 'peace dividend' expected when the Soviet Union collapsed proved quite small. The tough criteria set for membership of the monetary union made it hard for governments to sustain even temporary deficits in order to kick-start their economies during the crisis. And because Maastricht had made the convergence of interest rates a requirement, many governments were left with practically no room for manoeuvre to deal with the economic crisis. If they failed to devalue their currencies against the Deutschmark, they had to raise their interest rates in the midst of the crisis, while unemployment rose and production capacity stood idle.

After Denmark's voters rejected the Maastricht Treaty in June 1992, people grew nervous. The date for the French referendum drew near. On financial markets, confidence in fixed rates was declining rapidly. This created opportunities for currency traders to profit from the devaluation of the weaker currencies. In September 1992, fixed exchange rates had to be abandoned for the Finnish markka, the Italian lira and the British pound. Barely nine months after Maastricht, monetary union appeared to be no more than a faint hope.

Yet despite all the hurdles and prophecies of doom, the euro did arrive. Promptly on 1 January 1999, the single European currency was implemented as a virtual currency, and its coins have been jingling in the pockets of Europeans since 2002. No one has failed to notice its arrival, not least because of the alleged price increases. People complain about how expensive life has become since the euro was introduced. Even central banks admit that perceived inflation in

2002 was relatively high, despite the fact that measured price increases were low.

However, the euro project, so successfully implemented at a technical and administrative level, offers little cause for celebration. True, interest rates are low and so is inflation in most of the eurozone. However, interest rates are fixed at the same level throughout the eurozone, so that deviations in inflation from the European average cannot be targeted specifically. This has consequences for member states' economies and jobs. Before 1999, sceptics had already joked that EMU stood for 'Even More Unemployment'. As the economic cycles within the European Union are not synchronized, fiscal policy is the only tool member states have left to smooth out country-specific bumps in demand. When the Stability Pact was added to the Maastricht Treaty, however, it sharply curtailed the use of fiscal policy as a member state's last resort, particularly in times of economic slowdowns, as has been evident since early 2003. A country that has exhausted its debt capacity according to the Stability Pact and is struggling with slack demand cannot do much. If it is lucky, it can implement painful structural reforms, and it might find itself in better shape at some distant point in the future.

Since 1999, European economies have been diverging, not converging. Many countries are struggling with the new debt limit of 3 per cent laid down in the Stability Pact. To the surprise of many, not just 'weak' southern members of EMU but core countries like Germany have struggled with the 3 per cent deficit requirement. Germany and France have exceeded the limit for three consecutive years, triggering a growing crisis that threatens to kill off the pact (if not de jure, then de facto). In March 2005, the Council agreed a reform that makes the rules more 'flexible'. For example, member states will avoid the Excessive Deficit Procedure (EDP) if they experience any negative growth at all (previously −2 per cent), can draw on more 'relevant factors' to avoid an EDP and will have more time to clear up problems if they do move into an EDP.

Developments since 1999 have shown that the critics mostly had it right. Asymmetric shocks – affecting some countries, not others – are a very real danger. Interest rates in recent years have been too high for

Germany, which was in or close to recession for much of the period 2000–05. Other countries such as Spain may be overheating, with an unsustainable housing and credit boom. Because of EMU, a member state with above-average inflation has lower real interest rates – the exact opposite of what would be desirable to smooth the economic cycle. Is the problem just one of temporary adjustment, or is Europe having to learn to live with a grave problem that will not go away?

The failure to implement structural reforms in the past now appears to be proving harmful. In the United States, workers simply abandon a troubled region (such as the infamous 'rust belt' around Detroit) to seek employment elsewhere. Europeans seem to prefer to stay put even when they are unemployed, though admittedly it is easier to move within the same country and in an area that speaks the same language. What's more, although European unemployment rates may not have risen overall since the introduction of the euro, individual countries such as Germany are suffering badly. For the third time in a dozen years, monetary union has contributed to a situation in which economic policy is unable to stimulate growth. A comparison between the drop in unemployment rates in eurozone and non-eurozone EU states suggests that monetary union has given no additional economic stimulus (Figure 1.5) – but rather the opposite has been the case.

The dissolution of EMU does not appear practical for a number of reasons. It would be likely to create huge instability in financial markets, cause an explosion of interest rates on government debt for the weaker member states, and put an end to Europe's reputation for successful political initiatives. It could also create very large mismatches in bank and corporate balance sheets. So far Europe has wasted much of its political energies on a project that produces some convenience for travellers but major headaches for economic policy without delivering convincing returns. With limited ability to use either monetary or fiscal stimuli to keep the economy close to capacity – as the United States does regularly, and with vigour, as documented after 2001 – the European Union should seek other ways of keeping growth on track.

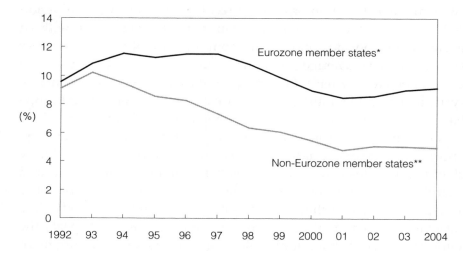

* Belgium, Germany, Finland, France, Greece, Ireland, Italy, Luxembourg, Netherlands, Austria, Portugal, Spain.
** Denmark, UK, Sweden.
Source: OECD Labour Force Statistics database.

Figure 1.5   Unemployment rates within the EU-15 since 1992

Where Europe stands now

Europe is not doing well. Almost five years after the proclamation of the Lisbon agenda, a committee led by Wim Kok concluded in November 2004 that not much progress had been made. The Kok report heavily criticized the member states' lack of commitment and the repeated triumphs of national interests. The Lisbon objective of 'becoming the world's most dynamic and competitive knowledge-based society' by 2010 is now widely accepted as over-ambitious. Yet the goal itself is clearly worthwhile. What can be done to achieve it as quickly as possible?

There appears to be a lack of serious debate today about what Europe should do. SEA and EMU have produced disappointing results, and except for calls for 'structural reforms' there is little sign that a course towards clear improvements is being charted. More ominously, in the wake of the failed large-scale plans and projects, a sense of unease prevails in many quarters in the boardrooms of corporate Europe, at the heart of Brussels' bureaucracy and in political circles. At the same time, the sense of crisis does not seem to be accompanied by any sense of urgency, and there appears little evidence of a readiness to change.

In this book, we want to show how Europe can wake up: how it can find its way back to higher growth in the economy, in productivity and in employment. In Part I, we attempt a more precise analysis and diagnosis of the current crisis as a point of departure.

The focus of the following chapter, 'Europe's real crisis', is the development of our argument that Europe has failed primarily in real economic terms and for reasons that are rarely publicly discussed. Europe is probably not as socially progressive as is commonly believed – a surprising finding. Second, Europe's future is not secure. Only the first small steps have been taken so far to address the looming demographic challenge of a greying population. And, third, Europe is less productive than the United States – the gap is larger than many observers think. Europe isn't even playing catch-up.

How can Europe's potential be transformed into real growth? In Chapter 3, we discuss the extent to which the US template for success fits Europe. We argue that Europe certainly can and should copy some good ideas from the US, but not all. The right approach is intelligent cherry picking: in other words, taking only those ideas that are compatible with European goals and values. In our view, Europe is capable of unifying social justice and growth, and of combining affluence, culture, environmental protection, retirement security and an impressive standard of living for the working population. To do so, however, it must accelerate productivity growth and increase employment significantly.

However, this journey is not just about money. What of the other requirements? There is no consensus at present on the balance of objectives and the right way to measure successful economic and social policy. For example, the widespread assumption that Europe pays too high a price for its quality of life in terms of lower economic output does not appear to us to be accurate. True, the old continent lags behind the United States in terms of hard factors such as per capita economic output. However, it seems to us that the soft factors such as environmental quality and leisure almost make up the deficit.

To start a discussion about these topics, Chapter 4, 'Economic indicators and the right measures', offers a quality-of-life index that could serve as a compass for European economic policy.

Soft factors notwithstanding, considerable improvements can still be made. As our comparison of the European average with the best-performing country in each case shows, Europe should not be satisfied with what it has achieved in the non-material categories. Furthermore, and for a number of reasons, Europe's economic situation has to be considered less secure than that of the United States. Our index addresses these subtleties in calculating success metrics and thus overcomes the inaccuracies inherent in using gross domestic product alone as a frame of reference. Perhaps most importantly, it is not only more accurate, but it also makes it possible to measure progress in areas that Europeans consider central to their quality of life.

2

Europe's real crisis

Europe's cities pulsate with culture and life, and people enjoy long holidays by the Mediterranean, in Tuscany or in the Maldives. Almost everyone has a car. The main accessories of modern life – colour televisions, DVD players, stereos, laptops, fashionable clothing – are readily available to large parts of the population. Working hours are short, life expectancy is high and outstanding museums, leading theatres and world-class orchestras are never far away. The trains are fast, the roads smooth and the poor are looked after by generous social security systems. Whichever way we look at it, life in Europe is not bad at all. Most people, in most parts of the world, would give a lot to be allowed to live here.

Despite the high visibility of some of the problems outlined in Chapter 1, this is certainly the prevailing perception that Europeans have of their continent: a rich, socially progressive, culturally exciting and amazingly pleasant place to live. All the joys of living life in Europe blind many to the cracks appearing in the façade. The situation is much more critical than it appears: our idyll is at risk.

Europe's economy is in worse shape than people believe. In the longer term, this will endanger our standard of living. The welfare state offers less protection from poverty than we realize – and will potentially cope even less well in the future. In addition, demographic pressures are creating the need for unenviable choices. Europe will have to make a tremendous effort if it wants to maintain what it has achieved.

To treat the problem, we need to understand its origins. It turns out, for example, that common views about the causes of the malaise do not stand up to scrutiny. For more than a decade, many Europeans have tended to blame their burgeoning welfare state for most economic ills, as the flipside of the otherwise highly valued social benefits. Almost the contrary seems true of both perceptions. The welfare state is neither the main cause of poor economic performance, nor is it fulfilling its social task well enough. The real heart of the problem seems to lie elsewhere: in poor economic productivity, which will become even more problematic in the face of the aging European population and, many would add, the threats from globalization.

DISAPPOINTING GROWTH RATES

Europe's economic growth record in the last 10 years compared with the United States has disappointed. Yet its true failure is deeper. Given Europe's starting level after the Second World War, it should be growing much faster than the United States. Output and therefore income per capita is still lagging behind by a third. Output per hour worked – that is, labour productivity – is a good way of looking at the issue. As in the post-war years, Europe should be shaving a few percentage points off the US advantage every decade. In a transparent world where state-of-the art technologies can travel at ever higher speed, and will do so if competitive pressures are sufficiently high, convergence ought to be as universal as a law of physics. This natural process has gone into reverse, constituting the European Union's real economic failure.

In the decades after the Second World War, Europe raced to catch up in terms of economic performance. In 1950, the per capita economic output of Spain (based on GDP) was 77 per cent lower than that of the

Index (USA = 100)

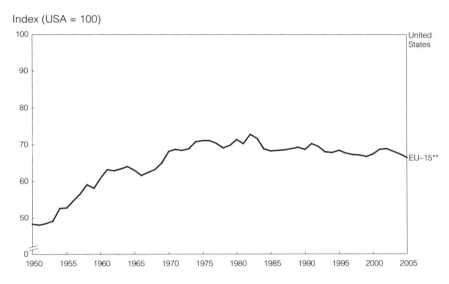

* Measured as GDP per capita, USD at PPP.
** 1950–89: West Germany, 1990–2005: All Germany.
Source: Groningen Total Economy Database.

Figure 2.1   Income per capita, EU-15 and the United States, 1950–2005*

United States, while France was at a little more than half the US level. By 1985, however, France was less than a third behind, and in 1998 late starter Spain produced about half of the GDP per capita of the United States

Economic historians define the 1950s and 1960s as a golden age of growth and full employment. The United States grew at a rate of 2 to 3 per cent per annum; many countries in Europe achieved rates of 5 to 6 per cent. In Germany, this was the era of the *Wirtschaftswunder* (economic miracle), when Minister of Economics and later Chancellor Ludwig Erhard could credibly promote 'prosperity for all'.

By the 1980s, the race had ground to a halt – long before Europe managed to catch up with the United States. In the 1990s the US economy achieved an acceleration in productivity and output growth. It had managed to grow labour productivity by about 1.4 per cent per year in the two decades before 1994. Thereafter, its rate of productivity improvement accelerated to 2.2 per cent.

Where there is no starvation, little corruption and no revolutions or wars, convergence in economic performance is the norm.[1] While it is true that we are far from a world in which all countries are slowly but surely heading towards exactly the same level of economic perform-ance, there are 'convergence clubs': groups of countries with stable legal systems, comparable infrastructures and similar human resources that are converging over the long term. Because Europe is starting from behind, it should grow faster than the productivity leader, the United States, by realizing the growth potential that results from the gap between the two levels. Instead, it is actually falling behind.

If the United States continues with 2.2 per cent productivity growth, Europe would need to increase productivity by 2.7 per cent a year to catch up with it in 40 years. A full 1 percentage point lead (growth at 3.2 per cent) would reduce this period to 20 years. This suggests that eliminating the gap within the next few decades is a daunting task. We shall use the simple metric of 'labour productivity times labour input (supported by capital productivity)', which will allow us to unpack the problem into discrete symptoms and diag-nose the sources of the gap. The growth rate of the variables then reveals whether and to what extent Europe is on course for conver-gence.

Why does Europe find itself in such a difficult situation? Is another key characteristic of the old continent, its huge welfare system, the prime economic problem, as many experts claim? If not, what is the main problem? Moreover, how much do Europeans get for all that welfare spending? We examine these issues in the next sections, dispelling the myth of the destructive and the myth of the generous welfare state in turn.

IT'S THE PRODUCTIVITY, STUPID

As noted above, Europe's real crisis is that it produces one-third less than the United States per capita, and that the gap is not becoming smaller. Why is the old continent producing so much less than the United States? The statistics are far from perfect, but they allow us to pin down the orders of magnitude involved. One main reason is that labour productivity is lower by 16 per cent (all figures in this paragraph refer to the year 2004). The other cause of low output is that Europeans work less, with labour input per head of population in the EU-15 about 20 per cent lower than in the United States. Figure 2.2 summarizes the main factors. We will argue that the single largest cause of lower output is low labour productivity. However, we also need to better understand the other part of the equation – labour input – and differentiate between deliberate choice and poor economic performance, such as the possible negative economic impact of the welfare state.

Labour input is low because Europeans are less likely to work than Americans, and because each of them works less. Europeans of working age are less likely to be employed – either because they cannot find work or because they are not seeking employment.[2] For every 100 inhabitants, the United States has 47 employees. In Europe, there are only 44. This factor alone is responsible for cutting labour input by 6 per cent. We will argue later that this is the principal way in which the welfare state is causing problems.

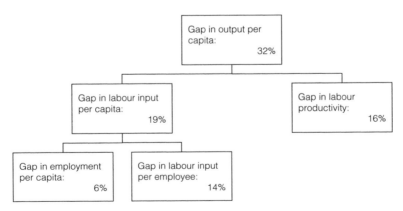

* Gap against US figures indexed to 100. Gaps at higher level of aggregation are calculated by multiplication of the respective EU-15/US ratios, eg, gap in output per capita = 1-(1–0.19) x (1–0.16), i.e., are not additive.

Sources: Groningen Total Economy Database; OECD Main Economic Indicators 2006; OECD Labour Force Statistics; Eurostat; Alesina, Glaeser and Sacerdote, 2005; IW Köln; own calculations.

Figure 2.2 Explaining Europe's 32 per cent output-per-capita gap compared with the United States, 2004*

Labour input also suffers because each employee in Europe works fewer hours – on average, by 14 per cent each year. Each employee puts in about 1,564 hours per year. The United States equivalent is 1,819. European vacations are long, maternity benefits and sick leave schemes are relatively generous, and the average working week has often been curtailed in recent years. All these differences contribute to the low number of working hours per employee. We argue that shorter hours per employee are largely neutral or even welfare enhancing (if they reflect deliberate choices).

Yet even if Europeans worked as long as Americans, total output would still be lower because Europeans produce less per hour worked, as mentioned above. For the EU-15, the weighted average of output per hour worked in 2004, adjusted for purchasing power differences, was about 16 per cent lower than in the United States. There are good reasons to think that, measured correctly, the true gap in labour productivity is even bigger.

If we consider the years 1994–2004, using the latest estimates, output per hour showed 2 per cent growth for the United States, and 1.7 per cent for the EU-15 (Daly, 2006). Crucially, European labour productivity statistics are too good to be true. Look at the official output per hour, and France and the Netherlands beat the United States. Germany comes close. Unfortunately, the figures are not actually comparable with those of the United States for a number of reasons. First, the figures do not account for the effects of high unemployment. Since only the most productive individuals work, Europe's labour statistics look better than they would if employment rates were high. Second, large parts of the recorded output – such as the government sector – do not in fact reflect economic output.

Europe's high productivity in the statistics is derived partly from the fact that less productive workers are the first to lose their jobs. If they had jobs, many unemployed would be less productive than those currently employed. Overwhelmingly, they have low skills and limited experience. A country that introduced a very high minimum wage, for example, would almost automatically show a big jump in GDP per hour worked – by effectively excluding a large part of the population. On top of unemployment, early retirement plans and disability benefits make it particularly attractive for the less efficient to exit the labour force. The employment rate of workers aged 15–64 is approximately 65 per cent in the EU-15. In the United States, it is 71 per cent. Some of this reflects preferences and other factors, such as the lack of opportunities for child care that might enable women to join the labour force. However, if the average person not employed in the European Union were 30 per cent less productive than those employed, this would lead to an overstatement of true productivity by approximately 4 per cent.

The problems do not end there. Measuring the output of the service sector is notoriously difficult. Government services are a particular problem. For businesses, economic output is measured by market outcomes – the difference between the value of goods and services sold and their inputs. This technique does not work for teachers, police officers, fire fighters or tax collectors. Government workers do not sell their services. The statisticians simply add up their salaries and assume that the sum is equal to the total value of their services. Every salary rise in the public sector thus increases measured output. Education in Germany and France, for example, where teachers are well paid, is about 1.5 times as 'productive' as in the United States.

When the public sector accounted for only 2 per cent of GDP, the measurement of output in the government sector did not matter much. Today, it produces big distortions. Governments employ large numbers of people. In 2005, Portugal, for instance, had 0.9 million employees on the government payroll, almost a fifth of the country's total employment. Germany, even more strikingly, had a total of 38.9 million employees, no fewer than 4.2 million of whom were employed by the state – almost 11 per cent of total employment. When calculating an economy's productivity, simply adding in the salaries of government employees now makes a big difference.

To avoid the problem, we could just measure and compare the productivity of the business sector alone. This shows Europe in a worse light. Excluding the government sector reduces GDP per worker by about 2–3 percentage points.

Another option is to drop the focus on overall macroeconomic figures and to compare individual sectors. The results are much more robust. When interpreting, we have, however, to keep in mind that one economy as a whole can be less productive than another for two reasons: either because every sector is less productive, or because the economy is weaker in the more efficient sectors. Europe lags behind the United States for both reasons.

One recent study by McKinsey Global Institute (MGI) analysed sectors of the economy in depth and produced some sobering findings: individual sectors in Germany and France are trailing dramatically behind the United States (McKinsey Global Institute, 2002). The official statistics paint a far less disturbing picture. According to these, economic output per hour worked in Germany is 88 per cent of the US value; and in France 108 per cent – including civil servants, teachers, the police and the low-wage sector (Figure 2.3). However, if this figure is adjusted for the two major distortions discussed above – the 'productivity' of government employees and the greater tendency for workers with lower productivity to be excluded from employment – the result for Europe is much less favourable: Germany reaches just 85 per cent of the US level and France 95 per cent, although both have a higher capital intensity. In the sectoral analysis by the MGI, German productivity lagged 22 per cent behind the United States and France 15 per cent. In the period analysed, Europe was ahead in segments of the retail sector and in mobile telephony, but there were shortcomings in the automotive industry, goods transport, electricity generation, banking and the clothing industry. Europeans also lacked productivity in fixed network telecommunications (Figure 2.4).

In quite a few sectors, good news is on the way. In road freight, fixed telecoms and banking, Europeans are catching up. In other sectors, such as food retailing and electricity generation, the gaps are large and growing.

The reasons for large and growing productivity gaps tend to be many and varied. Yet one factor appears to be common to them all: a lack of intense competition, followed by all kinds of problems such as sub-optimal production processes or fragmented industries, limited application of new processes, and less focus on high value-added products. Retail banking, with large state-owned and cooperative sectors in addition to the private sector, is not governed by the normal rules of market economies. Food retailing suffers from

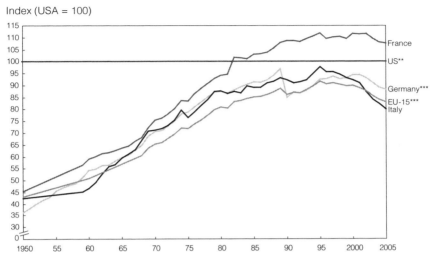

Index (USA = 100)

* Measured as GDP per hour worked, USD at PPP.
** US: 1951–58 no data available, linear progression assumed.
*** 1950–89: West Germany, 1990–2005: All Germany.
Source: Groningen Total Economy Database.

Figure 2.3 Output per hour worked, 1950–2005*

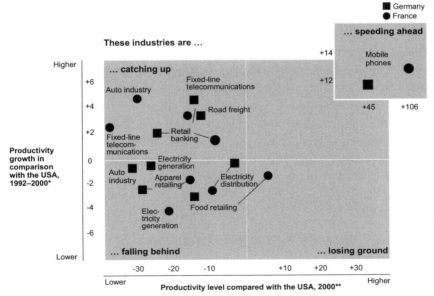

* Automotive industry and utilities, 1992–99; retail banking, 1994–2000; retailing 1993–2000
** 1999 for automotive industry and utilities.
Source: McKinsey Global Institute, 2002.

Figure 2.4 Productivity performance: Germany and France versus the United States

many barriers to entry, especially where planning permits are issued by municipalities. There may also be some cyclical factors at work. The extended boom of the 1990s in the United States, fuelled by strong demand, naturally facilitated a rise in productivity, especially in industries with high fixed costs. Economies of scale thanks to higher overall utilization of capacity are part of the recipe for success. This is where interactions between IT adoption and high demand come into play. Many sectors have invested massively in computing in recent years, especially in the United States. This increases fixed costs and leads to high productivity during periods of high demand.

To sum up, labour productivity – a long-standing source of pride for many European policy makers – does not look as high as the official figures suggest once adjustments are made for certain biases. The existence of large gaps is confirmed by industry-level studies. However, the official statistics also seem to confirm that nearly half of Europe's output gap compared with the United States is the result of lower labour productivity.

In Europe, low output per hour worked also spells low output per unit of capital. In the past, European economies often used greater quantities of capital than the United States. This increased labour productivity, but it is not a road to riches. Capital is costly. Depreciation has to be paid for. Today, despite using at least as much capital as the United States in many of its member states, Europe has failed – as we have seen – to raise labour productivity to US levels. This also means that for each unit of capital expenditure, it produces less than the United States. This makes investment unattractive, and contributes to a lack of economic dynamism.

THE MYTH OF THE DESTRUCTIVE WELFARE STATE

Once upon a time, in the 1950s and 1960s, Europeans worked hard and growth rates were high. Then entitlements grew, and more people started to use or abuse the system. Welfare spending and payments through government-run insurance schemes today are larger than all other government spending on services, investment and all other costs put together. Valuable resources that could be invested in infrastructure and education go directly towards immediate consumption. Welfare systems offer income for not working, even where people could help themselves. More than one observer has wondered just how much longer such a system can go on. The total share of government receipts in GDP is staggering – almost half of all resources generated in Europe are spent or allocated by the government. In Sweden, the share of government receipts in GDP has reached 57 per cent.

Many instinctively feel that, as the state takes an ever larger share of the pie, incentives must suffer and growth has to falter. It stands to reason that the larger the 'wedge' driven between pre- and post-tax returns by taxes and contributions, the less incentive there is for entrepreneurship, hard work, employment of low-skilled people and thus for wealth creation altogether. Contribution rates for unemployment insurance and taxes to finance social-payment transfers started to skyrocket. It seemed that fewer and fewer people could see the point of working. For more and more companies, employing unskilled or only semi-skilled workers became too expensive relative to their productivity. Europe's growth started to slow down, and vigorous economies driven by the rationale of the market suffered as more people started to chase entitlements. Labour markets became ossified: workers could not be fired, and so nobody was hired. Unemployment increased yet further. One of the reasons that Europe is poorer than the United States is the heavy hand of the tax office, financing a burgeoning welfare state that makes work unappealing. More than one European government believes that the painful path of 'structural reform' alone can solve Europe's economic ills, and numerous editorial writers have chimed in.

However, as the American writer H L Mencken once joked, 'for every complex problem, there is a solution that is simple, neat, and wrong'. We contend that popular interpretations of the welfare state's economic consequences frequently fall into this category. The reason is that, while the welfare state undoubtedly produces negative incentives for some, the costs simply are not large enough to account for most of the output gap compared with the United States. The main problem, as we saw above, is a yawning labour productivity gap – regardless of the welfare state's impact. Labour input plays a big role, but factors other than the welfare state are probably more important, especially Europeans' deliberate choice to work fewer hours. Better regulation, higher competitive intensity and greater efforts by business are likely to be more important in closing the productivity and output gap with the United States. 'Structural reforms' are necessary, especially in the face of demographic change. However, they are not the 'silver bullet' that will magically cure Europe's main economic ills.

The impact of the welfare state is often taken to include the effects of social transfers, generous social insurance, numerous, detailed, rigid labour regulations, strong unions and wide-ranging entitlements to vacations, sick leave and maternity leave. For our purposes here, the welfare state is defined in the narrower sense as principally involved in transfers, entitlements to sick leave and maternity leave, social insurance payments and the labour taxes levied to finance them. The government as a regulator of work practices and the like can also have an effect, as can union bargaining in many countries. Although we take these aspects into account, they are not what we mean when we talk about the welfare state in the narrow sense.

According to our analysis on that basis, the welfare state is indeed mainly responsible for changes in the employment/population ratio: that is, in the number of people who work. However, only a third of Europe's labour input gap of 19 per cent comes from the fact that fewer people work. The rest reflects each employee putting in fewer hours, and for that, other factors bear more of the blame (Figure 2.5).

Fewer Europeans than Americans work, relative to the size of the population of working age. That gap consists of two parts of almost equal size: unemployment and labour force participation. Many argue that the welfare state does keep employment down if the relative rewards of work compared with drawing unemployment benefits or, say, early retirement payments are not high enough. In addition, the higher non-wage labour costs are, the more employers become reluctant to employ the low-skilled. Unemployment is higher in Europe than in the United States: 14 million Europeans are out of work (some 8 per cent of the labour force), compared with only 8 million Americans (5 per cent of the labour force). With American

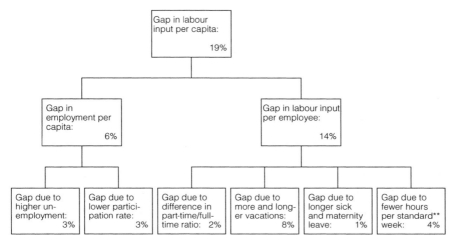

* Gap against US figures indexed to 100. Gaps at higher level of aggregation are calculated by multiplication (see footnote Figure 2.2).
** Hours effectively worked by a full-time employee in a standard working week, ie excluding weeks not or partly worked.
Sources: Groningen Total Economy Database; OECD Main Economic Indicators 2006 database; OECD Labour Force Statistics database; Eurostat data; Alesina, Glaeser and Sacerdote, 2005; IW Köln; own calculations.

Figure 2.5 Explaining Europe's labour input gap compared with the United States, 2004*

levels of unemployment, Europe could add some 5.3 million people to the payrolls, boosting labour input by 3 per cent.

Lower labour force participation also plays a role in the labour input gap. It accounts for the other half of the difference (some 3 per cent): discouraged workers, early retirees, mothers not finding a way to combine family life and a job, or people influenced by the effects of cultural differences, including a preference not to work.

How much of the total 6 per cent gap in employment comes from the supposed deleterious effects of the welfare state, including labour market regulation? An upper bound on the effect of the welfare state through this channel would probably attribute all additional unemployment to it. About half of the effect from lower labour force participation could be added to this, giving 4.5 per cent.

The correct figure is likely to be somewhat smaller, around 4 per cent. Unemployment is not just driven by the welfare state, even though it may play an important role. Replacement rates – the percentage of pay given to the unemployed – have broadly remained constant in most countries. Granted, the duration for which they can be drawn has tended to increase, but it seems that the generosity of Europe's welfare systems overall has grown more slowly than unemployment. (OECD, 2006a; Blanchard and Wolfers, 2000).

What is true is that Europe's system finds it harder to cope with shocks or increasing speed and depth of structural change than the United States' 'tough love' school of looking after the less fortunate. Once economic disturbances like the oil price shocks produce unemployment, it takes a long time to fall. This is clearly costly, but it is not a structural design flaw that can explain the whole gap. Higher rates of long-term unemployment may be the result of generous replacement rates, but the higher rates of transitory unemployment are less easy to attribute to it. In addition, some of the differences in the labour force participation rate are not driven by the welfare state, but by factors such as a lack of child care provision, cultural preferences and differences in the need to have a second income because of high property prices.

Our best guess therefore assumes that no more than two-thirds of the overall 6 per cent difference in employment ratios is the result of the welfare state. This would mean that the welfare state causes a reduction in output of possibly 4 per cent – not much compared with the 32 per cent income per capita gap. This is not intended to diminish the importance of the unemployment problem. Nevertheless, higher unemployment (and lower labour force participation) only explains a small part of the total gap in output. This argument is reinforced by the fact that, as we argued before, those outside the labour force and the unemployed are probably less productive than those in work.[3] This also reduces the welfare impact of the lower employment/population ratio. (For overall unemployment figures, see Figure 2.6.)

The biggest part of the labour input gap comes from fewer hours being worked per employee. This is influenced much less by the welfare state. Each employed European works markedly less than his or her American peer – 14 per cent less. This is responsible for two-thirds of the total labour input gap. Some of this is simply the result of more part-time employment. Europeans, when employed, are

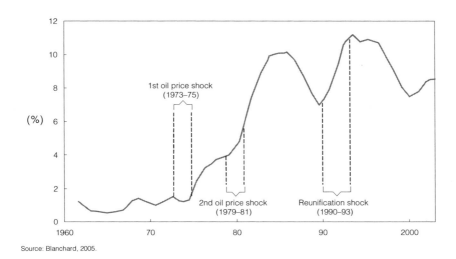

Source: Blanchard, 2005.

Figure 2.6 Unemployment rates in the EU-15, 1961–2003

more likely to take part-time jobs. This shaves about 2 percentage points off total labour input.[4] Those sceptical of the welfare state would attribute this to bigger tax wedges and the like, while other observers would see more part-time employment as the result of different preferences (such as the German penchant for women looking after their own small children, hence limiting their working hours). We therefore attribute a maximum score of 1.5 per cent to the welfare state (upper bound), which causes a commensurate reduction in income per capita. Our best guess estimate, however, actually attributes zero to the welfare state.

Also, Europeans on average work for fewer weeks in the year – about 42 instead of 46 weeks.[5] The welfare state is responsible for part of this. It reduces labour input by enforcing rules for sick leave and maternity leave which, on average, shave 0.7 of a working week more off in Europe than in the United States. A much bigger effect comes from vacations (and other time off). Germans, on average, have 39 public holiday and vacation days per year, Italians enjoy 39.5, and the French 35. Americans, on the other hand, are entitled to only 19.5. These differences cost Europeans approximately 8 per cent of the comparative labour input.

What is behind these numbers? European countries regulate the minimum vacations per year, while the United States does not. Yet most job contracts go far beyond the legal minimum, suggesting that long vacations are a bargaining result, and not driven by government fiat. It could be that high taxes alter the labour–leisure trade-off, in which case the welfare state plays a role. Nobel Laureate Ed Prescott argued that all of the decline in hours worked in Europe since 1970 (Figure 2.7) comes from higher taxes. For this to be true, workers would have to cut the hours they offer sharply when taxes rise. This, most academics have concluded, is not likely. Most estimates suggest that hours supplied do not respond very elastically (Alesina, Glaeser and Sacerdote, 2005).

Therefore, we believe that a genuine taste for leisure is responsible. Nor would this be unusual. As countries get richer, people work less. This has been the case since 1850. It implies that Europeans reduce their labour input by 9 per cent because of fewer working weeks, of which 1.4 can be attributed to the welfare state directly (as a best guess). This leaves 7.6 per cent for leisure preference and the effect of tax wedges. An upper bound would probably attribute half of the

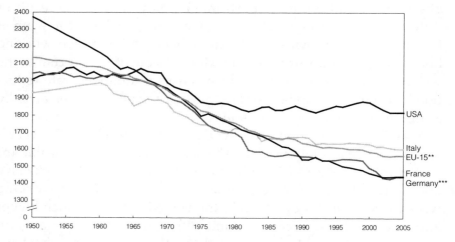

* Annual hours incl. paid overtime, excl. paid hours that are not worked due to sickness, vacation, and holidays.
** Employment weighted average, 1950–89: West Germany, 1990–2005 All Germany.
*** 1950–89: West Germany, 1990–2005 All Germany.
Source: Groningen Total Economy Database.

Figure 2.7   Annual hours worked per employed person, 1950–2005*

difference in weeks of vacation between the United States and Europe to the welfare state's indirect effects, on top of the effects of maternity and sick leave. This would imply that welfare cannot be responsible for more than 3.8 per cent of the reduction of labour input through fewer weeks of work (upper bound).

Labour input in Europe is further reduced by the full-time employee's shorter standard working week. In the United States, the negotiated hours per week still stand at 39. Some European countries have gone for 35-hour weeks, producing an average on the old continent of 37. In addition, factors such as overtime or special work-break agreements influence the hours effectively worked by a full-time employee in a standard working week. The difference in these between Europe and the United States is a bit smaller. Labour input is about 4 to 5 per cent lower in Europe compared with the United States because of all of these factors. Reductions in hours mostly arise from workplace bargaining. We assign 50 per cent of the difference to the disincentive effects of higher taxes; this would add an impact of 1.8 per cent at best guess. The maximum impact of welfare state and labour market regulation is thus no more than 3.6 per cent.

The imputed negative effects of the welfare state end here. Labour productivity is probably, on average, neither increased nor reduced by the welfare state. Since it forces the least productive out of work, measured productivity will go up when this effect starts to bite. The state as a regulator can seriously hinder productivity, for example by enforcing outdated labour regulations or by giving more bargaining power to unions that insist on job protection and the like. Slower structural change is partly a result of labour market regulations lowering productivity. On average, we assume that these factors cancel out. The MGI sectoral studies regularly show that other factors, especially product market regulations such as ease of entry, competitive intensity and the like, are much more important determinants of productivity.

The total tally for the effects of the welfare state on labour input and income per capita is summarized in Table 2.1.

This means that, under the most likely scenario, labour input is some 7.1 per cent lower as a result of the welfare state including labour market regulations. This pales by comparison with the gap in

Table 2.1 Reduction of labour input through the welfare state and the labour market

Reduction due to:	Best guess %	Upper bound %
Welfare state		
Longer sick and maternity leave	–1.4	–1.4
More and longer vacations		–3.8
Less employment per capita	–4.0	–4.5
More part-time work		–1.5
Labour market		
Fewer hours per week	–1.8	–3.6
Total impact on labour input*	**–7.1**	**–14.0**
Share of total output gap	**22%**	**44%**

* Total impact is calculated by multiplication (see footnote Figure 2.2).

Sources: Groningen Total Economy Database; OECD Main Economic Indicators 2006; OECD Labour Force Statistics; Eurostat; Alesina, Glaeser and Sacerdote, 2005; IW Köln; own calculations.

labour productivity, which stands at a staggering 16 per cent. Even the upper bound, calculated under strong assumptions, is smaller than the productivity gap. Europeans pay for their welfare state in the form of lower per capita income – but the negative impact of the welfare state is much smaller than might be expected.

THE MYTH OF THE GENEROUS WELFARE STATE

Europeans care a great deal about social justice. In general, they value redistribution of wealth and the lowering of income differentials. They also see it as a key function of their governments to protect them from a large number of risks.

At irregular intervals, the International Social Survey Programme asks several thousand interviewees about their perception of actual inequality and their personal preferences, that is, how large they feel the differences in income should be. It concludes that the majority of interviewees worldwide would like to see more equality. Furthermore, as a rule, democracies achieve a higher degree of redistribution. Almost everywhere in Europe, people believe that greater redistribution in favour of the disadvantaged is crucial.[6]

There is also some evidence that equality makes people happier. A Harvard study examined cross-country differences in general life satisfaction, and found that in European countries in particular, greater income differences are associated with growing life dissatisfaction (Alesina, DiTella and McCulloch, 2003). Americans, in contrast, seem to care less about income differences. Differences are particularly pronounced on the left of the political spectrum and among the poor. These segments report themselves less happy in Europe when inequality is high, while results for comparable groups in the United States do not seem to change much under the same circumstances. Continental Europeans regularly tend to respond in surveys that they would prefer more generous benefits (for, say, the unemployed), in contrast to Americans and the British. European welfare states could only become as big as they have because they basically deliver what people want – and because politicians have been able to win elections by promising ever larger benefits.

And big they have become. Most of life's risks – from unemployment to health care, from old-age poverty to widowhood and invalidity – are covered by government programmes in most European countries. Provisions often go far beyond basic living standards. In most continental European countries, state pensions dominate old-age income, and virtually everywhere health care is mainly the preserve of government. The 20th century saw a rapid rise of the state's role as the 'insurer of last resort'. In the wake of every economic, natural or political disaster, more responsibilities were shifted onto governments.

That said, how does the European social welfare state actually perform? What is the right yardstick to measure its performance? The prevailing opinion says that in Europe the poor are better off, which means those with average and higher incomes have to live with a considerable tax burden. Economic output may suffer somewhat, but the consensus is that protecting the weakest is principally a question of distribution. What is more, the social process continually produces new burdens – from higher pay raises for lower-paid groups in every round of wage negotiations to changes in the contribution thresholds for those earning better incomes and tax breaks for those at the bottom end of the income distribution. We will examine here whether these assumptions are actually true.

Relative poverty

One way to approach the issue is to look at relative poverty: the percentage of citizens who live below a specific 'poverty line', usually half the median income. Unsurprisingly, European welfare states do a good job in preventing this kind of poverty. By taking from the (relatively) rich to give to the poor, they reduce relative poverty rates markedly. Europeans cut poverty rates by two-thirds through their benefit systems. The United States manages only a reduction by a quarter, and ends up with the highest poverty rates in our sample of rich countries.

The European welfare system also meets its own objectives with respect to pensioners – at least up to now. Fewer than one in eight European retirees is obliged to manage on less than half the average income. In the United States, on the other hand, one in five is left with less than half the average worker's income after a longer working life.

Some member states have made considerable strides in the fight against poverty in recent years. OECD figures show that between the mid-1980s and today, Ireland, Spain and Sweden cut poverty rates by between 55 and 83 per cent (Förster, 2005). Social progress in this dimension has been more than twice as fast in Europe as in the United States.

Spending is high, and reductions in relative poverty are substantial. Is the performance of European welfare states what we should expect, or is the very large reduction bought at the cost of increasingly diminishing returns? Europeans use 18 per cent of their GDP for non-health social spending, and get a reduction in average poverty of 16 per cent in return. The United States spends 9 per cent and receives a reduction of 6 per cent in return. Per unit of GDP devoted to transfers, Europe actually gets a bigger poverty reduction than the United States – despite having fewer 'easy wins' than the States. One of the reasons why the European welfare state hasn't sunk the boat yet is that it is relatively efficient. It can do better, as we will discuss in our recommendations, but it is far from a poor tool.

There is another aspect that appears to demonstrate the advantages of the European system. Poverty is particularly tragic when it is not just a transitory phase but instead becomes permanent. In the United States, nearly one in every three people living in (relative) poverty is stuck in that position. Even six years after becoming impoverished, they are still unable to earn more than half the median income. In Germany, this is only true of 17 per cent of the poor, in Sweden of 14 per cent and in the Netherlands of 13 per cent. Because of the lower overall prevalence of relative poverty, this means that in Europe only 1 per cent of citizens are permanently poor, whereas in the United States the figure is 5 per cent. This flies directly in the face of prevalent myths about the United States and European systems. Many observers assume that the US system ensures greater mobility: those who are poor do not remain so for long in a dynamic economy where the incentives to work are strong. The statistics speak a very different language. In terms of mobility out of relative poverty, Europe is both fairer and more dynamic than the United States.

Absolute poverty

However, the evidence in Figure 2.8 on relative poverty may be too sanguine. How do the poorest on each continent compare in terms of absolute available income? In his 1971 book *A Theory of Justice*, Harvard philosopher John Rawls argued that we should compare welfare in different countries by looking at how the poorest segment of the population is treated. The argument is that, if we had to choose where to live (behind a 'veil of ignorance', not knowing whether we would be rich or poor), we would choose the society where being at the bottom of the heap is not too painful. His theory is hotly debated. However, we do not need to subscribe to all of the implications to examine the absolute level of income at the bottom end of distribution. How well off are Europe's poor in reality?

Based on Rawls's simple criterion, Europe overall does a lot less well than the relative poverty rates suggest. In purchasing-power-adjusted terms, the US poor – the lowest 5 per cent[7] – are about 5 per

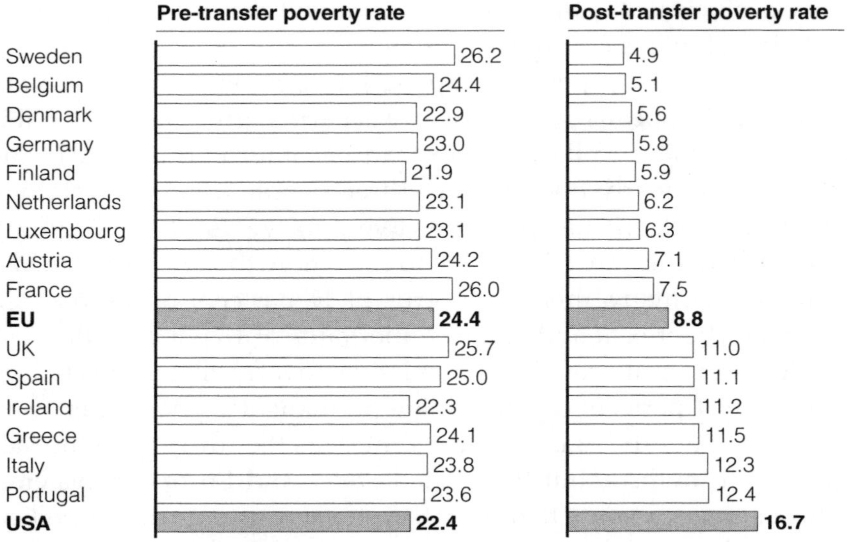

	Pre-transfer poverty rate	Post-transfer poverty rate
Sweden	26.2	4.9
Belgium	24.4	5.1
Denmark	22.9	5.6
Germany	23.0	5.8
Finland	21.9	5.9
Netherlands	23.1	6.2
Luxembourg	23.1	6.3
Austria	24.2	7.1
France	26.0	7.5
EU	**24.4**	**8.8**
UK	25.7	11.0
Spain	25.0	11.1
Ireland	22.3	11.2
Greece	24.1	11.5
Italy	23.8	12.3
Portugal	23.6	12.4
USA	**22.4**	**16.7**

Source: Collado and Iturbe-Ormaetxe, 2005.

Figure 2.8 Relative poverty in Europe and the United States, 2000 (%)

cent better off than their European peers. Only a few of the richer European states (the Scandinavian countries, Germany, Italy, France and the Netherlands) manage to give their poorest citizens incomes that are about one quarter higher than the United States. The bottom 10 per cent[8] are about 10 per cent worse off in Europe. Here, Germany and Denmark manage to offer substantially more than the United States, but most European countries do not. Even in the most generous and richest of European welfare states, incomes in the 20th percentile from the bottom of the distribution are only about equal to the US level. There are some additional factors not captured in Figure 2.9. European countries make public services available to the poor that their counterparts in the United States lack – quality education, easy and safe public transport, and decent universal health care. Yet it is clear that even the most generous welfare states in the richest economies of Europe do not manage to put markedly more money into the pockets of their poor.

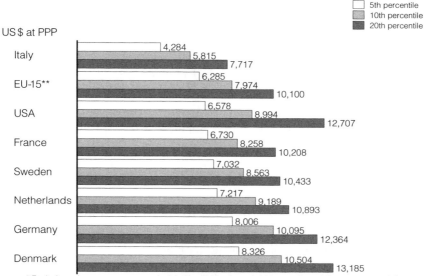

Figure 2.9   Equivalence income per person after cash social transfers, 2000*

How socially oriented is Europe?

When it comes to relative poverty, Europe's welfare state delivers the goods. Poverty is reduced massively and effectively. Yet it is generating disappointing results in absolute terms. On average, not even the poorest 5 per cent are as well off as in the United States. This is even more surprising upon further reflection. Europe spends about US $3,730 per head of population on non-health social transfers. The United States spends US $2,647, about one-third less. Despite its much lower per capita GDP, the EU commitment to social justice is so strong that transfers per head of population are higher in absolute terms. And given how much is spent, it is disappointing that the poor are still as poor as they are. Obviously, the welfare state can become much more efficient at channelling expenditure to the purposes that ought to be highest on the list. We present recommendations for this in Chapter 8.

Observers who believe that the welfare state is the main or even sole root of Europe's problems are nearly as mistaken as those who believe that globalization must inevitably undermine European living standards. Europe clearly needs to shape up for two reasons: its future demographics and global challenges. While the former have almost no redeeming features, the latter area contains as many positives as negatives. We first turn to the challenges and opportunities of international trade in goods, services and capital.

THE MYTH OF GLOBALIZATION DANGERS

Who is afraid of globalization? According to recent European newspaper reporting and televised economic affairs programmes, the answer is – everyone. If Chinese workers toil for a week for less than a European earns in a day, how can European companies producing in the old continent compete? Will the relocation of production go on for ever? Will the fall in the number of jobs ever come to an end under these circumstances?

Initially, only manufacturing and blue-collar workers were affected by globalization. Today the Third World is beginning to compete in services too. From call centres in India to sophisticated design work by Russian engineers, there is now a global system of service outsourcing. This kind of 'offshoring' has brought home the reality of worldwide competition to white-collar workers as well.

However, we believe that globalization in all dimensions is only a threat to a sleeping Europe. For a dynamic one, it will be a unique opportunity. The more aggressively Europe seizes it, the better it will do. There is not even a danger from 'social dumping' to a reformed, but still European-style welfare state, which will make it easier to cope with globalization and become a true source of competitive advantage.

What is new in trade?

Trade between different peoples is older than the Bible. Why it is economically beneficial has often been explained. If countries specialize in those areas where they are relatively better, and leave the rest to others, everyone gains. Comparative advantage is as often invoked as it is misunderstood. You do not need to be the world's most productive provider of data-inputting services to benefit from specializing in this area – what matters is whether you are better at it than anything else you might be doing.

Take the example of a couple, as used by former Stanford economist John Taylor. Imagine that Jack is terrible at doing everything: working for money, doing the housework. It's not that he can't cook a nice goose, but it takes him forever. He is married to Jane, who is great and fast at everything she touches: she has a great job as a lawyer, and she is the best cook you will find. What should they do? Clearly, Jane is better at everything, but it would not be efficient for her to do everything. Her income as a lawyer might suffer if she spends too much time doing the dishes. If they split all work down the middle, Jack will earn a few miserable bucks stacking shelves in a supermarket, and Jane will cook some great meals very quickly. However, this is not the best they can do. If Jack can get all the housework done, he will free Jane to do best in her career as a lawyer. This is the division of labour in operation. Their household income will be much higher, and the housework will still get done. While not all couples will want to approach the issue in purely economic terms, the economic logic is compelling. Each partner should do what he or she is better at in relative terms. Jane is a terrific lawyer, and only great as a housekeeper. Jack is terrible as a 'home maker', but slightly less terrible than as a worker.

Countries benefit hugely from following this logic: produce what you are best at, and import the rest. That is what trade has always been based on. The entry of large, poor countries like China and India has often been portrayed as a radical discontinuity, but it is not. There is nothing about trade that requires countries to be at similar levels of economic development. Europe will continue to do well at producing machine tools, luxury cars, haute couture and top-flight financial advice, as well as more and more badly needed services. It should not weep over the loss of jobs in textile manufacturing and steel production. It is perfectly true that Europe has a number of industries that will find it hard to compete head on with, say, cheap

Chinese manufacturers. That they will go out of business is, however, not a problem in longer-term European economics overall, although we do not underestimate the suffering of those living, for example, in areas whose prosperity is closely linked to the 'migrating' industries.

Structural change has been synonymous with economic growth for the last two centuries at least. Few people wept about the loss of jobs among carriage makers once car manufacturing took off, and people understood that such dynamics ultimately produced more and better job opportunities. Why regret the decline of the domestic charcoal industries, which cut down large forests all over Europe from the Middle Ages onwards, once cheap oil could be imported and provide more people with jobs and purchasing power? In overall economic terms, what German textile manufacturers have lost is more than made up for by the exports of German printing-press producers and automotive manufacturers.

Europe is doing surprisingly well in the global game of selling to China. China's success on world markets is in turn fuelling a surge of exports from Europe. In 2004, the European Union sold goods worth €48 billion to China. The United States managed a mere €34 billion. The European Union has more than doubled its exports in the last five years alone. Germany in particular, with its specialization in machine tools and other intermediate inputs, has done spectacularly well. Europe as a whole is well positioned to reap even greater rewards in the future. As China, India and other countries around the globe industrialize and become richer, European goods will be in high demand. Luxury goods in particular are a European speciality, and will see a gigantic surge in demand once a wealthy middle class emerges in these developing countries.

Europe still runs an overall trade deficit with China, as it does with other countries such as Russia, Japan, Norway, Korea and Taiwan (Figure 2.10). Some observers regard this as a sign that globalization is causing a giant 'sucking sound' across the border (in the words of former US presidential candidate Ross Perot), with jobs disappearing overall. A closer look shows that EU trade with the rest of the world is almost exactly balanced – the aggregate trade deficit is less than 1 per cent of GDP. EU deficits with the Far East are compensated for by big surpluses with the United States. If the United States ever closes

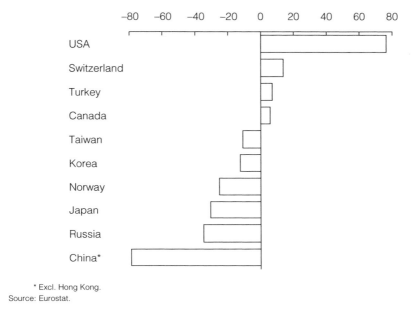

* Excl. Hong Kong.
Source: Eurostat.

Figure 2.10 Trade balance of the EU-25 with the rest of the world, 2004 (€ billion)

its trade gap, Europe may start to have a problem. It would do well to produce goods that appeal to Asian consumers and firms, as we argue in Chapter 7.

Even on a narrow 'mercantilist' measure, trade is not a problem for the European Union, but a source of strength. To put it another way, if the European Union was really losing 'competitiveness', it would not run a minuscule trade deficit. That almost no net demand is 'lost' to the rest of the world is comforting. What about the often-claimed gains in productivity from international trading? It is tricky to pin them down in the data. Rich countries on average trade much more than poor ones. This need not prove much. Countries that become richer trade more: they buy more from abroad, and being rich probably means they produce something special and valuable to sell. Whether the connection was actually causal long remained largely a question of belief. However, many have been convinced partly by the fact that there is one channel through which countries trade more without being necessarily richer – geography. Economies trade overwhelmingly with partners that are nearby. This is not related to being rich, except that it produces additional trade. The effect is pretty large. For every 1 percentage point extra in the ratio of trade to GDP, productivity increases by between 0.5 and 1.5 per cent (Frankel and Romer, 1999). This means that for Europe to achieve any of its ambitious aims, it must embrace deeper integration into the global economy.

The benefits, of course, don't stop with higher productivity. What is the value of variety? Picturing the contrast between drab supermarket shelves in the former Eastern Bloc and those of the West makes us realize just how much we appreciate having a wide range of choices. Many goods cannot be produced domestically, either because market size is insufficient, or because climatic conditions are inappropriate. Even large blocks like the European Union and the United States benefit from trade in such commodities. Calculations for the United States suggest that trade leads to greater variety, which consumers value a great deal. They buy 16,390 kinds of goods from abroad, according to Columbia University economists. The expanding range of these products produces a value that is equivalent to lowering prices by 1.2 per cent per annum. For the period 1972–2001, the gains for US consumers via this channel alone were equivalent to an across-the-board price cut of 28 per cent (Broda and Weinstein, 2004). This means that real GDP, if it were properly measured, grew by almost a third simply because the United States imported goods and varieties from the rest of the world. Almost half the gains in living standards during the period can be attributed to this channel alone. A world of countries exporting and importing is just richer – in terms of both size and variety.

If trade in goods is nothing to worry about, what about the recent trends in offshoring? Since this is the source of much recent anxiety, it merits a closer look.

Offshoring

A recent survey showed that 40 per cent of Western Europe's 500 largest companies have already begun moving their service operations to low-wage countries (Aggarwal, 2004). What actually happens when firms move their call centres and IT support abroad in this way?

Research by MGI reveals that even when white-collar jobs are affected, net gains outweigh the losses. This is particularly true for the United States, but it is also, broadly speaking, correct for Europe. There are two effects: direct consequences for the workers and firms involved, and the general impact on the economy as a whole. We shall first look at the direct effect. Even here, the vast majority of gains are captured by the countries that outsource. The balance becomes even more positive when we consider the picture as a whole, as shown in Figure 2.11.

The direct effects look better for the United States than for, say, Germany. The United States claws back US $1.12–1.14 directly for every dollar of cost moved abroad. Its firms save money. Its suppliers sell IT products to the call centres and other service providers, and profits from the subsidiaries doing the work are repatriated to the United States. Crucially, that country is good at redeploying labour.

US $

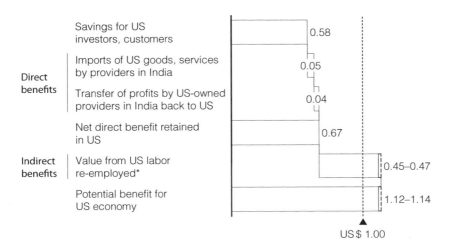

* Estimate based on historical re-employment and wage levels.
Source: McKinsey Global Institute, 2003.

Figure 2.11 Value potential to the United States from US $1 offshored to India, 2002

For each dollar of spending moved overseas, the United States gains 45–47 cents through the value of re-employed workers.

Comparable figures for the whole European Union are not available, only for a few countries. However, it is highly likely that outsourcing can be favourable here as well. Much outsourcing goes to Eastern Europe, not India. This ensures that the new value added is created in the European Union. Also, European countries export heavily. On average, they have trade-to-GDP ratios that are at least twice as high as those of the United States, and many items are capital goods. This ensures that as labour is moved abroad, firms in the European Union get orders to equip the new labs, factories and call centres. Finally, Europe is also good at exporting consumer goods that will be in higher demand in the countries doing the outsourcing work . As their own workers get richer, they will start to demand the cars, watches, scarves and wines that Europe excels in making. Europe also re-employs much of the labour released through offshoring. According to the OECD, its re-employment rates are about 20 per cent lower than US ones, but the wages of those who do find work are higher than before. In the United States, they are often lower (OECD, 2005a). This suggests that Europe may gain a little less from re-employed labour, but should gain more from the location of outsourcing firms, from consumer spending and equipment investment. In both the United States and the European Union, there is little reason to think that per dollar moved abroad, people at home are impoverished. This is only the case when a country has nothing to export or if there are massive obstacles in the way of the redeployment of labour.

Why welfare states and globalization can go hand in hand

How can countries whose social security systems add 40–50 per cent in costs to already sky-high wages compete globally, particularly against competitors with minimal labour protection, low wages and rapidly improving infrastructure and education levels? Everybody knows the importance of unit labour costs: the cost of wages and other labour-related expenses relative to productivity. Here, Europe is nowhere near as far behind as journalists and the general public often fear.

One largely unknown fact is that countries that are highly integrated into the global economy also have bigger welfare states. Many of the world's most open economies are in Europe: the Netherlands, Sweden, Germany, Finland. Their trading volumes have grown much faster than output, while their welfare states did the same.

Economists are only just waking up to the remarkable resilience of big welfare states at a time of massive globalization. Why has the simple logic of a 'race to the bottom' (in other words 'social dumping') simply not – or not yet – taken effect?

Social spending and openness

Two factors are probably involved: social insurance and the 'taxing' of foreigners. As commentators always remind us, globalization produces net gains. Winners gain enough to compensate the losers. Microsoft's labour force earns enough from obtaining patent protection as part of a trade package to compensate for unemployed textile workers in Southern Carolina. Nevertheless, the theoretical possibility is not enough to elicit widespread support. For the potential losers to accept more trade, they must have some assurances that they will actually be compensated. Countries with large welfare states could be good at this, by definition. Here, workers faced with misfortune know that they will not fall through the cracks. In the United States, on the other hand, they will lobby for steel tariffs, for anti-dumping duties, non-tariff barriers and the like. Europe is effectively making it easier to shoulder the social dislocation that comes from globalization by using its supposedly generous welfare system as a shock absorber as long as it leads to change and does not perpetuate unemployment. Incentives to take new jobs, and not remain in the welfare safety net, should be put in place.

The second mechanism is more subtle. By taxing country-specific inputs to production, such as labour, governments add to the price of end products. If these are sold abroad, foreigners end up paying some of the tax bill. The harder it is to find ready substitutes for a country's products, the stronger this effect will be. In other words,

Europeans earn their welfare state by producing novel goods that the rest of the world is keen to have. Customers buying Volkswagens anywhere in the world are in part paying for the high labour contributions levied by the German state. There are clearly limits to this process. Even if these cars are unique, consumers will switch eventually to another brand if prices become too high. There are those who argue that Volkswagen has reached that point.

The more countries export their products, and the more unique they are, the easier it becomes to raise taxes and make foreigners pay for some domestically provided government services, especially social services. Europeans with their high taxes on labour and large trade share are benefiting from the highly differentiated types of products churned out by their industry. There is no reason that this process should go into reverse in the future, as long as Europe's products are distinctive and come with plenty of pricing power. Our proposals about category definition in Chapter 7 aim to exploit this mechanism yet further.

Important reforms are needed to prevent the burden of Europe's welfare state from becoming too large, as the ageing population demands more support and poor incentives mean that some younger and potentially abler people are discouraged from working. Yet globalization is not necessarily a factor in its troubles: normally, increased trade has spelt prosperity. So has a shift in industry structures, nationally and globally. It leads overall to a corresponding shift in the need for labour rather than the destruction of jobs.

Why a low-wage-sector strategy is not promising

The bogeyman of cheap competition from abroad regularly leads to calls for wage restraint. There are those who argue that in a global world there is no way for the market to give low-skilled workers decent wages. The government should instead step in and structure a special 'low-wage sector' where those with fewer skills can eke out a living, aided by transfers.

While we do not advocate higher wages, however, a race to the bottom in terms of unskilled wages does not seem to us to be necessary either. Highly productive export sectors tend to set wage rates in a country, and the better Europe plays the globalization game, the higher wages will be. The relatively less skilled can still be employed, and at similarly decent wages, as long as labour markets work reasonably well.

Do plumbers working in Stuttgart do anything differently from the ones in Shanghai? The differences are probably less than the gap in wages. A few yuan suffice in China to keep a dexterous man in good shape; his Stuttgart colleague would starve on a similar rate of pay. Higher productivity and wages in Germany pull up everybody's pay, including that of the less skilled. In much of the non-traded sector, producing everything from security services to education, functioning plumbing, entertainment, hotels, restaurants, domestic services, hairdressing and psychological advice, there is no competition from abroad. If the export sector is sufficiently buoyant, demand will be high enough to produce plenty of jobs in these service sectors. All of them are labour intensive. Wage rates will benefit from the value creation in these sectors in line with productivity in export industries. This will provide decent jobs for many who will not be able to work in the most advanced sectors. For this 'Porsche and plumbing' strategy to work, immigration must be prevented from driving wage rates for the unskilled (domestic and newly immigrated) to unacceptably low levels. It also requires that some of the disincentives to finding work – by paying relatively high absolute amounts to families on welfare, for example – are dismantled. Negative income taxes helping those who work but do not earn enough for a decent living could play an important role in this. The community should pay people for work, not for not working.

On balance, globalization will make it easier to preserve European living standards. The same cannot be said of the coming demographic challenge, which is the single biggest reason that Europe urgently needs to reconsider the way it operates.

EUROPE'S TICKING TIME BOMB

The yawning productivity gap – not globalization or the welfare state – is the key problem facing Europe today. The problem is all the more acute because the future will bring a radically new challenge: population ageing. For any given level of productivity, Europeans will live less well. Because of this, if nothing changes, Europe is going to grow old and poor. The demographic shifts facing the member states of the European Union over the next 30 years are going to give new meaning to the term 'old continent'. These changes have now become virtually unstoppable, and even massive immigration could only alleviate the effects.

Few people would dispute that rising life expectancy is in itself a good thing. The economic problem arises from the expanding proportion of senior citizens relative to the next generation, or from the years after retirement relative to the years before retirement in each individual's lifetime. The specific design of most European social security systems exacerbates the situation. In continental Europe, government-run pay-as-you-go systems generate much of pensioners' incomes. In the future, they will have to take ever more away from ever fewer contributors – employees and their employers – and give ever less to pensioners.

This is because Europeans seem to have largely stopped having children. In every country in Europe, birth rates have fallen below replacement levels. At the same time, a high standard of living and medical progress have increased life expectancies. Consequently, a smaller and smaller number of people between the ages of 15 and 64 will have to feed an unusually large number of older people. By 2030, in Germany and Italy, there will only be two people of working age for each pensioner. In Sweden, the Netherlands, France and Belgium, the ratios will not be much better (Figure 2.12). The average European population over 65 as a percentage of the overall population will rise from 15.8 per cent in 2005 to 28.8 per cent in 2050.

The demographic imbalance will cause particular problems. Europeans focus obsessively on inequalities between rich and poor, but often think little of treating individual cohorts very differently. To highlight the disparity in the distribution of the burden, economists have developed 'generational accounts'. These show the value of taxes minus transfer payments that individuals of different generations will pay or receive on average over their remaining lifetimes under the assumption that the current rules do not change. The

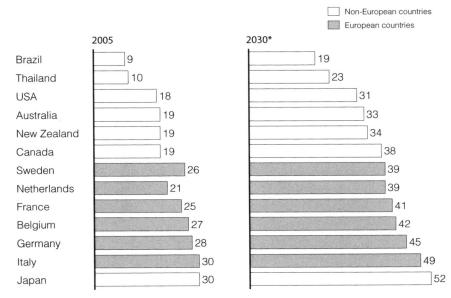

* Data for EU-25; under the following assumptions: average birth, normal mortality, and normal migration rates.
Source: UN World Population Prospects.

Figure 2.12 Population over 65 as a percentage of the population between 15 and 64 years of age

sustainability of the system is reflected in the amount the new-borns have to pay – and in a comparison between this and any birth year further back. Figure 2.13 illustrates this for the United States and Germany in 1995.

Best placed are those who were 65 years old. In Germany they could assume that they would draw over US $200,000 more (adjusted for price increases) than they would have to contribute. By comparison, those who were 20 years old were at a severe disadvantage: they would, all else being equal, each pay US $300,000 more than they would receive. The imbalance is similar in the United States, although the disparities are significantly smaller. Social security also works as a pay-as-you-go system there, but is smaller in relative terms, and it also built up a reserve for the coming demographic transition. The net profit for a 70-year-old pensioner in the United States is somewhat over US $100,000, while 20-year-olds will have to write off approximately US $170,000.

US $ thousands

Net amount received

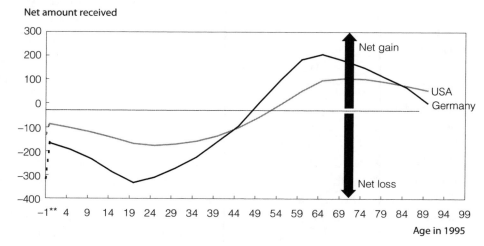

* Expected transfer payments minus taxes.
** −1 summarizes the payments and claims of all future generations.
Source: Kotlikoff and Leibfritz, 1999.

Figure 2.13   Net future payments per capita by respective generation,* 1995

Although these figures are quite impressive, they themselves do not allow any conclusion to be drawn about the sustainability of the pension system. It is self-evident that in a system which transfers money to the very young – children, students – and to the old, those who are just starting to work have to face the biggest net payments, and those who are retired will have the biggest net gains.

The size of the disparities (and, as many would argue, the level of injustice) may be seen from the net amounts payable by the generation born in the base year 1995. In the United States, they will have to pay on average US $86,300 over their whole life; in Germany, this figure is almost twice as high: US $165,000. If we look at the future development by summarizing the net gains and losses of all people born in the years after 1995, assuming there is no change in the legal framework, the challenge becomes palpable. In the United States, they will have to pay US $130,000; in Germany, the figure is over US $310,000 per person.

To finance such transfers in Germany, the rates of social security contributions for pensions alone would have to jump to over 40 per cent of income by 2030; taxes and other social security contributions would come on top. Alternatively, if contribution rates were frozen at today's level, pensions paid out would drop from 70 to 40 per cent of average income.

There is no simple, universally applicable and easily acceptable solution. Longer working lives or higher immigration, taken together, would help to solve the problem, but they both have disadvantages. Either they cannot generate enough money (numbers employed) or they produce social and cultural problems (immigration), or they just cut benefits (extending working lives), and in addition they are all tough to implement.

Lasting improvements can really be achieved only by three approaches that are far removed from tinkering with the existing system: first, introducing a stronger funded component into the system that provides pensions, health care and long-term nursing care in old age; second, faster growth in productivity; and third, an increase in employment.

A larger funded component can help because many entitlements for people retiring in 2030 and beyond are still accumulating today. If people currently in the labour force could be compelled or encouraged to invest an additional portion of their income in the capital markets to fund part of their retirement expenses, they could retire with substantial reserves. This would in turn lower the burden on the small cohorts working after 2030.

The Mannheim-based economist Axel Börsch-Supan has calculated that a gradual switch in Germany from the pay-as-you-go approach to a funded pension system would initially lead to a cost increase of approximately 15 to 25 per cent over the current contribution level (to around 22–25 per cent of earnings). But this would allow pensions to remain constant until 2040, while contributions would remain stable at their new, higher rate, as well. For the United States, economists Martin Feldstein and Andrew Samwick conducted a similar analysis. They calculated that increasing the Social Security tax, currently at 12 per cent, to a rate of 15 per cent could actually bring about a reduction in contributions in 2040, with pensions remaining at the same level

(Gruber and Wise, 2001). Even if the capital market returns used in these calculations are a little too optimistic, savings can help defuse the demographic time bomb.

Higher productivity growth can also help to stave off the looming choice between slashing payments to pensioners, increasing contributions from workers or both. For this to work, one of the key elements of state pension systems will need to be modified: the link between pensions and the real pay of current workers needs to be weakened. This link is alien to a funded system, under which interest-bearing investments are made to provide income in old age, and pensioners share in economic progress only to the extent to which their savings generate earnings. In the redistribution systems of continental Europe, however, pensions increase mainly as a result of productivity gains by current workers.

A model calculation for Germany demonstrates some of the effects. If pensions and pension age limits in Germany were to remain unchanged despite the ageing of the population as a whole, contributions towards state pensions would have to rise from today's rate of just below 20 per cent to approximately 44 per cent in 2030. In our model calculation, we consider the increase only in the resulting pension contributions and calculate a net income 'after pension contribution'. Taxes and other deductions will naturally still have to be paid as well, but because they will not be changed significantly by the ageing of the population, they are ignored in this model.[9]

Without productivity growth, the increase in pension contributions would reduce net incomes to 70 per cent of their 2003 level – a drop of almost 30 per cent and a hardship that is difficult to imagine (see Table 2.2). With productivity growth at a rate of only 1 per cent a year over this period, the increase in pension contributions would be largely offset, leaving workers in 2030 with just under 94 per cent of the net income in 2003 – nearly the same amount. Boosting the average productivity growth rate to more than 1.2 per cent a year would completely prevent a reduction in the absolute income level (after pension contributions). Achieving an average productivity growth rate of 2 per cent a year would be sufficient to boost the economic output of each working person by 70 per cent by 2030. Even if pensioners participated fully in this increase in economic

Table 2.2 Scenarios for pension levels in 2030

	Productivity growth per year		
	0%	1%	2%
2030			
Income (gross)*	1.00	1.35	1.81
Pension contribution rate	0.44	0.60	0.80
Income (net)	0.56	0.75	1.01
2003			
Income (net)**	0.80	0.80	0.80
Change in net income vs 2003	**−30%**	**−6%**	**+26%**

Index: 1	= gross income 2003
*	Includes employer-paid share
**	1.0 gross minus 0.2 pension contribution rate

Source: Own calculations.

output by receiving higher pensions, the productivity gain would still be large enough to put 26 per cent more into workers' pockets (Table 2.2). This would be equivalent to an annual increase in net incomes of 0.9 per cent, although this is a far cry from the fat years after 1950, when incomes rose by 2 to 3 per cent a year. Only productivity growth can prevent the unenviable trade-off between falling incomes for pensioners or smaller take-home pay for workers.

Managed properly, more rapid productivity growth has the power to cushion much of the blow that will come from higher dependency rates. If an ageing Europe manages to grow faster, using the same amount of resources, it will be able to deal with the heavy burden of an ageing population.

PRODUCTIVITY GROWTH: THE MOST IMPORTANT WAY OUT

Many Europeans today believe that their welfare state is producing massive distortions and is costing them a great deal in terms of economic efficiency, that globalization is about to threaten their standard of living, and that growth rates in the last 10 years compared with the United States have been disappointing. A root-and-branch set of reforms, they feel, is necessary to stem the decline in 'competitiveness'.

Our analysis puts the emphasis elsewhere. The challenge may be every bit as large as Eurosceptics believe, but for very different reasons. Europe grew only a touch more slowly in the last 10 years than the United States. The welfare state is not so much of a problem to overall economic performance as is often asserted, and globalization can even be good news. If all of this is true, why change?

The simple answer is that Europe's gap in terms of absolute output is still shockingly large. A mistaken focus on labour productivity, combined with the problems in the national income statistics, distorts perceptions of Europe's true performance. If we take capital and labour together and eliminate the biggest distortions in the figures, Europe has an overall output gap of 32 per cent and a productivity gap of 16 per cent compared with the United States. Given how far behind the old continent is, it should be growing much faster than the US economy – and it is not. Productivity improvement is a matter of urgency because of two fundamental problems.

First, Europe's welfare systems do not put as much money in the pockets of the poor as Europeans would like. Despite massive transfers, not enough help ends up in the right hands. While reductions in relative poverty look pretty good, absolute incomes at the bottom end of the distribution are no better than in the United States, despite higher per capita spending. This is not a proud achievement. Europe will have to rethink how it manages the job of the welfare state: improving the lot of the poor. Second, without drastic countermeasures, demographic changes over the next decade are going to thrust many people into poverty.

Europe is poorer than the United States. Lower productivity is the more important cause. Labour productivity lags, but capital productivity is also far behind. Lower labour input is another component of the equation, but it is conceptually ambiguous, as the sections on the welfare state showed. Europe does not make itself poor mainly as a consequence of its welfare state, as conventional wisdom claims. It is above all poorer because it is not using its resources as intelligently and sparingly as it should. The largest part of the output gap – and the one that matters for welfare – is driven by poor productivity. Given that Europe is about to face a historically unique challenge, it is high time that it addresses this issue.

All in all, productivity growth in Europe needs to accelerate significantly. Without a higher per capita economic output, the rapid ageing of Europe's population threatens to reduce either pensioners or workers to poverty. This sums up and explains the goal. If we are to get beyond wishful thinking, Europe needs to find a strategy for faster productivity growth and higher employment.

Comparisons between Europe and the United States, in which the latter appears as the winner in numerous ways, often seem to imply that the solution to Europe's problems lies in simply copying the US approach. However, this route is neither feasible nor desirable. In the next chapter, we will consider what Europe can learn from the United States – and what it should ignore in order to keep the values that constitute its identity.

3

Why the US model is not suited to Europe – and what we can learn anyway

Many observers feel that the US economic model is vastly superior to the European one. It has market forces instead of state intervention, bond and equity markets instead of bank loans, and flexible labour markets with low unemployment instead of rigid rules that produce millions of unemployed. Venture capital finances innovative start-ups. Thanks to the United States' leadership in high tech, most of the rising sectors in the world economy are US dominated. This leadership is maintained because of world-class universities, generous industry R&D funding and helpful government support. In short, it is perceived as a country where risk-takers are encouraged, knowledge is diffused rapidly, individuals bear the consequences of success or failure, and economic dynamism emerges naturally and in abundance.

Thumbnail sketches like this are always somewhat overdrawn, of course. High tech is not an exclusively American domain, and there are many successful European entrepreneurs. Nonetheless, key aspects of the US model do include flexible labour markets, an abundance of entrepreneurial spirit, strong capital markets, a smaller state apparatus and a vigorous civil society.

For the last decade or so, the US 'model' has served as a template for many reformers in Europe: to combat the Old World's ossification, they feel that Europe could do worse than approximate US practice in terms of labour and capital markets, redefining government responsibilities and other changes. Others view the prospect of 'Americanization' with dismay. To them, the US model spells callous disregard for the poor, short-term profits at any price, a decaying infrastructure and top-flight research in the midst of semi-illiteracy. In this chapter, we try to sort through some of these points. Before we can do so, we need to give some thought to the role that economic 'role models' play in discussions of economic policy.

In the early 1990s, the 'tiger' economies of East Asia were considered a model for the future. Before that, in the late 1980s and into the early 1990s, Japan was widely regarded as unbeatable. During the 1950s, some economists argued that the investment rates and rapid growth of the Union of Socialist Soviet Republics demonstrated the superiority of central planning. In retrospect, the failings of each model are clear. At the time, the first titbits of bad news cropped up while the press and the public were still extolling their favourite system's virtues. The flaw though was not in the models themselves, but the extrapolation of successful pieces of them to the economy as a whole. Methods such as *kaizen* are then often proposed as the ultimate solution to all management problems. The other, more insidious flaw in this thinking is that it leads to imitation. No economy ever overtook another simply by copying.

Europe can learn from the United States in some specific areas, although we would never advocate wholesale transfer of the entire system. To understand which features could be usefully applied in Europe, we analyse the US model and its internal coherence. We then discuss the substantial challenges facing that system, and conclude with a section identifying the possible lessons from the US model.

THE UNITED STATES AS A MODEL: A BRIEF SURVEY

It is of course impossible to describe the US economy in just a few pages. It could also be argued that any relatively well-educated newspaper reader already knows how things work on the other side of the Atlantic. Nonetheless, we would like to make a few empirical observations about the US economy to help us arrive at a better understanding of which elements of that model might possibly be useful for Europe.

The more closely we inspect the US economy, the less clear the differences seem to be. In case after case, Europe has a surprising number of similarities with the United States, even in terms of its pension system. Some contrasts do emerge, however, especially when it comes to government services and transfers, the labour market and capital markets.

A smaller government – and a better one?

Ronald Reagan raised gales of laughter when he famously claimed that 'The nine most terrifying words in the English language are, "I'm from the government and I'm here to help."' Compared with the Europeans, people in the United States seem to have more reservations about federal government and all state authority. Despite this, the United States is not that different from most European countries in the degree to which the state intervenes in many areas of life. US government spending as a share of output is quite high – much higher than it was 50 or 100 years ago, and much higher than in the majority of countries around the globe. Just as on the European side of the Atlantic, the state runs schools and builds roads, provides a social safety net, offers retirement benefits, regulates capital markets, subsidizes agriculture and invests in research and education. At its core, when it comes to what economists call 'government consumption' – spending on state employees, police, defence, schools, roads and interest on debt – differences are small. Europe uses 22.5 per cent of GDP for these things plus investment and debt service, the United States 21.6 (see Figure 3.1).

	USA	EU	Difference, EU to USA
Public			
Interest	2.7	2.9	0.2
Defence	4.2	1.8	−2.4
Culture, education, research	6.4	6.5	0.1
Subsidies	0.4	1.2	0.8
Other	7.9	10.1	2.2
Expenditure other than social	21.6	22.5	0.9
Social expenditure such as active labour market policies, social services,** health, pensions, social insurance for non-pensioners	14.8	25.0	10.2
Public total	**36.4**	**47.5**	11.1
Private* **	**14.1**	**4.3**	−9.8
Total	**50.5**	**51.8**	1.3

* Latest years available.   ** For families, disabled, pensioners (eg, nursing homes).
*** Thereof spending on research and education: USA 3.8%, EU 1.8%.
Sources: OECD Economic Outlook database; IMF Government Finance Statistics database; OECD Education at a Glance statistics database; OECD Main Science and Technology database; OECD Social Expenditure database; OECD Society at a Glance 2005; own calculations.

Figure 3.1 Comparison of expenditure, European Union versus the United States (as % of GDP)*

Differences largely have to do with the amount of spending on social cost. Here, Europeans appear to splurge in comparison, adding 25 per cent to government expenditure compared with merely 15 per cent of GDP in the United States – establishing Europe's image as a 'welfare superstate'. While no European state (except Ireland) spends as little as the United States, 15 per cent is a long way away from a minimalist state.

What is more, social spending in the United States does not stop there. Once we look at total social expenditure, rather than just the part spent by governments, differences become very small. As recently as 1980, European countries spent substantially more (by as much as 4 percentage points), but the United States has caught up. According to the OECD, it now has greater social expenditures than the European Union.

Two factors are responsible for this. Spiralling health care costs, as well as the growing funding costs of pensions, have driven up the US

Table 3.1   Public and total social expenditure, 2001
Percentage of GDP at factor costs*

	Public social expenditure		Total social expenditure	
	Gross	Net	Gross	Net
Denmark	34.2	26.1	35.8	26.9
Sweden	34.1	27.1	38.2	29.7
Belgium	30.9	26.5	30.9	26.5
Germany	30.6	28.1	33.3	30.1
Austria	29.6	23.6	31.4	24.9
Norway	27.0	22.4	29.4	23.8
UK	25.4	23.3	30.6	27.5
Netherlands	24.6	20.6	31.7	25.5
Iceland	23.4	20.8	25.1	21.7
OECD-18	**23.2**	**20.2**	**25.9**	**22.2**
Czech Republic	22.2	20.0	22.2	20.0
Spain	21.7	18.8	22.1	18.9
New Zealand	21.1	17.7	21.7	18.2
Canada	20.9	19.5	26.0	23.5
Slovak Republic	19.8	18.1	20.2	18.5
USA	**15.7**	**17.1**	**26.7**	**25.6**
Ireland	15.3	13.5	15.8	13.9
Mexico	13.1	13.4	13.3	13.4
Korea	7.1	7.1	12.3	11.6
European Union	**26.2**	**22.3**	**28.4**	**23.9**

* Since adjustments are required for indirect taxation, net social expenditure is related to GDP at factor costs.

Source: OECD (ed), 2005.

total. Second, accounting for social expenditure is often unsystematic. If benefits are taxed, for example, total costs to the government are much lower than headline figures suggest. Scandinavian countries in particular tend to make large payments and then claw back a great deal through taxation (both by taxing welfare payments and by VAT). The distinction between gross and net costs lowers the European average by a healthy 4.5 percentage points. In the United States, the difference is a mere 1.1 per cent. Properly measured, there is little difference in the share of GDP allocated to social expenditures (see Table 3.1).

The key difference therefore does not lie in how much is spent, but in who does the social spending and how the buying of social services is organized. The role of the private sector in the United States is undoubtedly much greater. It finances 33 per cent of social spending in the United States, whereas the comparable figure in Europe is a mere 6 per cent.

In addition to higher taxes, Europeans pay very substantial social security contributions for pension, health and home care, unemployment insurance and other benefits. They receive fairly comprehensive health and home care services in return. Private health care spending is therefore a mere 2.1 per cent of GDP in addition to 6.7 per cent from government. Americans pay massively for health care, and receive decent coverage in exchange – if they are covered. In the United States, citizens and employers together add 8 per cent to 6.6 per cent of GDP government spending on health (OECD, 2005b).

When it comes to other parts of social spending, differences are also much smaller than many think. Total pension spending (public and private, excluding direct income support for the elderly) was 10.8 in the United States and 10.2 per cent of GDP in Europe in 2001 – the latest date for which the OECD has published figures. For this, the US retirees will receive a higher level of income than their European peers because the demographic imbalance is smaller. Of all pension expenditure, 56 per cent was government spending in the United States, and 91 per cent in Europe.

Also, unemployment and social insurance benefits are not that different in percentage terms. Single people, for example, receive 56 per cent of their salaries in the initial months of unemployment in the United States, whereas the figure in the European Union is between 29 and 85 per cent (an average of 60 per cent).[1] The big difference lies in the duration of payments. In Finland, for example, benefits remain at 51 to 67 per cent even after many years, whereas in the United States they drop to only 7 to 12 per cent after six months. In the European Union, the overall level remains between 24 and 61 per cent (an average of 44.2 per cent) of the reference level in the case of long-term unemployment. However, in some European countries such as Greece, benefits are reduced to the level of welfare after an initial period of 12 months. The duration of payments varies a great deal between EU countries: while Belgium, for example, pays benefits without limit of time in most cases at a level of up to 60 per cent of previous income, Italian unemployed lose their initial benefits after 180 days (OECD, 2006a).

The United States puts heavier pressure on the unemployed to find work (a key element, for example, in President Clinton's welfare reforms and in pilot projects such as Wisconsin Works) than most European countries do – with the surprising exception of countries like Denmark or Sweden. The evidence suggests that welfare reform has, in fact, encouraged a return to work. It has not helped to alleviate poverty, but it definitely has helped to boost GDP. Much as some European observers like to depict the United States as a dog-eat-dog economy, a closer look instead reveals a social safety net that would be familiar to most Europeans, featuring a lower total level of benefits, derived from commensurately lower burdens on taxpayers. It is a true safety net, containing no aspect of a daybed.

There are two readily identifiable features of this aspect of the US model, revealing both dos and don'ts for Europe. First, the US system uses incentives wherever possible. This seems to have benefits when it comes to the labour market, but works less well and does not appear to be such a good fit with health care. Second, the US government itself is not particularly efficient in its administrative role. Given that it spends about the same proportion of the economic pie as its European peers for the services it provides, the quality produced is often low. We shall come back to these points in greater detail in Chapter 8. Our conclusion is that is that US government does not offer an attractive role model for Europeans. However, US solutions have some important features that could improve the European system. Let us look at some aspects of the US model in more detail.

Pensions

The ageing of society is putting a great strain on publicly funded pension systems in Europe. The United States is facing a similar challenge, but its current system is more geared to focusing resources on the poor, which it does by limiting the size of the state pension and creating opportunities for wealthier individuals to invest for themselves.[2]

On the face of it, the United States also has a basic three-pillar model. According to the most recent statistics (from 2002), 67 per cent of the income of households with members over 65 years of age comes from the state pension system, 6 per cent from assets, annuities and capitalized pensions, 12 per cent from employment income and 5 per cent from other sources.

Averages can be misleading, however. The *New Yorker* once published a cartoon showing a beggar, a workman and a multi-millionaire standing next to one another and captioned: 'Average income per year: US $1.8 million'. Pension wealth in the United States is marked by unusually large disparities, making averages less than meaningful. Breaking down the sources of income for households in which at least one member is over 65 years of age into five income segments, as in Figure 3.2, quickly reveals the sharp divergence of the typical retired household from the arithmetic average.

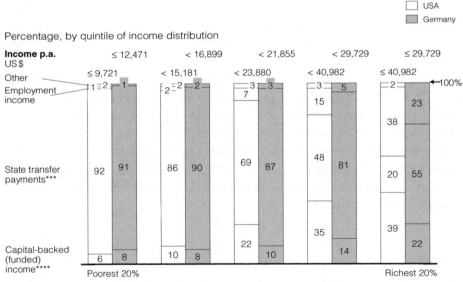

☐ USA
▨ Germany

Percentage, by quintile of income distribution

* USA: individuals over 65 years of age or households in which at least 1 person is over 65; Germany: people in households in which the head of household is over 65 or a head of household between 60 and 64 receiving a pension; Differences to 100% due to rounding errors.
** Quintile boundaries from 1993, adjusted for inflation and purchasing power for the reference year 2002.
*** Statutory pension insurance and welfare.
**** Private savings, house and property assets, company pension plans.
Sources: Schnabel, 2003; Social Security Administration, 2002.

Figure 3.2   Origin of income of population over 65*: United States (2002) and Germany (2002)

For the lowest 40 per cent of households (the two quintiles on the left), around 9 of 10 available dollars stem from Social Security, the US pay-as-you-go pension system. In the third quintile, just over two of every three dollars are from Social Security. Even in the fourth quintile, this share is still almost half the total household income. In short, for 20 million of the 25 million retired households in the United States, the state's European-style, pay-as-you-go system is by far the most important source of income. The 'typical' (median) retired household receives over 70 per cent of its income from Social Security, the US equivalent of a typical European statutory pension system.

Looking at the same factors for Germany, it becomes clear how much the differences are often misunderstood. For the poorest 20 per cent of retired households in the United States, state support is actually even more important than in Germany, and for the next-poorest 20 per cent, the situation does not change all that materially. It is not until we reach the middle of the income distribution that retired households in Germany become significantly more dependent on government pensions. In Germany, the proportion of other, non-governmental income does not increase significantly from the first to the third quintile, whereas in the United States, it increases from 9 per cent to 32 per cent. Households in the top 40 per cent in terms of retirement income in the United States rely considerably less on Social Security than their German counterparts depend on the statutory pension system (Figure 3.2). They also work a great deal more until a much older age.

What this means is that the pay-as-you-go system is concentrated on the segments of the population where it belongs sociopolitically: on the lower-income groups, which are not in a position to accumulate appreciable private reserves in anticipation of retirement. For more than half of all US retired households, the notion that capital-backed components, including savings, company pensions and real estate assets, play a greater role in retirement planning than in Europe is more myth than reality.

Yet no part of retirement planning changed as much between 1983 and 1998 as individual retirement savings plans. Only 12 per cent of Americans had such plans in the early 1980s, while nearly 60 per cent have them today. What is also striking is that this has been accompanied by a sharp decline in the role of defined benefit plans. In 1998, less than half of households with members over 47 years had defined benefit plans; in 1983, nearly 70 per cent of such households had this type of plan. In the meantime, the United States has seen the rise of the defined contribution plan.

Defined benefit plans link entitlements to employee income. Employers carry a high risk by relying on investment income to fund the pensions. With *defined contribution* plans, employers add some funds to the employees' own contributions. The match varies significantly, from one cent for each employee dollar, to US $4.90, with the average match around 70 cents.

In theory, defined contributions should serve to limit workers' current consumption. However, exemptions in the US model seem to feed current consumption in some cases. Employees can obtain direct loans on these funds, they can use them if they become unemployed or to buy a house. For example, 19 per cent of those eligible for loans out of 401(k) plans (named after Section 401(k) of the US Internal Revenue Code) had outstanding loans in 2004 (Holden and VanDerhei, 2005). All three options serve to increase current consumption rather than savings.

Special vehicles for retirement savings could be beneficial in Europe. They would allow public resources to be focused on those with the greatest need and would encourage a long-term view. The US model can be improved. Many countries, from Germany to the United Kingdom and Spain, have already introduced tax-privileged schemes along the line of US 401(k) plans. It is doubtful whether the way forward lies entirely with such defined contribution plans, however, as they shift all risks onto employees. Without a generous state pension as a safety net, this can create very unfavourable outcomes. As the pensions crises at many companies after the crash in 2000 showed, firms are ill-suited to managing the risks of defined benefit plans, which have vast liabilities when markets falter. Nevertheless, plans along the lines of 401(k) create additional problems. Employees, left to their own devices, often make poor investment decisions. Worse, many companies encourage their workers to invest in the firm's own shares. This creates an unwise concentration

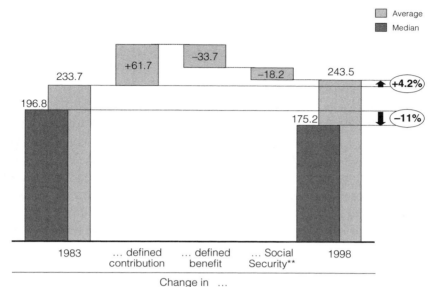

* Defined contribution + defined benefit + Social Security.
** Change in expected future Social Security benefits.
*** 1998 Prices.
Source: Wolff, 2002.

Figure 3.3 Pension assets* of US households with members in the 47–64 age bracket, 1983 and 1988 (US $000)***

of risk: workers face both unemployment and a fall in pension assets if the firm runs into trouble.

Levels of support in the United States also leave many question marks about the overall performance of its pension system. The poorest 20 per cent of pensioners in Germany – despite Germany's lower GDP per capita – live markedly better than their American peers. To be in the bottom quintile, they have to earn less than US $12,000. In the United States, the figure is less than US $9,000. Despite a vigorously growing economy, the typical US household is today worse off in terms of pension assets than it was in 1983 (Figure 3.3). By 1998 (the latest available data), 18.5 per cent of households headed by a person approaching retirement could expect incomes below the poverty line. This share actually increased during the 1990s, up from 17.2 per cent in 1989. The share of households unable to replace half of their pre-retirement income rose sharply, from 29.9 per cent in 1989 to 42.5 per cent in 1998. The share was even higher in 1998 among African-American and Hispanic households, at 52.7 per cent. It is therefore no surprise that the United States has poverty rates among the elderly that are twice as high as in the OECD as a whole. Fully one-quarter of pensioners lives below the poverty line. In Germany, Finland and France, the figure is 10 per cent, and in the Czech Republic and the Netherlands a mere 2–3 per cent (Wolff, 2002).

For most of the population, the US pension model has a large pay-as-you-go component. But since the system is much less generous than European equivalents, many households are left behind. The resources freed up for private saving are overwhelmingly used by wealthier households to build bigger nest-eggs. The poor are, once more, in a bind. Europe can learn from the things that have not gone to plan in the United States. By and large, individuals are often over-whelmed by having to make sensible choices about their pension plans, and do not save enough even when match rates are high. A pension system as low-paying as the US model leaves many house-holds unacceptably poor by official poverty standards. A combina-tion of relatively generous, tax-financed state pensions and compulsory saving in low-cost, responsibly managed defined contri-bution plans, in contrast, could probably help significantly in solving Europe's pension problems.

Health care

The United States spends more on health care than any other OECD country. This is true in absolute values, per capita and as a proportion of income: 14.6 per cent of GDP. The proportion consumed by health care in the United States is 1.5 times higher than in the EU-15's systems. In absolute terms, the gap is even bigger: US $5,287 dollars per head versus US $2,361 or, for example, US $2.762 in France. No other system in the world is anywhere near as costly. At the top, the quality of services provided is second to none. World-famous institu-tions like the Mayo Clinic regularly perform small miracles. The opposite end of the spectrum is equally extreme. Nearly 46 million people do not have health care coverage, except when they need emergency treatment (OECD, 2005b). Many of the poor (especially the working poor) do not receive regular health check-ups, dental care or help with everyday minor injuries. The high number of uninsured leads to wrong or late medical treatment and causes inefficiencies through needless visits to emergency rooms.

Average performance measures for the US health care system are not impressive. Life expectancy is 77 years – one more year than in Cuba, which spends US $200, a mere 6.7 per cent of GDP (at US $3,000 per head). Infant mortality rates in the two countries are identical and are 40 per cent higher than in Europe. Even in the most privileged sectors of society, infant mortality is consistently higher despite the resources available.

The low efficiency of the US model stems largely from partial coverage. To be insured, Americans need a job. But not everyone with a job is covered. This system is unique in the OECD. No other country among the world's rich or modestly well-off nations devotes as few resources to its poor. The absence of universal coverage contributes directly to higher costs. Uninsured individuals seek help in costly emergency rooms when their health problems become overwhelming. In many cases, a primary-care physician could have treated the problem much less expensively if consulted earlier. The lack of preventive care produces additional public health problems by keeping poor people who are ill on the streets much longer than is healthy for the rest of the population; this has led, for example, to the resurgence of communicable diseases such as tuberculosis.

For health care, the efficiency of the private sector is doubtful. The publicly administered, privately delivered Medicaid and Medicare systems in the United States have administrative costs of approximately 4 per cent a year, compared with about 12 per cent of non-benefits expenses for privately administered plans (Krugman, 2005).

The US model displays many inefficiencies. Europeans with their vastly cheaper, more efficient and equitable universal coverage approach cannot learn much from the United States. Their systems have different problems and therefore need different solutions.

Labour market: McJobs instead of joblessness?

In the United States employers have a great deal of flexibility in hiring and firing. In most cases, employees experience this flexibility as a pattern of 'hire and fire and hire'. With every crisis and every shift in the relative importance of the industries making up the economy, a large number of jobs are lost. Measured over the long term, an average of 3.2 per cent of all American workers lose their jobs each year.[3] In Europe, this figure ranges from 0.4 per cent (the Netherlands) to 1.4 per cent (Finland).[4] At the same time, however, the US economy also creates a huge number of new jobs. On average, someone who loses a job in the United States remains jobless for 'only' four to five months. After that, unemployment benefits are cut considerably. Similar figures in Europe are to be found in Norway. In Germany, the average length of unemployment is over 9 months, in France 14 months and in Spain 17 months (OECD, 2005c).

The greater flexibility of the US labour market does not automatically ensure lower unemployment rates: that comes from its more dynamic growth and more plentiful offering of new jobs. However, flexibility does guarantee that the economy can adjust more quickly to structural changes, even when such changes are associated with regional shifts over thousands of miles. Unproductive, increasingly obsolete jobs are artificially propped up only in rare cases. American workers typically accept new job offers relatively quickly, even if they are in a different industry and a different region. This helps to accelerate productivity growth. In the United States, unemployment is something that afflicts many once in a while, but it hardly ever lasts long (Blanchard and Portugal, 2001: 203–04). Almost half of all jobless Europeans are unemployed for over a year. In the United States, fewer than 8 per cent of those without jobs fail to find new ones within 12 months.

On the whole, US workers work longer hours for less pay than their European counterparts. Two to three weeks of annual vacation is the norm, and as we saw in Chapter 2, the labour force participation rate is high throughout the country. In 2004, 75.6 per cent of all

US citizens of working age were members of the workforce, compared with only 70.9 per cent in the EU (OECD, 2005a). Furthermore, low-wage jobs are more common in the United States. Of all white- and blue-collar workers, nearly 25 per cent earn less than two-thirds of the median income. In contrast, only 6 per cent fall into this category in Sweden, 15 per cent in France and 19 per cent in the United Kingdom. The main reason for this difference is higher minimum wages in Europe: the statutory minimum wage in France is 61 per cent of the median income, while it is only slightly over one-third of the median income in the United States (OECD, 2002).

The key differences between the two systems can be summarized in somewhat general terms as follows: relatively poorly paid work is common in the United States, along with a very high labour participation rate, while Europe has a significantly lower employment rate combined with relatively generous minimum wage levels. The US partly produces involuntary overwork, and the EU partly produces involuntary unemployment.

The high labour participation rate in the United States is not solely the result of the flexible labour markets. Shorter training periods (both at university and outside) also play a role; and while the retirement age when Social Security benefits become available has remained largely constant for the past 20 years, laws against age discrimination have done away with compulsory retirement. In addition, many retirees continue to work to supplement their incomes. In Europe, early and complete retirement has become increasingly widespread. In the mid-1960s, French men retired between age 67 and 68. By the second half of the 1990s, this was down to 59, and similar developments have occurred in many other European countries, including Italy, the Netherlands and Germany. In the United States by contrast, the retirement age according to OECD figures from 1994 to 1999 was 65: actually higher than in the 1980s. There were only minimal differences in the retirement age for women, who retired at 64 on average.

By and large, the greater flexibility of the US labour markets offers more advantages than drawbacks. This is not, as is often

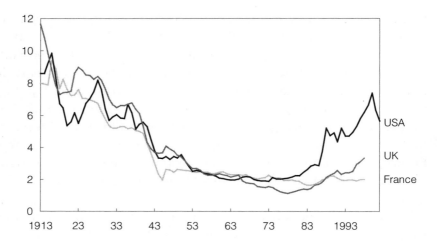

Source: Piketty and Saez, 2003.

Figure 3.4 The top 0.1 per cent income share in France, the United States and the United Kingdom (% of total national income, disregarding capital gains)

assumed, because it contributes directly to a reduction in the unemployment rate, but because it benefits economic growth, structural change and productivity, and because it alleviates certain social hardships such as long-term unemployment. Europe should take note of the advantageous elements in the US system, but also look to best practices in home-grown European role models, for example those of Denmark, Sweden and Finland.

Inequality

Princeton professor Paul Krugman recently argued that, in the past 50 years, a predominantly middle-class society had turned into a more or less unfettered plutocracy. The rich and very rich are increasingly separating themselves from the rest of society. They live in separate residential areas with private police. Umberto Eco once described these trends as 're-feudalization': as in medieval Europe, security today in the United States depends on the patronage and protection of the local rich. Their children overwhelmingly attend private schools and universities to which the less wealthy have access only occasionally through merit scholarships or affirmative action (Krugman, 2002; Eco, 1993).

Who are the recipients of the vast wealth the United States produces today? The United States has a more pronounced income divide than most European countries. The income of the top 20 per cent of the US income pyramid was more than eight times higher than that of the lowest 20 per cent in the 1990s. The top 0.1 per cent of income earners (those earning at least US $277,000 in 2000) now take home a staggering 7 per cent of total incomes (Figure 3.4), up from 2 per cent as recently as 1973. Add in capital gains and the figure rises to 18 per cent of total incomes. Median workers' earnings today are about as high they were then. The share of the pie going to the bottom half has therefore shrunk considerably. Income inequality in the United States today is more extreme than it has been at any point since 1929.

The situation in Europe is somewhat more egalitarian: the 20 per cent of Europeans at the top end earn 4.4 times more on average, and not eight times as in the United States.[5] Top earners in Europe have not increased their share of the pie. When these facts are set alongside the data on absolute poverty (see Chapter 2), it becomes clear that the difference between US and European income distribution lies at the top of the income pyramid, not the bottom.

Another interesting aspect is the way in which income disparity in the United States changed during the boom. Between 1996 and 1999, the real income of the upper 20 per cent of households increased by 10.8 per cent; people in the lowest 20 per cent experienced almost the same increase at 9.3 per cent. From 1999 onwards, the gap began to widen again. This suggests that the demand for highly skilled workers in technical fields is not to blame for the widening income disparity in the United States, since the income gap only resumed its growth when the technology boom ended. Instead, it appears that the trend towards increasing economic disparity in the United States can be slowed only during phases of unusual economic expansion that include a large reduction in unemployment. And even with full employment, the basic trend would not be reversed, but rather preserved at its extraordinarily high level. Because of the dramatic differences in income levels in the United States, a very considerable

portion of productivity gains and increased economic output benefits only those already at the top of the income pyramid.

While the disparity in US incomes is dramatic, the situation for
assets is even more startling. The top 1 per cent own over 20 per
cent of the country's assets: there are approximately two million
households with average net assets of US $3,391,000. The richest
400 Americans, as calculated by Forbes, are growing richer faster
than anyone else. During the long boom of the 1990s, top earners in
particular enjoyed significant asset growth. After deduction of all
debt, a US household in the top 10 per cent of earners held average
assets of US $2.5 million in 2004, which was 72 per cent more than
in 1989 (Figure 3.5). For the upper middle class (top 40 to top 10 per
cent of earners), the increase amounted to 61 per cent, whereas all
the rest, the bottom 60 per cent of earners, saw their net assets rise
by only 36 per cent during this period.[6] In 1989, the richest 10 per
cent of households had approximately 15 times the net assets of the
poor and middle-class households; in 2004, 19 times.

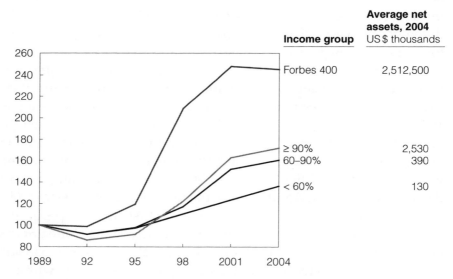

[*] Raw data in real 2004 USD, total financial and non-financial assets less debt.
Sources: Federal Reserve, 2004; *Forbes*, various issues (1989–2004).

Figure 3.5 Change in net assets in the United States by income group

In contrast to beliefs commonly held by Europeans, it seems that many of the rich in the United States did not get richer at the expense of everyone else. There is nothing to suggest that Lawrence Page and Sergey Brin of Google became richer at the expense of disadvantaged Americans. Nor is there any convincing evidence that the link works the other way around: greater inequality is not good for growth. The richest countries in the world, in general, have more egalitarian income distributions than the poorest (and the United States is one big exception to this general rule). Nor is growth higher if income differences are large or getting bigger. Societies can decide how much inequality they want to accept, without too much concern for any indirect effects on economic efficiency.

Inequality is, however, a particularly critical issue when it undermines social fairness and efficiency. The United States is in danger of approaching that point. Where large parts of the population are denied basic health care and receive only a rudimentary education, the rich getting richer appears problematic. A common line of argument is that high economic inequality is acceptable in the United States, and compatible with fairness, because everyone has a chance to go from 'rags to riches'.

The reality is different. One lens for examining the issue is intergenerational mobility. If the offspring of rich families end up rich almost automatically, and the children of the poor rarely have a chance to actually get ahead, something has surely gone wrong. And that is precisely what has been happening in the United States. Mobility used to be high. In the 1950s, 1960s and 1970s, one in four of the sons of fathers in the bottom 25 per cent of income made it to the top 25 per cent. Today, this number has fallen to 1 out of 10. In the United States today the rate of upward mobility is less than half of what it was under Eisenhower, Kennedy and Nixon (Bernstein, 2003).

Comparative studies of intergenerational mobility are conspicuous by their absence. The few facts we have suggest that the United States does not (yet) have unusually high levels of social ossification. European countries fare as badly or worse, according to a study by the University of Utrecht. Americans from families where the father had a low occupational status were 44 per cent more likely to attain a high status themselves than Germans (Borghans and Groot, undated). The disappearance of 'Horatio Alger' stories about working one's way up from dishwasher to business owner has made the United States more like European countries. Combined with unusually high inequality, however, a lack of upward mobility has some worrisome implications. One of the great reforming Prime Ministers of Britain, Benjamin Disraeli, spoke of 'two nations' to describe the vast social differences created in the United Kingdom by the Industrial Revolution. The United States today appears to be returning to a world that would have been familiar to Karl Marx, Teddy Roosevelt and Disraeli. The rich get richer and rule the country, the poor stay poor, and the two groups' paths hardly ever cross at school, the university or the workplace.

An additional reason why inequality matters is the risk it creates for people who face a temporary shortfall in income. While relative positions are transmitted in a very stable fashion from parents to children, individual incomes in the United States now fluctuate more from year to year than ever before. Many families experience sudden and catastrophic declines in economic status, often as a result of losing a job or falling ill. According to Bruce A. Moffitt, the Krieger-Eisenhower professor of economics at Johns Hopkins University, incomes in the United States used to fluctuate by 16 per cent a year. Today, this figure is closer to 30 per cent. Among the poorest 20 per cent of households, income volatility today is as high as 50 per cent. This means that on top of low and declining average incomes, the working poor in the United States face very substantial risks of seeing their wages fall. Risk-adjusted, the American dream has faded over the past three decades and for large parts of the US population, so there are no positive lessons here.

Capital markets instead of bank loans?

Capital markets still play a much greater role in the United States than in Europe. Frankfurt or Milan, say, are nowhere near as important to the German and Italian economies as Wall Street is to the US economy. This general perception is backed by the fact that, even at the end of 2004, the US stock market was still worth more than the entire annual output of the US economy. In continental Europe, the corresponding ratios are often only half that. This is partly because of the different importance of two key capital market functions, financing and corporate governance.

The differences in the *financing function* are often overstated. On both sides of the Atlantic, most investment is financed through retained profits and write-downs. The difference lies in the detail: that is, in the mix of bank loans, corporate bonds and stock, as well as other forms of equity. At the end of the 1990s, only 12 per cent of the gross capital accumulation in the United States was financed via the stock market – a fairly small contribution compared with the other sources of financing, but still substantially more than in the United Kingdom (9 per cent). One area in which capital markets are crucial in the United States is start-up financing. NASDAQ initial public offerings (IPOs) long encouraged venture capitalists to pour funds into promising start-ups. Here, Europe has been catching up. However, since the launch of its own NASDAQ-style markets coincided with the bursting of the tech bubble, it has much more work to do to repair damage in terms of investor trust.

Wall Street's role is significantly more important than the financing figures suggest because US capital markets exert much more influence on corporate governance than do their European counterparts, partly because of the greater importance of equities. US bond markets also perform many of the same functions as banks in many European countries. The corporate governance structures associated with bank loans differ significantly from those associated with capital market financing. Universal banks, the dominant form of intermediation in the 19th century, created a combination of direct shareholding and debt financing. This model also shaped the industrial policy of the so-called 'Deutschland AG' with its closely interwoven networks of capital ownership and interlocking directorates. In Europe, the capital markets have a major role in corporate governance only in the United Kingdom.

Differences between the United States and the United Kingdom on the one hand, and continental European countries on the other, are heavily influenced by historical and legal factors. An extensive study by Harvard economists Rafael La Porta and Florencio Lopez-de-

Silanes explored the links between financial system development and legal systems. States influenced by English common law typically have large liquid stock markets with capitalization equal to approximately 60 per cent of GDP. In countries where French civil law was the basis, stock market capitalization was equal to just over 20 per cent of GDP (La Porta *et al*, 1997).

From the financial market perspective, the defining difference between the two main systems lies in the relative weighting of investor and creditor rights. Countries influenced by common law tend to grant greater rights to investors, such as requiring companies to issue only shares with uniform voting rights, to set up special mechanisms to protect 'oppressed minorities', to permit proxy voting by mail and to allow cumulative voting in board elections. These rights, dubbed 'anti-director rights' by La Porta *et al*, are found twice as often in common-law-based countries as in states following the French civil law tradition.

The situation is reversed for creditors' rights. For example, in countries with codified law, companies (or shareholders) can rarely sell assets when they are faced with insolvency. This protects creditors from inheriting only the worthless portions of the company after a bankruptcy.

For example, takeovers in the United States used to be much more likely to occur via the capital markets than through direct 'back room' negotiations as is common in much of Europe. However, even in the United States, hostile takeovers have always been the exception rather than the rule. Changes in operating performance – both at firms actually taken over and at those threatened by a bid – were quite impressive. Hostile takeovers do not affect successful companies that are creating employment and shareholder value. Empirically, the reverse seems to be true: in the vast majority of cases, takeovers affect firms that have failed all of their major stakeholders, destroying jobs and shareholder value. By removing the management responsible for the mess, takeovers lay the foundation for turning these firms around.

Even during the big US takeover wave of the 1980s, most acquisitions were actually friendly. Up to now almost half of the S&P 500 companies have introduced 'poison pills' that make hostile takeovers next to impossible. Nearly all US states now have provisions on their books that allow firms to make themselves immune to 'corporate raiders'. At the same time, a series of spectacular acquisitions in Europe, such as those at Mannesmann and Telecom Italia, have resulted in an apparent closing of the gap in corporate governance systems. Still, the share of exchange-listed companies in Europe is smaller, which is why the capital markets are substantially less influential in steering European corporate governance. Empirical studies indicate that a smoothly functioning corporate governance system pays off: in North America and Western Europe, investors are willing to pay an average premium of 12 per cent for stocks of companies with exemplary corporate governance (McKinsey & Co, 2002). These studies also show that firms exposed to the dangers of takeovers tend to improve their operating performance, and that poison pill defences encourage the 'quiet life' for managers.

Of particular interest is how much more marked these differences became during the course of the 20th century. In 1914, Germany still had more listed companies per million inhabitants than the United States. Major crises, inflation, two world wars and the Great Depression all led to reductions in the influence of the markets on the continent. Over the same period, the United States moved in the opposite direction: steadily strengthening and improving market mechanisms, particularly in the capital markets.

In response to the Great Depression, the administration of Franklin D Roosevelt oversaw the formation of the Securities Exchange Commission (SEC) to supervise the stock market, the outlawing of insider trading and the creation of a comprehensive body of regulation that largely prevented excesses and problems until the 1990s. Another significant measure was the separation of banks' lending and capital market operations under the Glass-Steagall Act. As a result, specialized investment banks formed (which would later – following the major waves of innovation on the financial markets – increasingly act as catalysts for a strong capital-market-based economy) and removed the rationale for US universal banks such as JPMorgan, whose empire at the height of its expansion was comparable with that of Deutsche Bank in Germany.

The somewhat arbitrary separation of lending and capital market operations under the Glass-Steagall Bank Act of 1933 first led to a wave of innovation in conjunction with the deregulation of the 1970s and the application of modern IT systems. Almost as soon as fixed fees for stock trading were eliminated, pressure to innovate rose, generating the now-familiar world of derivatives and complex financial transactions, asset-backed securities and junk bonds, leveraged buyouts and swaps, credit derivatives and reverse floaters.

Today, following the repeal of Glass-Steagall, banking structures are again becoming more similar. The United States is evolving its own brand of universal banks, from JPMorgan Chase to Citibank. They often dwarf their European equivalents like Deutsche Bank, and compete fiercely as investment banks with large balance sheets. Citibank's market capitalization is twice as large as that of the largest European bank, UBS. Whether this will have knock-on effects on the financing mix is unclear at this stage.

One would hardly want to suggest that Europe copy Wall Street-style governance wholesale: the scandals in the United States since 2000 showed that Gordon Gekko's motto ('Greed – for the lack of a better word – is good') had been carried much too far in real life. In industries where fraud was rampant, the indirect consequences were often painful. Massive misallocation of capital and ill-advised corporate restructurings occurred in a hopeless bid to match the 'performance' of companies like WorldCom.

Whether recent regulatory tightening, epitomized in the Sarbanes-Oxley Act, can restore a modicum of trust is unclear. It has certainly proved effective in keeping foreign firms from listing and in encouraging others to delist. Also, as the bursting of the technology bubble demonstrates, there is a downside to the virtues of a capital-market-centred financial system. The impact of the collapse was felt much less in Europe because of the smaller role of the capital markets in financing, retirement and corporate governance.

There are, however, valuable lessons to be learnt about raising financing for new sectors and companies, and about the disciplining effects of takeovers. Before the bubble, NASDAQ provided venture capital for high-tech start-ups in abundance, for example. Here, Europe has to make up for lost ground. Europe could become world class if it invigorated the market for corporate takeovers. The benign effects of KKR-style takeovers vastly outweigh the costs. This is because in contrast to common mythology, takeovers tend to sharpen firms' performance. More importantly, when the threat of a bid – hostile or friendly – hangs over managers, they do whatever they can to improve performance. This occurred in the United States as the big takeover wave crested. The effect has since disappeared as a result of poison pill defences. Europe could decide that it is not the job of financial regulators to protect managers against the consequences of their own failings, and make the European market for corporate control the most open in the world.

Citizenship and the civil society: also-rans in the quality of social life

When the young French assistant judge Alexis de Tocqueville took an extended leave of absence in 1831 to visit the United States, what impressed him most was the spirit of citizenship that he found. Everywhere he went, people felt they had a stake in the state's activities. Nowhere was this phenomenon more pronounced than in the non-political associations and organizations that he saw as being as integral to people's lives in the United States as their daily bread:

> Americans of all ages, all conditions, and all dispositions constantly form associations. They have not only commercial and manufacturing companies, in which all take part, but associations of a thousand other kinds, religious, moral, serious, futile, general or restricted, enormous or diminutive. The Americans make associations to give entertainments, to found seminaries, to build inns, to construct churches, to diffuse books, to send missionaries to the antipodes; in this manner they found hospitals, prisons, and schools. If it is proposed to inculcate some truth or to foster some feeling by the encouragement of a great example, they form a society. Wherever at the head of some new undertaking you see the government in France, or a man of rank in England, in the United States you will be sure to find an association.

> (de Tocqueville, *Democracy in America*)

Similarly, French writer Simone de Beauvoir's memoir of her four-month tour of the United States in 1947, published in English as

America Day by Day, also recounts her astonishment at the friendliness of the tax authorities, people's willingness to help one another, and the strength of the civic society in general.

Trust, helpfulness, honesty, a tendency to settle disputes without litigation or violence, the ability to quickly identify common interests: this is what sociologists today call 'social capital'. These intangible qualities allow people to cooperate with one another without difficulty. When de Tocqueville visited, the United States seemed to have it in abundance.

Social capital and all key parameters measuring growth and prosperity are highly correlated. If the normal trust variable in OECD countries averages, say, 38, this value for 'transition' countries considered by the OECD is on average only 20. The specific causal relationship between social capital and prosperity remains undefined. Intuitively, the answer is clear: the ability to interact and trust one's peers reinforces a range of other dimensions of transactions and exchange. It is easier to increase output in places where cooperation is facilitated by abundant social capital.

By and large, the United States continues to be a country with many associations and organizations, 'civic spirit' and helpfulness. In international rankings, the United States still scores relatively highly in terms of trust between people. People in the United States belong to an average of 1.5 associations and organizations each, nearly double the number for the average EU citizen. In Spain the figure is 0.3, in Italy 0.5, and even in Germany it is just 1.1. Only the Scandinavians exceed the Americans in their penchant for joining clubs and societies (OECD, 2002: 107).

That said, the qualities that impressed Tocqueville have been steadily waning in recent decades. In 1960, 55 per cent of all Americans still believed that they could trust their fellow citizens in general (the alternative on the questionnaire was 'You cannot be too careful,' and participants chose one or the other answer). In 1998, only 32 per cent believed this, and among young people only a quarter trusted their fellow citizens. With good reason: no other country in the OECD has higher incarceration rates. In the United States, 546 people per 100,000 inhabitants are behind bars. In Scandinavia, this number is usually 60 to 70, Germany somewhat more than 90, and in the UK up to 130.

A similar trend towards loss of trust is evident in social activities. Sociologist Robert Putnam summarized it succinctly in the title of his book *Bowling Alone* (2000). In 1974, 17 per cent of all Americans were still responsible for a specific function in an association or club; by 1994, only 8 per cent held such positions. The informal solutions to disputes that Tocqueville described have given way to a flood of litigation. Between 1900 and 1970, the share of lawyers in the work-force remained relatively constant at about 400 per 100,000 employ-ees (at the same level as doctors). Since 1970, however, the proportion of lawyers has more than doubled. The share of doctors has remained approximately the same. In the United States, many of the brightest minds now specialize in redistribution through the courts, with dubious or plainly negative economic consequences.

We are aware that Europe is no stranger to social disintegration. Even if the prefabricated concrete high-rises in the Parisian banlieue or the Neuperlach district of Munich do not look like projects in the Bronx, the Old World is also fighting crime, distrust and a gradual disintegration of civil society. Luckily, the situation in Europe has not deteriorated anywhere near as much as in the United States. Income disparity ratios are not as extreme, and Europeans work hard at inte-grating minorities, supporting disadvantaged groups, and keeping key public services like security and education accessible to all.

The United States can teach Europe to some extent about the good that private organizations and associations can do, the remnants of the civic spirit that impressed Tocqueville.

The coherent US system: myth or model?

Complex as reality often is, the differences observed can be reduced to a single common denominator: the emphasis on individual rights and responsibilities. Collective mechanisms are largely extensions of individual self-interest. In general, collective responsibility and group mechanisms, whether in salary negotiations or political deci-sion-making processes, are less common on the whole in the United States, and where they are found, they are less important. We would identify this as a systematic difference in the concepts of the United

States and Europe, encountered in many areas. However, it does not constitute an alternative model.

On the whole, however, it can be said that the United States has a more consistent overall model that is more clearly focused on economic value creation in its institutions (for example, the leaner state), in its incentives (for example, in the labour market, retirement planning), and in its corporate governance via Wall Street. This overall model is quite coherent, and is supported by a broad societal consensus that economic success should be an integral part of what the United States stands for, as reflected in the cliché 'from rags to riches'.

However, this coherence lies more in the general tendency to prefer a market-oriented solution. The solutions in each area create their own challenges: flexible labour markets and low wages, efficient public pensions with a growing demographic crisis, or market-based corporate governance that can be systematically undermined. That said, parts of the US approach may be applicable to the European problem. Before turning to the question of transferability, we examine the long-term challenges in the United States in greater detail.

SUCCESS ON A SHAKY FOUNDATION? THE UNITED STATES IN 2006

Before we go on to discuss transfers in the 'Selective learning' section below, let us check on sustainability. Recessions in the United States after 1945 have all followed more or less the same choreography: at some point during expansion, the productive capacity of the country is used to the full, all available workers are employed and prices are increasing. The unions start to demand pay increases. The Federal Reserve increases interest rates and private demand cools. Investments become more expensive, and demand for capital goods also tails off. Employment and capacity utilization fall, and a recession unfolds. Price pressures gradually wane. The Federal Reserve can lower interest rates again, and pent-up investment and consumption ensure the next boom.

The crisis in the US economy after 2001 was different. Throughout the 1990s, inflation remained relatively low and the Federal Reserve did not raise rates significantly. This slump more closely resembled the speculation-induced crashes of the 19th century, such as the financial market crisis (*Gründerkrise*) in Germany during the 1870s and 1880s. Curiously, the current recovery also has some unusual features. Economic growth is strong, inflation is low and productivity growth is high. At the same time, employment growth has remained unusually slow, and growing imbalances threaten to undermine the expansion.

We would like to highlight two specific and related macroeconomic challenges facing the United States in the new millennium: a low savings rate, leading to a ballooning current account deficit, and a housing bubble.

Low savings, excessive consumption and foreign funding

'Shop till you drop' is flippant shorthand for a favourite American pastime that is also a hugely effective driver of growth and prosperity in the United States. In 2004, consumption absorbed approximately 71 per cent of the national income. In fact, private households have largely stopped saving money. The household savings rate in 2004 was only 1.8 per cent of disposable income, one of the lowest figures in US history and also the lowest in the OECD. In the 1990s, the overall savings rate (that of households, companies and the government) slipped further and further below the rate necessary for investment. In 2004, only two-thirds of the gross investment rate of 19.6 per cent could be financed from the overall savings rate, which amounted to only 13.4 per cent. The rest came from abroad. In the years of budget consolidation under Bill Clinton, the steep drop in the household savings rate could be justified by growing budget surpluses; this has changed radically since 2001. US citizens are no longer saving (see Figure 3.6), companies are increasingly borrowing, and after a temporary phase of surpluses, the government has plunged steeply into the red again.

In other words, the United States is increasingly importing significantly more goods and services from the rest of the world than it

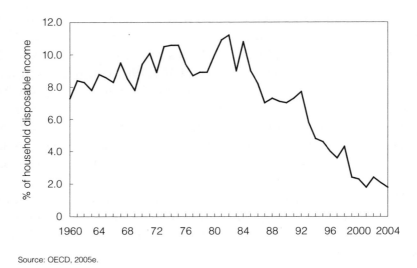

Source: OECD, 2005e.

Figure 3.6   Savings ratio of private households in the United States since 1960

exports. The current account deficit (the sum of the balance of trade in products and services plus the balance of earned income and investment income plus the balance of current transfers) is growing all the time. The increase in the trade deficit is not solely attributable to the well-chronicled years of decline in the manufacturing sector, where even relatively low-skilled workers generally earn respectable wages. Even the flagship US service sector cannot compensate for the economy's weakness in the export of goods despite annual surpluses of between US $67 billion and US $48 billion from 1994 to 2004.

The huge surge in consumption since the late 1990s was made possible by a seemingly unlimited willingness by other countries to grant the United States credit and to purchase more and more US assets, such as stocks, government bonds and land (Figure 3.7).[7] Although the United States held a net interest in foreign assets until well into the 1980s, the situation has now been reversed drastically: today over US $2.5 trillion (net) in US debt issues, companies and real estate belongs to the rest of the world.[8] This corresponds to 21 per cent of the country's GDP. In 2005, the United States borrowed the equivalent of 6.5 per cent of GDP from abroad to maintain its level of consumption and investment.

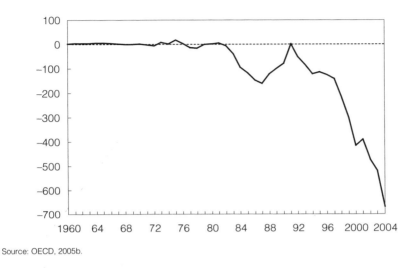

Source: OECD, 2005b.

Figure 3.7   US current account balance of payments 1960–2004 (US $ billion)

However, high foreign debt and an increasing balance-of-trade deficit do not automatically lead to an economic downturn. As long as the status quo remains unchanged – as it has done for many years – there is no problem. One thing that has clearly helped the United States has been a favourable asset–liability mix. While the rest of the world puts its money into the United States in terms of treasury bills that yield only a few per cent, US assets abroad are often equities or profitable foreign direct investment (FDI). As a result, despite being a net debtor, the United States actually has a surplus in its investment income account.

However, what will happen if the rest of the world ever loses its appetite for US stocks and bonds? If US $2.2 billion is no longer flowing into the country every day, other 'variables' as trading volumes or FX rates have to adjust; for example, the dollar exchange rate will deteriorate. The strengthening of the euro since the summer of 2002 shows how quickly the tide can turn. It is a godsend for US manufacturers, while major European exporters are suffering a setback, or at least will do so in the long run.[9] A falling exchange rate is always problematic if the higher import prices fuel inflation in the domestic market and trigger a wage–price spiral. However, because the level of US integration with the global economy is relatively low (compared with European countries for example), and spare capacity is high to boot, even a rapid decline in the value of the dollar probably would not lead to a significant increase in inflation. A more likely scenario could be that foreigners pay in the form of a decline of their portfolios in the United States, which in their home currencies would be worth a lot less.

This effect is greater, and potentially more problematic, because of the low savings rate. If the capital inflow stops, then US households and companies will have to finance investments and government debt. The resulting adjustment can take three forms in any combination: lower investment, smaller deficits or a higher savings rate.

The potential scope of this problem is difficult to quantify. If government and corporate spending remained constant and the capital inflow from abroad suddenly dropped by half, demand in the United States would shrink overnight by 6 per cent. Interest rates would have to rise very sharply to curb private consumption and to motivate individuals to save money. Investment spending would fall, and Washington (which has shortened the maturity of its debt aggressively in recent years) would have to cut spending right, left and centre. This scenario would lead to a cooling of the economy. However, it is unclear whether the imbalances in consumption, the savings rate and the trade deficit should be corrected in one fell swoop, inevitably leading to a recession, or whether the imbalances should be eliminated gradually, step by step, which would result in a few years of unsatisfactory growth rates. How the United States will return to saving remains an open question for the time being.

A housing bubble

In recent years, house prices in the United States have soared. In 2000, the median home cost US $133,000. A mere five years on, it cost US $209,000, a rise of 57 per cent. For quite some time, there has been lively debate about the extent to which these price increases were justified by fundamentals. Incomes have increased and interest rates have fallen. Calling anything a bubble is a tricky exercise: it implies that prices are too high relative to what a sophisticated observer thinks they should be, but the observer may be wrong.

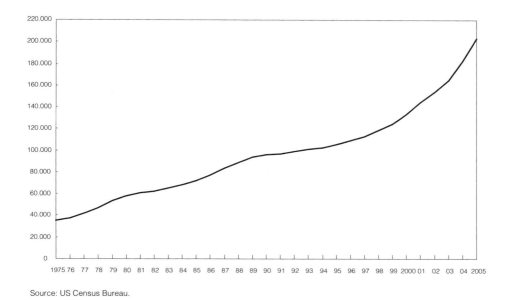

Source: US Census Bureau.

Figure 3.8 Median house prices in the United States, 1975–2005

In the case of US housing, the then Federal Reserve chairman Alan Greenspan remained sanguine for a long time. His argument went like this: fundamentals are strong, and higher house prices simply reflect this. Since inflation is under control, interest rates have fallen. And there are a lot of savings available. Real interest rates are now around 1 per cent. They used to be 2–3 per cent five years ago. Since most of the value of a house arrives at some point in the future, lower discount rates going forward makes the same house much more valuable now. Of course, in some 'hot spots' like New York and California, prices were going up at rates that were hard to justify. But for the country as a whole, a bubble was unlikely.

This argument always had a somewhat problematic ring to it. The areas where even Greenspan accepted that prices were overheating matter enormously in the aggregate: California and New York alone account for 17 per cent of the total value of housing in the United States. The fact that Kentucky, Nebraska and Oklahoma do not have much of a bubble is not that important: they account for 1.5, 0.6 and 1.3 per cent of housing values in total. Overall, the areas classified as suffering from a bubble (according to a valuation model by HSBC) generated 48 per cent of US GDP in 2005, and the rise in prices in the bubble areas has been extreme. California homes now cost more than twice as much as they did five years ago (US $456,000 as opposed to US $211,000).

Incomes have not kept up. For the 25 years between 1975 and 2000, house prices were almost constant at a multiple for the median home of three times household earnings. Today, the ratio is 4.5. In New York, it is approaching six; in California, it has reached nine.

Permanently lower interest rates would make it easier to finance bigger mortgages with the same income. Yet it seems unlikely that mortgage rates will stay where they are, at historically low levels. In the United States, many mortgages used to be fixed-interest, 30-year contracts. If this were still the case, only future home buyers would have to worry if rates rose. Unfortunately, however, mortgage rates are now often linked to short-term interest rates. According to the Federal Housing Finance Board, in 2004 approximately one loan out of three was of the adjustable rate type, up sharply from only a few years earlier. In addition, more and more households are using exotic structures like interest-only mortgages and 'back-loaded' contracts that only start the repayment of principal after a few years.

Also, speculation is becoming a major reason for investments in real estate. Robert Shiller of Yale University, whose book *Irrational Exuberance* (2000) warned against the dangers of the NASDAQ bubble just as the market was nearing its peak in 2000, found that home buyers almost everywhere in the United States expect price increases for the next 10 years, and rates of increase as high as 15 per cent per annum. The vast majority name investment and expectations of rising values as a principal reason for their real estate purchases. While nobody can confidently predict that prices will collapse – and real estate prices tend to move more slowly than share prices – it seems likely that house price appreciation will have to come to an end. In a best case scenario, nominal prices stagnate for years, while rising incomes and prices rid the market of the worst overvaluation. In the worst case, prices fall quickly and for years, as they did in California from 1991 to 1996.

What would the consequences be for the US economy? The bubble is very big, if the pessimists are right. Overvaluation of 35–40 per cent is likely. The parts of the United States affected by sky-high house prices produce about half of US GDP, or the equivalent of Germany, France and the United Kingdom combined. The problem is that the US economy relies on a buoyant housing market to a surprising extent. High prices have fuelled a boom in house building, providing a large number of jobs. Five per cent of workers and 12 per cent of the self-employed work in construction, a total of 9 million people. Employment gains in construction were much faster than in the rest of the economy. And currently, the United States builds 2 million houses a year, while the number of households has been rising by only 1.4 million.

The other side of the coin is home equity withdrawals. Households that saw the value of their homes appreciate have often 'taken out equity' by remortgaging. This sustained consumption growth during the recession, when investment spending collapsed. If house prices stall, few home owners will be able to use their houses as sources of cash any more. At the same time, all those households that made equity withdrawals in the past will still have to service the additional debts.

The current sanguine guesses are that a collapse of the US housing bubble would cost approximately 3 per cent of GDP growth. If this drag materialized over a 5–10 year period, its consequences would be negligible. If, on the other hand, the bubble collapsed rapidly, it could tip the United States into recession. If house prices fell and some families failed to service their mortgages – as a result of short-term variable mortgages combined with rate hikes – the negative equity trap would start to bite. Houses would be seized by lenders and sold for less than the purchase prices. In the United Kingdom in the early 1990s, they were often sold for less than the mortgage value, leaving former home owners still saddled with debt, and without a house. It is easy to see how this could lead to a self-reinforcing downward spiral, with falling house prices dragging down private consumption and a good part of the banking system.

An optimistic scenario would see a gradual transition for the United States, without a crisis in either the housing market or the banking sector. A pessimistic scenario puts the imbalances in the current account together with the housing bubble. If the rest of the world changes its investment policy and ceases to fund US consumption, and long-term US interest rates rise sharply, this could trigger a collapse of the housing bubble. The slowdown in growth, combined with problems in the financial sector, could then lead to greater problems in the current account as more and more foreigners lose their appetite for holding US assets. The adjustment needed could be wrenching. A drop by 3–5 per cent of GDP caused by a collapsing housing bubble and a 4–5 per cent adjustment in the current account could spell the biggest recession since the Great Depression. While the US economy over the last 10 years has performed well overall in terms of employment, output and productivity, it has done so at the expense of macroeconomic sustainability. The next 10 years will not see a repeat of the fabulous gains in jobs or house prices. The only question is whether the slowdown will be gradual and well managed, or sharp and protracted.

The two major imbalances we have highlighted suggest that US growth performance over the last 15 years was not as good as the statistics suggest. The United States may be able to enjoy the good life for a few years while running up foreign debts. Housing bubbles are fine while the party lasts and everybody feels rich. Neither trend is sustainable. We need to adjust the US macroeconomic record for the temporary growth benefits that these imbalances have created. Sooner or later, the United States will have to pay for them in the form of markedly slower growth, lower consumption, less investment and more savings, which will drag down employment. The best the United States can hope for is a gradual unwinding of these problems. There is no reason for *schadenfreude*, however: the stock market crash was no less dramatic here. Furthermore, in Europe, the crash and crisis after 2000 occurred in an economy with higher unemployment, lower returns and significantly less flexibility, and instead of the legacy from the new economy bubble that the United States carries, as we have seen Europe has to shoulder the future burden of an ageing and declining population.

SELECTIVE LEARNING INSTEAD OF OMNIBUS SOLUTIONS

What can Europe actually learn from the US model, on both the positive and the negative side? There is no point in transplanting policies that rely on American legal systems, economic traditions and civic culture for success. Luckily, however, there are few interdependent components to be considered. There is no law of economics that links capital market-based financing with a hire-and-fire labour market, or private schools with massive investments in military research. The American model consists mainly of a bundle of individual policies and practices. Some could be transferred, adapted and used in the European context.

Streamlining the state

There are a few arguments in favour of remodelling public services along US lines. Where government taxes less, it also offers markedly less. Differences in basic spending on security, education and infrastructure are small. We would argue that Europeans largely receive value for money for the 20 or so per cent of GDP that go on these services. US welfare spending is dramatically lower. And results are very different, too: lower transfers spell many more people below the 'relative' poverty line. At the broadest level of aggregation, there is not too much for Europeans to copy or learn. Benefits to be gleaned should focus on the incentives to work and the strengthening of private solutions and market mechanisms in the various social systems.

Labour market

The US model results in a high level of job losses in times of crisis and in troubled sectors. At the same time it also creates more new jobs. Its great benefits are twofold. First, it facilitates productivity growth through reallocation effects. Second, it is actually more socially equitable by redistributing unemployment widely, for shorter periods of time. Europe, by contrast, creates a semi-permanent class of unemployed whose self-esteem, abilities and economic prospects are often irreversibly damaged by years of joblessness. In this sense, the US model of 'hire and fire and hire' would be good not only for productivity, but also for society. Flexibility itself will not cure unemployment, but it can help to deal with it in an equitable manner.

The relatively low level of support for those out of work in the United States may not be the best solution in a European setting, however. If incentives need to be sharpened, other means than simply cutting back on support to the disadvantaged are already available. For example, Denmark's Flexicurity makes unemployed people members of a programme that forces them to attend public service or training for re-employment at 8.00 am every morning. The US model in some cases forces people to accept job matches that are not ideal, leading to rapid turnover. This creates negative externalities and low rates of on-the-job learning. A genuine fusion of the two approaches could combine US-style flexibility with a generous package of income support and some non-monetary incentives to return to the workplace as soon as possible.

Retirement planning

In public debate, the issue of privately funded retirement planning is largely misunderstood. The solution considered typically American applies to the top 40 per cent of retired households; for the rest, the state is the principal source of income, just as it is in Europe. Yet how attractive is this approach really for the upper 40 per cent?

Depending on the returns achievable on the capital markets, the level of benefits afforded a typical recipient household in the US system is relatively good. The upper 40 per cent of retired US households live significantly better than their counterparts in Germany, for example. When the markets were performing well, many retired people were actually pleasantly surprised to find that their savings had crossed the magic line into true wealth. However, when the markets plunge, retirees start to suffer. New Corvettes are replaced by more years behind the desk or on the shop floor. A growing concern for many is the future of their employer-based pension plans, as insolvency threatens both new- and old-economy companies.

The US pension model fails on one of the key criteria for success in any pension insurance system: preventing poverty for large groups of society. The level of assistance granted to the poor is considered more or less important depending on the basic ethical values of a given society.[10] An increasing number of US citizens are threatened with a descent into poverty in old age. Capital-backed retirement funding via 401(k) plans and the like has so far not yet worked effectively. The median household today is worse off than it was 20 years ago.

There are specific changes that could benefit the European worker. Tax deferrals improve the public welfare as long as the returns received by individuals on the capital markets are higher than the yield on government bonds (see also Stenzel and Voth, 1997). The state de facto lends money to the contributors so that they can invest in securities for the long term. That creates a strong incentive for citizens to actively save for retirement. This is how the main attraction of any capital-backed process takes effect: active individual saving decouples the insurance system from demographic developments.

The US 401(k) plan has problems. These can actually be resolved. The main issues – over-investment in a single asset category, stocks and over-borrowing by households using their accumulating assets as collateral – can be dealt with through better regulation that leads to more appropriate products. Where people are not saving enough voluntarily, they must be compelled to do so. Europeans are much more at ease in using such measures than Americans typically are. Individuals should also be forced to invest their funds in a diversified, sensible portfolio.

Excessive borrowing against retirement funds can be limited by taking away the right to borrow and providing better information. Instead of informing investors only of the total value of their investments, companies could be required to convert the total into a projected monthly benefit payment rate. In this way, the state could help to ensure that people are not tempted to go on a spending spree when they see how much money they have in their retirement accounts. Combined with reasonably generous pay-as-you-go public pensions, capital-backed systems could work in Europe. In this way, Europe could copy the more attractive aspects of the US model without having to accept the negative consequences.

Corporate finance

The transferability of the US model of corporate finance and the importance of the capital market is likely to be limited. The La Porta studies (1997 and 1998) documented the impact of legal systems on financial system development. Regardless of how superior a financial system may appear on paper, the costs of switching an entire legal system are likely to be prohibitive. Legal systems are closely tied to their national cultures. Does anyone seriously want case law's collection of precedents (often hundreds of years old) instead of clearly codified legal standards to define what is right and wrong in continental Europe? Introducing case law in Europe would inevitably fail in the face of social and political opposition. The La Porta studies findings imply that the prevailing legal traditions will continue to limit any and all attempts to create a capital-market-centred corporate culture.

The capital market is important in the US model not only as a source of funds, but as a market for corporate governance. Granted, the weak market for hostile takeovers and the Enron and WorldCom crises indicate how poorly the stock market can sometimes function in overcoming the conflict of interest between shareholders and managers. Yet the traditional European model with golden shares for state companies, co-determination for workers and reciprocal stock ownership by companies has its own drawbacks. There are no simple solutions to the principal–agent problem.

Many incremental changes to European capital markets would nonetheless represent improvements. A vigorous market for corporate control across Europe would increase pressure on sub-optimal ownership and management to achieve true productivity-led growth through improved scaling and dissemination of innovations, and thereby solve many problems of economic ossification.

Our review of the US approach finds that there are aspects that can and should be copied and incorporated into the European model. Some important European challenges could be solved by emulating US solutions that are culturally and economically compatible. Yet imitation can only ever take us so far. On closer inspection, many of the alleged advantages of the US model turn out to be incompatible with European values, or much less attractive than one might think. Europe has to develop its own distinctive approach that enables it to maintain its quality of life and values. It needs its own internally consistent and systematic approach to economic revival. In the second half of this book, we describe what such an approach could look like. But as a first step, to guide us on the way, European politics needs a European-style compass that is compatible with its values.

4

Economic indicators and the right measures

What can't be measured can't be managed. Good policy needs clear targets. They are in short supply in Europe. There is widespread agreement that GDP alone is not enough as a yardstick, but there is no comprehensive, rigorous alternative that can guide policy. In this chapter, we propose a simple alternative that can guide future policy.

There is certainly no shortage of targets and measures: whether for competitiveness or consumer confidence, the quality of life in urban areas or car crash safety, there is something for everyone. Some of these are based on rigorous quantification. Others rely on judgement and rules-of-thumb. When it comes to measuring output, gross domestic product is the most widely used indicator. It is also known to fail spectacularly as a measure of the quality of life. This should matter a great deal to Europeans: many things that they deem important are actually not captured by it. All of these things could be pursued separately. However, we prefer to make the trade-offs between the various targets transparent and to aggregate them all into a single measure of the quality of life. The hope is that the new Quality-of-Life Index (QuaLI) that we present strikes a balance between comprehensive coverage and transparency, and can be used as a yardstick for policy.

ORIGINS AND LIMITS OF THE 'GROSS DOMESTIC PRODUCT'

GDP is the 'mother of all economic indicators'. It has a powerful hold on the public imagination, and influences economic policy decisions to a great extent. Like all good indicators, it focuses attention on something that clearly matters. GDP measures domestic economic output by adding up the value of all goods and services produced within a country, regardless of whether they are produced by nationals or non-nationals. GNP (gross national product), on the other hand, measures the economic output of all nationals, independent of whether the output is generated domestically or abroad.[1]

To understand national income accounting, we have to look at its evolution. Simon Kuznets is generally considered to be the father of the system. He was commissioned by the US Commerce Department in the 1930s to develop an extensive system for measuring economic output. The need for such a measurement system grew out of the First World War. With the war's vast mobilization of resources in all belligerent countries, enormous amounts of data were collected and compiled. Towards the end of the war, the British Ministry of Munitions and the German Ministry of War's Central Office for Raw Materials Management controlled a large part of the two economies directly. Yet there was still no comprehensive measure of output overall. This is the gap that macroeconomic accounting and its end product, GDP, now fill. Nobel laureate Paul Samuelson described it like this:

> Much like a satellite in space can survey the weather across an entire continent, so can the GDP give an overall picture of the state of the economy. It enables the President, Congress and the Federal Reserve to judge whether the economy is contracting or expanding, whether the economy needs a boost or should be reined in a bit, and whether a severe recession or inflation threatens.

> (Samuelson and Nordhaus, 1995)

During the Great Depression at the beginning of the 1930s, US President Herbert Hoover's advisers tried to gauge the state of the economy by analysing indicators such as train traffic, the order intake in the steel industry and the volume of mail. Using the results of their analysis, Hoover wrongly told a delegation of leading economists that the depression was over in the spring of 1931. In actual fact, it lasted another two to three years, and only finished long after Hoover had lost office.

Kuznets was commissioned to come up with better, more timely indicators of output. Annual calculation of the GDP was presented to Congress as a concept in 1937, began in earnest in the United States in 1942, and became a vital part of economic planning during the Second World War. Indeed, many historians believe that GDP, as a comprehensive planning tool, was one of the main reasons for US successes in out-producing its enemies in the number of ships, airplanes, tanks and other military equipment.

GDP and GNP have long since ceased to be semi-military planning tools and have become key concepts for economic policy. Journalists pounce on quarterly GDP figures; headlines proclaim the rise or fall of a country's economic fortunes on the basis on a few years of poor or strong growth. Yet the seemingly objective yardstick has its problems. Living standards often seem very different from what the national income statistics suggest. This is not just a question of which data are collected. There are systematic limits to comparability, even for something as homogeneous as money. When money is converted into goods, we must always specify which goods we mean. Yet basic national differences inevitably decree that the basket contains many items that are as dissimilar as apples and oranges: Spain's everyday table and sparkling wines are luxury goods for many of the British.

There are numerous serious drawbacks to GDP. It does not take into account capital consumed in the course of production, the adjustments it includes for price differences and changes in quality are difficult to quantify and often very problematic, unpaid work (such as housework) is not included at all, and the huge informal economy in many countries is only captured through guesswork, or in separate calculations without an integrated view.

GDP is even more problematic as a benchmark for the standard of living. The most extreme distortions arise when we measure goods that have no monetary value but are nevertheless central to the quality of life, such as leisure and the environment. Time taken for production is measured and included in the calculation, but no macroeconomic accounting system in the world includes adjustments to offset the growth-generating effect of a new suburb with a new road and more commuter traffic against all the extra hours that people now sit in traffic just to get to the office, plant or shop where they make their individual contribution to GDP. The same is true for the environment. The consumption of resources such as fresh air, clean water and an unobstructed view is not measured; the use of non-renewable resources such as oil is not fully captured. All of these factors are therefore inadequately considered in every single economic policy decision that focuses entirely on GDP.

These are not new problems. Government statisticians are well aware of the limits of their best-known indicator and therefore calculate what are known as 'satellite accounts' to record the value of housework or environmental consumption, for example. One strategy by which measurement can generally be improved is simply to recognize the weaknesses and allow them to be adjusted correctly. The second, more radical approach is to use a broad indicator that puts a number of other parameters on a par with GDP, facilitating a fairer evaluation.

BEYOND MACROECONOMICS

More than two millennia ago, Aristotle worried about just how useful money actually is. In the fourth chapter of the first book of his *Nicomachean Ethics*, he said: 'Wealth is evidently not the good we are seeking; for it is merely useful and for the sake of something else.' So what should take the place of GDP? Actually, there is no shortage of indicators. They fall into two main types. Some simply adjust GDP for whatever other factor they feel needs to be incorporated. Others derive composite indices of various outcomes that are unambiguously desirable (like longevity or low crime), and combine these according to some weighting scheme.

Recently, the OECD (2006b: 129–43) presented leisure- and inequality-adjusted GDP figures (see Figure 4.1). These take account of the fact that some countries – notably the United States – produce more because their citizens work more. This may or may not be a choice that people want to make, but it is very unwise not to account for the trade-off that exists. Few Europeans would want to double their income and end up working 70 hours or more per week, as their great-grandparents did during the Industrial Revolution.

Depending on how we value leisure – at GDP per hour worked, at the value of hourly compensation or less than that – the gap in output with the United States shrinks more or less dramatically for most European countries. In simple productivity terms (notwithstanding the biases we discussed earlier), Germany, France, Denmark and the Netherlands do pretty well. If the more realistic measure (hourly compensation) is used, no European country bar the Netherlands, Luxembourg and Norway comes close to US performance.

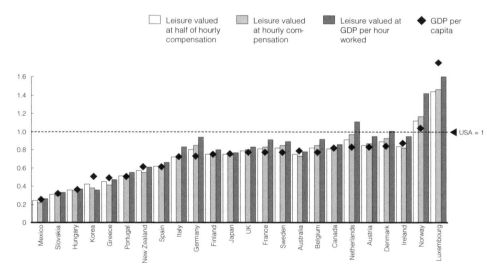

* Leisure time estimated as time endowment – time for personal care (common) – annual working hours (country-specific).

Source: OECD, *Going for Growth*, 2006.

Figure 4.1 GDP per capita adjusted for leisure time of workers, 2001* (ratio to United States at PPP)

The OECD also tried to take account of the fact that inequality can drastically reduce the utility from income. In a society where all money went to one individual and everyone else merely subsisted, there would be few smiles. Adding another dollar to the income of America's top 1 per cent of wage earners hardly adds to utility in the same way as it would among the poorest 1 per cent. The higher the weight on the poorest – that is, the greater our aversion to inequality – the smaller the adjusted household income becomes. How much we want to adjust for inequality is a value judgement. To demonstrate the implications of this judgement, the OECD uses a range of 'inequality aversion coefficients' and adjusts average disposable household income accordingly.[2] Figure 4.2 presents the results for selected aversion coefficients.

On the basis of the highest levels of inequality aversion, the United States still scores relatively well, as we would expect from our analysis of absolute poverty. Switzerland, the United Kingdom, France and Norway are now on par, while Germany pulls ahead of Italy. While

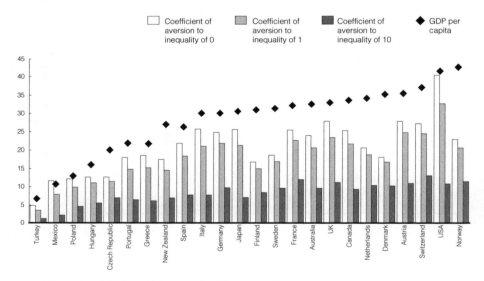

* Average household disposable income, adjusted for aversion to inequality and household size. A coefficient of aversion to inequality of 10 means high aversion to inequality, 0 means no aversion to inequality.
Source: OECD, *Going for Growth*, 2006

Figure 4.2 Disposable household income, adjusted for inequality, 2002* (US-\$000 at PPP)

adjustments based on inequality aversion appear ad hoc, they clearly address an important dimension that GDP itself fails to capture.

An altogether different way of going 'beyond GDP' relies on compiling composite indicators. A prominent example includes the Human Development Index (HDI). HDI is inspired by the work of Indian economist and Nobel Laureate Amartya Sen. He argues that it is not income that counts but 'functionings'. These are the skills that enable people to play a full role in society. Economic development that does not increase these capabilities is not considered a success, which is why Sen entitled one of his best-known books *Development as Freedom* (1999).

HDI has three components: longevity, educational attainment and income per capita. First, the observed maximum and minimum values across all countries are used as a range of potential achievements. Second, each country's position on this scale is expressed as a value between 0 and 1. This procedure is repeated for each subcategory. In the latest version of the HDI, the higher the income level, the lower the significance of income per capita (reflected in the use of a logarithmic scale for this variable). The crucial assumption is that an increase in income of US $1,000 per person per year to US $2,000 is much more important than an increase from US $20,000 to US $21,000. Income is factored into this calculation because it can be indirectly used as an indicator for access to other desirable goods.

Other indicators have followed a similar approach, adding political rights and civic freedoms, for example. The OECD produced a novel ranking that tries to get round a crucial problem with composite indicators: choosing weights. We may or may not agree that the variables being measured in a particular indicator belong there, but the weights assigned to them are necessarily arbitrary. What is the best trade-off between pollution and GDP? There is no 'right' answer.

The OECD picks 16 variables, social indicators from joblessness to mean student performance and suicide rates (it does not include GDP). It then uses a weight for each that can vary between 0 and 1. For each variable, the weight is assigned randomly, and country scores – called RCI in Figure 4.3 – are calculated. The result is recorded and another (random) test is performed. The OECD researchers repeated the exercise 10,000 times. This produces a range of outcomes, depending on the values one prefers.

The interesting thing is that these ranges contain a lot of information. Finland and Japan have very similar GDP per capita. Finland scores well on social indicators across the board, reflected in a narrow grey band. This shows that in this case weighting does not really matter much: Finland does well compared with its GDP. Not so Japan: here the average social score is lower. Also, the chosen weighting makes a big difference. For some weighting schemes, Finland and Japan are neck-and-neck; for others, Japan lags far behind. As Figure 4.3 shows, in somewhat less than half of the countries the median RCI is close to the GDP score; in the majority social and economic performance differ substantially, and in such cases the countries tend to fare better in social than in economic terms (Boarini, Johansson and Mira d'Ercole, 2006).

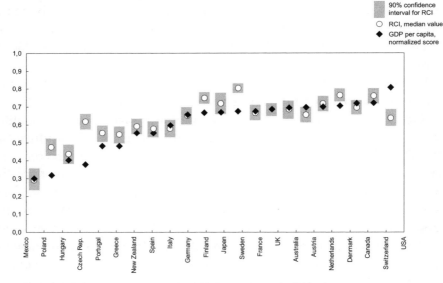

* Composite index is based on 16 social indicators; Random Composite Index (RCI) is the average of 10,000 randomly assigned weights for each indicator.
** GDP per capita, rescaled on a range given by the minimum and the maximum median values of the composite index.
Source: Boarini, Johansson and Mira d'Ercole, 2006.

Figure 4.3 Random Composite Index* of selected social indicators and GDP per capita***

Some countries do spectacularly well socially, given their GDP. The Czech Republic and Poland score much higher than we would expect, as do Sweden and Finland. Germany, the United Kingdom and France on the other hand are pretty much where we would expect them to be based on their GDPs. The United States is a real outlier. Given how much it produces, it scores amazingly poorly. According to the OECD, no choice of weights can redeem its generally poor outcomes in terms of health, education, crime, child poverty rates, gender wage gaps and inequality. When it comes to measuring outcomes other than GDP, the United States is mostly below the range for EU countries.

The OECD social indicator exercise is interesting, but it has its problems. The same categories are used more than once (for example, crime enters twice, through victimization and incarceration). Also, GDP is not used at all, as if material goods had no value. The attempt to capture factors beyond GDP is spirited, but discarding material goods entirely seems problematic, too. What seems to be missing is an indicator that is simple, intuitive and robust: one that goes beyond GDP while still reflecting European values. It should provide politicians in the OECD countries with a suitable measure that can guide policy aimed at improving the quality of life.

In one respect, all indices are the same: you only get out what you put in. The components of all indicators that consider more than just GDP select a subset of the possible range of variables. This is partly driven by personal preferences. GDP itself, of course, is no different: the assumption that the market prices of all goods reflect their importance is itself a value judgement. The same applies to the implicit assumption that the value of all goods that do not have a market price is zero. In the end, what holds true for businesses also applies to indicators: the good ones tend to survive. GDP and HDI combine aspects that appear to be important for people; the quality-of-life index we propose will have to prove its worth in a similar manner.

THE QUALITY-OF-LIFE INDEX

Our Quality-of-Life Index (QuaLI) has four components: material wealth, leisure, social justice and environmentally responsible economics. With this composition, QuaLI echoes the HDI notion that material goods become less important above a certain income level. The additional components reflect preferences in highly developed countries, where leisure time, social justice and a healthy environment are high on the list of priorities.

We deliberately sacrifice comprehensiveness for tractability. There can be no doubt, for example, that education and health are key determining factors in the quality of life; and it may also be desirable to integrate indicators such as crime and equality. We have deliberately decided against a broader, all-encompassing indicator in favour of a simple benchmark whose overall result is easy to trace back to its subcomponents, and which also covers what we believe are the most important aspects for Europeans. This means that the results can be easily interpreted, and differences can be attributed to performance in only a handful of indicators.

The weighting of the components is also a little arbitrary. We treat all the soft factors together on a par with economic output. A lower weight would probably not reflect the importance of income for modern societies. Time will tell whether our indicator is robust in terms of the weighting issues. In any case, we are convinced that economic output should not be weighted by more than 50 per cent. After all, Europeans appear to believe that the good life includes a short working week, a healthy environment and a fair distribution of gains (Figure 4.4).

Similarly, the three soft factors – leisure time, social justice and environment – do not necessarily merit equal weighting, but we believe that favouring any one of these factors over the others is likely to lead to even greater question marks.

We first describe the individual components and how they are calculated, outline the pros and cons of the indicator we have selected for measuring success or failure and then present the index as a whole.

Material wealth

Having lamented the shortcomings of GDP, we nevertheless use a closely related measure. Net national income (NNI) is our preferred

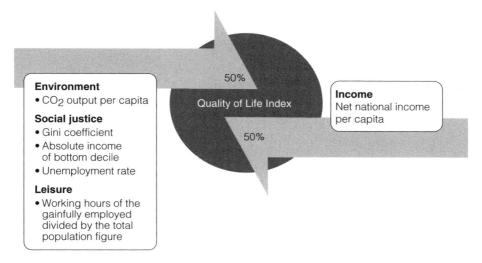

Figure 4.4 Components of the Quality-of-Life Index (QuaLI)

measure of material wealth. In contrast to GDP, we deduct capital consumption since it creates no immediate economic benefit, but is simply a means to an end. Replacement investments are certainly necessary, but only substitute worn-out machinery with new equipment. We use national income instead of domestic income to avoid problems in the cases of Ireland and Luxembourg, where much value added comes in the form of profits and wages from foreigners and foreign firms.

One final question concerns government services. Should we include them in our calculation of total output, given how poorly they are measured (see Chapter 2)? Since governments provide numerous important services that do contribute directly to the quality of life, and since we have no better way of capturing their value, we decided to make no adjustments.

We have chosen to use NNI per head since we are concerned with measuring the standard of living of people in a society. Of course, we use real values adjusted for inflation. We use purchasing power parities, not foreign exchange rates, to adjust for systematic differences in how much people can buy for their money.

To make this indicator useful for our group of countries, we award 100 points for the best performance (excluding Luxembourg to avoid biases because of its small size and superior but atypical economic performance) and zero for the worst, in each case with reference to the 15 EU countries and the United States. On this basis, Luxembourg is streets ahead of the others at 139 points, followed by the United States with 100 points (Figure 4.5). Portugal, the country with the lowest economic output of those considered, receives 0 points. The other EU-15 countries with the exception of Luxembourg also trail behind the United States. The UK scores just 66 points, while France reaches 51 points. The European Union as a whole is awarded 47, fewer than half of the points given to the United States for NNI. The NNI indicator is very well suited to the US society and economy, as it is good at the creation of material wealth and places less emphasis on leisure and environmental consumption, and possibly also on social justice.

Measured in terms of NNI, Europe does not fare very well. On the road from poverty to wealth that relatively developed countries follow, Europe is only half way towards what can actually be achieved and what the United States has already achieved.

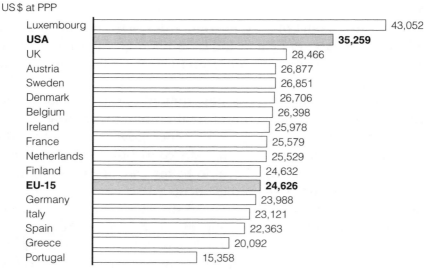

US $ at PPP

* NNI per capita 2005 estimate based on NNI per capita 2003 and GDP per capita growth rates 2003–2005.
Sources: OECD National Accounts database, 2005; Groningen Total Economy Database.

Figure 4.5 NNI per capita in the United States and members of the EU-15, 2005* (US $000 at PPP)

Leisure

Just how attractive is material wealth if it comes at the price of longer working hours? Harvard economist Juliet Schor argued in her best-seller, *The Overworked American* (1998), that the US business model systematically leads to a lack of leisure time, and that the majority of US workers would gladly forgo a good chunk of their income to have vacations of four to six weeks, as in Europe, instead of just two and a half weeks. In the OECD, only Czechs, Koreans and Icelanders work as long or longer.

In the European Union as a whole, the labour input per head of population is 20 per cent lower than in the United States. Each employee works 14 per cent less, and fewer Europeans work in relative terms. The French top the leisure list, working as much as 31 per cent less than the Americans, followed by the Germans, Belgians and Italians (Figure 4.6). The Europeans who work longest are those in Portugal, Spain and Greece.

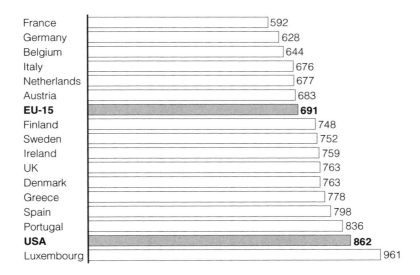

Source: Groningen Total Economy Database.

Figure 4.6 Annual working time of the gainfully employed per capita of total population, 2004 (hours)

On account of their extremely long working hours, Americans gain no points in this category: 0 instead of 64 for the 15 EU member states.

The differences in the working time put the US lead in production (NNI per capita) into perspective. In terms of production per capita, Europe is, on the whole, well behind the United States, but an important part of the difference is simply because of the higher consumption of leisure time in Europe. This is why per capita consumption cannot be the only measure for Europeans.

Both leisure and output enter our indicator. This could lead to problems. By giving different weights to these factors, we could introduce systematic biases: we might in effect implicitly tell societies to work harder, when their labour–leisure trade-off is entirely in line with preferences. To avoid this problem, leisure enters in the indicator with a weight that reflects European preferences for it. During the post-war period, Europeans reduced their working hours by roughly 1 percentage point every time that productivity increased by 4 percentage points.[3] In other words, of the potential gain in output of four units, three went on material goods and one on more vacations, shorter working weeks and more part-time work. This is exactly the weight we assigned it in the QuaLI: a ratio of 1:3 compared with output.

Social justice and employment

The term 'social justice' sounds odd in some ears. It is reminiscent of campaign rhetoric and envy. Yet it is crucial for many people who feel ill at ease when the gap between poor and rich becomes too wide. Traditionally, economists have feared that too much redistribution can dent incentives, leaving society as a whole worse off. Most studies show that this is not true empirically. Greater inequality does not help growth. So if average wealth does not rise more rapidly, why should one live with greater social differences?

Social justice enters our indicator in a number of ways. The Gini coefficient measures the degree of inequality across the entire income distribution (Figure 4.7). The coefficient would register zero for a society in which each member received exactly the same income, and a coefficient of 100 if one person had everything and the rest nothing. The Gini coefficient for the United States is 35.7; for the EU-15, it is 30.1. Denmark, Sweden and the Netherlands are especially egalitarian, contrasting with Portugal, Italy and Greece, which exhibit a relatively high degree of economic inequality. In addition to this – reflecting the spirit of Rawls' concerns as discussed in Chapter 2 – we look at the absolute income of the lowest decile. Finally, we study the unemployment rate, since unemployment – even without poverty – denotes a particular social and psychological hardship.

Ireland, the United Kingdom, the Netherlands and Denmark have particularly low unemployment rates – below the US level – whereas the other European countries lose points (Figure 4.8). In the 15 EU member states, the unemployment rate in 2004 hovered around 8 per cent, while in the United States it was 3 percentage points lower.

In terms of the absolute income level of the poorest groups, the United States is better off than the average of the EU-15, and fares much better than Portugal, Greece, Spain, Italy, Ireland and the

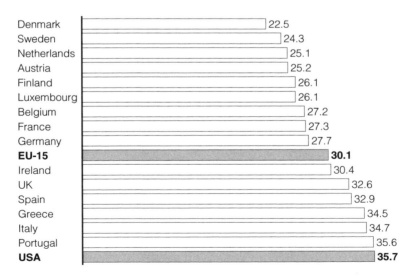

Source: Förster and Mira d'Ercole, 2005.

Figure 4.7   Gini coefficients, 1995–2000 (%)

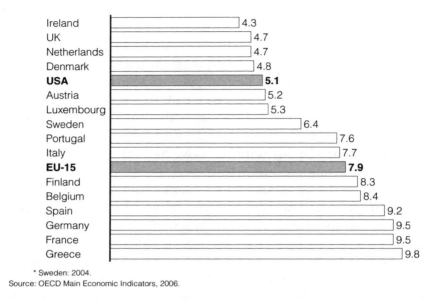

Ireland	4.3
UK	4.7
Netherlands	4.7
Denmark	4.8
USA	**5.1**
Austria	5.2
Luxembourg	5.3
Sweden	6.4
Portugal	7.6
Italy	7.7
EU-15	**7.9**
Finland	8.3
Belgium	8.4
Spain	9.2
Germany	9.5
France	9.5
Greece	9.8

* Sweden: 2004.
Source: OECD Main Economic Indicators, 2006.

Figure 4.8   Unemployment rates, 2005* (% of total labour force)

United Kingdom, which bring up the rear (Figure 4.9). In Germany the poorest 10 per cent of the population receive 12 per cent more than in the United States, and the Danes, Belgians, Austrians and Dutch also receive generous support.

Taken as a whole – that is, considering the three indicators together – the two economic blocks do not have the same levels of social justice. The European Union lags behind by about 16 per cent because of its lower score for higher unemployment rates and a lower income of the bottom decile.

Environmentally responsible economics

Few question the importance of the environment. Finding ways to account for it is nonetheless challenging. Carbon dioxide (CO_2) emissions are one suitable measure because they are released in all combustion processes: in coal-fired power stations and motor vehicles, for example. CO_2 is a particularly important issue because a growing number of experts believe that these emissions produce global climate change. The exact risks and causes of the change in the

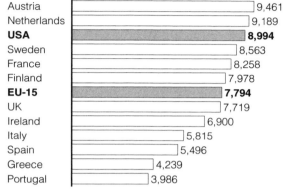

Luxembourg	15,169
Denmark	10,504
Germany	10,095
Belgium	9,666
Austria	9,461
Netherlands	9,189
USA	**8,994**
Sweden	8,563
France	8,258
Finland	7,978
EU-15	**7,794**
UK	7,719
Ireland	6,900
Italy	5,815
Spain	5,496
Greece	4,239
Portugal	3,986

* Equivalence income per person after social transfers, excluding health.
Source: Collado and Iturbe-Ormaetxe, 2005.

Figure 4.9   Absolute income of bottom decile after social transfers, 2000* (US$ per capita at PPP)

world's climate are fiercely disputed, and a monetary estimate of the consequences is scarcely feasible as most of the effects will not become apparent for a long time.

We use CO_2 emissions as an indicator of environmental responsibility. The connection with global climate change is only one key element of this equation. CO_2 emissions also lend themselves to the measurement of the consumption of fossil fuels in the total economic and consumption process. Using resources sparingly through well-insulated houses, fuel-efficient engines and the right price signals creates a good that is important for the whole of humankind; energy is saved for the future and the negative impact on the environment is reduced.

The US way of life (and production) is tremendously wasteful of fossil fuel. In 2003, CO_2 emissions in the United States came close to 20 tons per capita. In contrast, the European Union generated a mere 8.6 tons per capita, less than half of the pollution of its transatlantic counterpart (Figure 4.10). No single European country, with the

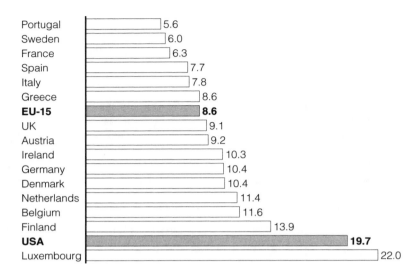

Source: International Energy Agency, 2003.

Figure 4.10   Carbon dioxide emissions, 2003 (tons per capita)

exception of Luxembourg, comes anywhere close to the US figures. Even relatively heavy polluters like Finland and Belgium only top the 12 ton mark.

Climatic differences are not the main reason for the poor showing of the United States. Nordic countries are not the smallest polluters, but at 6.0 tons per capita Sweden puts its Scandinavian neighbours Denmark (10.4) and Finland (13.9) to shame. A higher percentage of the US population lives in areas with extremely cold winters or very hot summers, so part of the difference is attributable to energy needed for heating and air conditioning. But even Australia and Canada, with a similarly extreme climate, pollute the environment much less than the United States.

Although, on the whole, the European Union has a much lower CO_2 emission than the United States, a number of European countries are still a long way from best practice. Luxembourg, Europe's largest polluter per capita, could reduce its CO_2 emissions by as much as 75 per cent if it emulated Portugal's thriftiness. All in all, the United States is at the bottom of the ranking (though some points ahead of Luxembourg) in this category and receives zero points versus 79 points for the EU-15.

The index as a whole

Where is life particularly sweet? And how can politicians make choices between competing goods in a way that reflects the values important to Europe's citizens? Two things become clear when we look at the quality-of-life scores of the two economic blocks (Figure 4.11).[4] First, the QuaLI Index confirms the OECD finding that life in Europe is pretty good. The combination of material wealth, environmental responsibility, tolerable – even though not optimal – social justice and ample leisure time is impressive. Second, Europe's Achilles' heel, material wealth, is about to get even more vulnerable.

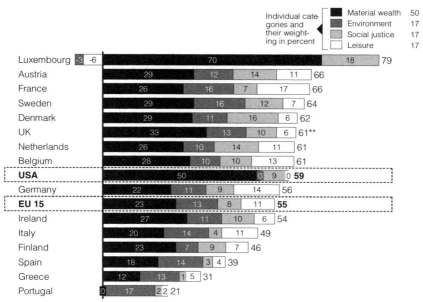

Figure 4.11 Quality-of-Life Index: EU-15* and United States (index points, individual categories by weighting)

This is where Europe flags compared with the United States, and because of demographic trends, the situation may get even worse.

We developed the QuaLI as an alternative to the exclusive focus on GDP. The US Commerce Department once praised macroeconomic accounting as the 'achievement of the century', but then that was quite early in the 20th century. With its strong focus on GDP, we believe that macroeconomic accounting can lead to over-simplification and – if applied uncritically – the wrong economic policy. When the world's climate suffers or leisure declines, an indicator that serves as a compass for politics ought to indicate a deterioration. GDP does not do this, but the QuaLI does.

According to the QuaLI, Europe on average is behind the United States overall. It has glaring deficits in terms of material wealth creation. These are compensated for in the other categories: our European-style indicator suggests that Europe is not as far behind overall as it is on material wealth alone. Nonetheless, some countries – Greece and Portugal, for example – perform badly in our index. Austria, France and Sweden emerge as particularly good places to live. The QuaLI also points to further deficits that policy makers would do well to address. For some it may be surprising that Europe does not score well in terms of social justice because of high unemployment, and because of the low incomes for the bottom 10 per cent in absolute terms. Here, too, more growth is an important part of the solution, driven by a faster increase in productivity together with higher employment. In Portugal, Greece and Italy, a more equal division of the economic pie would also be desirable. In terms of environmental quality, Finland and Belgium could aim for substantial reductions in emissions.

We can also see that Europe will have a hard time reaching pole position in the rankings, ahead of the United States, and staying there. Europe could do much better if it solved the main problem, its unsatisfactory levels of productivity and employment. There is a ray of hope coming from this. In line with the OECD's conclusions, Europe is much better at translating output into all the other goods that its citizens care about, from the kind of society we live in to the level of pollution in the air we breathe. As the Paris organization's results show, this is not the consequence of the particular indicators we chose: it holds for everything from crime rates to health, education and alternative environmental indicators. If efforts to improve output reduced the productivity gap between Europe and the United States by only half its current level, Europe would then come out ahead of the United States in the QuaLI.

The QuaLI is deliberately designed to reflect European values. It is a mixed bag for a reason: GDP alone is not enough, yet without economic output, there is no quality of life. There could be many permutations of the index components we have used. The QuaLI in its present guise has one advantage compared with, say, the OECD social indicator study: its simplicity. What matters is the sum total of the goods that Europeans value, and our indicator captures this in a way that could guide policy. The next chapters turn to specific initiatives that Europe can pursue to address its principal shortcoming, the deficit in the creation of material wealth, which is at the same time the basis for immaterial benefits.

Part 2

Europe's journey to the top

5

The power of unity

COMPLETING THE SINGLE MARKET

The creation of the single market was supposed to be Europe's crown-ing success. Europe would regain its competitive edge and employ-ment dynamics. It was generally expected that better integration would increase productivity in the European national economies. In 1988, the Cecchini Report on the 'cost of non-Europe' envisaged a series of interrelated changes.

First, because of increased competition, the prices of consumer goods and durable goods were expected to harmonize at a lower level. This would help release resources, which would lead to higher savings rates and flow into additional consumption. The state would profit too: once development projects were open to bidders through-out Europe, the costs of infrastructure such as airports and highways would fall. Second, European companies were expected to grow in size as a result of mergers and acquisitions. The United States had long benefited from the competitive advantage conferred by its size-able domestic market. Creating a similar-size market would let

Europe at least catch up with, or even overtake, the United States; after all, the EU has a larger population. Economies of scale would enable these new European giants to offer lower-priced products at home, and have their competitors in the world market trembling in their boots. Alongside the increase in size would come more innovation and an improvement in the quality of management. Finally, the increase in size would disproportionately raise profits and market values because large institutions often better understand the link between their profitability and the talents of their knowledge workers and other intangible assets.

On the whole, once market forces were unleashed and bureaucratic obstacles overcome, it was hoped that the advantages of an integrated market would be felt from the Adriatic to the Baltic, and from the Danube to the Tagus. The 1988 Cecchini Report expected gains of 4.3 to 6.4 per cent of the economic performance measured as gross domestic product of the European Union. The rest of the effects quoted in the report also read like a European's Christmas wish list: a drop in the unemployment rate of up to 2 percentage points, savings of 1.5 to 3 per cent in national budgets, and a 6 per cent decrease in prices for consumer goods.

Unfortunately, as we discussed in Chapter 2, the implementation of the single market is far behind schedule. We argue in this chapter that it is still the right concept and the fundamental prerequisite for Europe to reach its ambitious goals. Therefore, besides all further measurements we discuss later, implementation needs to progress faster and more vigorously. We will also identify the most important areas it should now focus on.

1992 AND THE CONSEQUENCES

If lack of access to an integrated, large market with its efficiency advantages was a problem before 1992, and if the Cecchini programme had been implemented successfully, small member states should have reaped unusually large benefits. They should have seen an acceleration of growth compared with their bigger peers in the European club – and they did. Figure 5.1 compares the

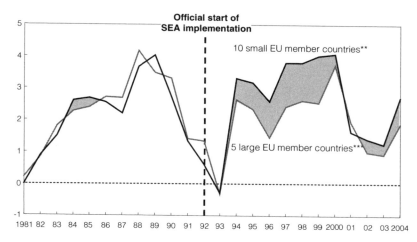

* Weighted by gross domestic product.
** Austria, Belgium, Denmark, Finland, Greece, Ireland, Luxembourg, Netherlands, Portugal, Sweden.
*** France, Germany, Italy, Spain, UK.
Sources: Global Insight: World Market Monitor database.

Figure 5.1 GDP growth* before and after the introduction of the single market (%)

GDP growth rate in small and large member countries before and after the introduction of the single market. Until 1992, the development of both groups was largely parallel, with slight advantages for the smaller states in the mid-1980s and slight advantages for large national economies towards the end of the decade. Since 1992, however, a large and relatively constant gap has separated the two groups: the smaller states are growing by up to 1.5 percentage points more quickly per year. It would be in line with anticipated trends if the gap decreased over time, as the effect of full access to the single market as an exceptional growth factor starts to fade.

Increasing synchronization between European national economies would also be expected as a result of the 1992 programme. When an extremely heterogeneous group of states slowly but surely grows into a single economic block, these states' main macroeconomic indicators should also converge. However, with the exception of the convergence of inflation rates – driven by monetary union and the global trend toward greater price stability – the macroeconomic differences between European countries have remained.

Low levels of synchronization are not surprising. Labour markets remain largely segmented. This is especially disappointing given that the creation of the single market was supposed to contribute greatly to labour force mobility. However, where improvements were not of a purely formal legal nature (for example, the recognition of degrees in regulated professions such as medicine and pharmacy), they mostly served to increase the mobility of that portion of the labour force that was already mobile and attractive. Very little has been done that boosts the mobility of the problem groups, such as employees with few qualifications who are either very young or very old. Fewer than 2.5 per cent of Europeans live outside their native country, but still within the European Union. The other EU countries are therefore about as unlikely to employ them as equally rich countries overseas. In the United States, by contrast, barely 30 per cent of the inhabitants reside in the state in which they were born.

Regulatory prerequisites

The administrative machinery has functioned fairly well. The creation of enactments worked more or less smoothly. By April 2003, a total of 1,530 directives and 377 regulations aimed at producing a single European market had come out of Brussels. A good portion of these then went through the legislative process in Strasbourg, which then leaves implementation to the member states.

At this point in the process, activity slowed. On average, 6.3 per cent of all regulations had still not been implemented by the member states in 1997, a full five years after the start. This also partly explains the rather disappointing economic effects of the integrated market. By the summer of 2002, however, the average share of non-implemented regulations had fallen to just 1.8 per cent (European Commission, 2002: 5). However, that included some of the most crucial ones, especially in the area of the capital markets.

Getting to the integrated market was often surprisingly difficult. Citizens, the EU Commission and businesses often had to take legal action in order to make the borderless European Economic Area somewhat more of a reality. There were 1,100 lawsuits for violations of single market regulations pending in 2005, in comparison with only 700 in 1992. However, such lawsuits are the tip of the iceberg. Before a case goes to the European Court of Justice, businesses and citizens suffer years of delays at the hands of national authorities, costing untold amounts of money.

There are many examples that show how difficult it is to implement European decrees in member states. For instance, almost without exception the member states have transposed into national law all aspects of the 'single European passport' for financial services. A business admitted by the UK's Financial Services Authority in London may also open a bank in Sicily. At least that is what it says on paper, but these regulations are not put into practice. After all, it is the central bank or the department of finance that grants an investment bank approval as a primary government bond dealer, for example, and one can imagine that a country would not want to entrust its bonds to a bank that is regulated abroad. The scandal that erupted in Italy in the summer of 2005 – ultimately leading to the resignation of the central bank governor – illustrates this well. Foreign banks were trying to snap up an Italian one. The governor, in what newspapers called a brazen violation of EU rules, national laws and the spirit of European integration, was allegedly caught on tape coordinating Italian banks that were about to come to the rescue to keep the foreigners out.

The recent bid by the German electricity generator E.ON for the Spanish utility Endesa is also instructive. The Spanish government came out publicly against the bid because it saw its preferred outcome – Endesa as a national champion in the energy sector – threatened. According to the spirit – and many would say, the letter – of European competition policy and the single European market, such a thing should be unthinkable today, 20 years after the Single European Act legislation got under way. It highlights how common government meddling still is. It seems likely that non-nationals would face major problems in any attempt to take control of Electricité de France (EDF), and foreign banks may not find other markets any easier to enter than Italy. In many areas of policy making, Europe appears as far from being an integrated market as it was a quarter of a century ago.

The continuing debate on the European regulatory framework for financial services also serves to demonstrate the difficulties of implementing European decrees in member states. Following the official completion of the financial services action plan (FSAP) in 2004, the Commission published a green paper in May 2005 in order to further accelerate the integration of Europe's financial markets.

The white paper that grew out of the ensuing public debate in December 2005 emphasized the need for coherent and timely implementation in each member state. The only segment in which the single market commissioner considered additional regulations refers to the investment trust market, where national regulations still weigh upon cross-border consolidation. Financial services regulation thus seems to be an illustrative case of lagging industry consolidation as a result of inflexible and misguided regulation. However, awareness is beginning to spread that 'gold plating' through additional regulation on the national level might significantly slow down the necessary integration process. From the Commission's point of view, timely implementation will be a main concern for the years to come and national governments will be closely guided.

It is difficult to say what percentage of the single market regulations have actually been put into practice. The impressively long list of regulations may be less a testimony to work accomplished than a symbol of the Sisyphean task of implementing the single European market.

Counting directives is all very well, yet some of the potentially most important ones have failed in recent years. When the takeovers directive, originally destined for completion in 1993, made its way to the EU parliament in 2001, the parliament rejected it. Only three years later, in April 2004, did the European institutions finally manage to agree on a compromise aiming to establish standardized rules on takeover bids. The resulting directive, however, is a shadow of the commission's initial proposal. In this context, Article 12 of the directive is most likely to provoke debate, as it allows any member state not to implement those parts of the directive that prevent certain defensive measures, including the provisions that forbid the board of the offeree company to frustrate a takeover without authorization of the general meeting of shareholders.

And this is no idle thought. In early 2006, the French government proposed to permit so-called 'poison pill' defences that would make takeovers all but impossible. This could trigger retaliation from other European countries. Italy has already announced that it will introduce similar measures if France does. Few European countries will sit on the sidelines if their own firms are snapped up by EDF and French banks, which would themselves be protected from foreign bids. Europe is in serious danger of losing what was once its main advantage: its ability to force measures onto the member states that are politically difficult to sell at home, but beneficial overall.

A last example of national interests undermining the cause of further integration concerns the services directive. At the beginning of 2004, the European Commission presented a draft directive (also known as the Bolkestein directive) on the creation of an internal market in services, which has since provoked widespread debate among all concerned stakeholders. Representing roughly 75 per cent of jobs, the service sector clearly has an important impact on Europe's economic prosperity. Excessive red tape is rightly at the top of the Commission's agenda. The proposed directive covers all services (except those provided free by national authorities). The main idea, as for the single market in goods, is to enable a service provider from one member state to set up shop elsewhere in Europe. Just as with financial services, a 'single European passport' should enable a provider to operate everywhere, be regulated and registered once, and trade throughout the European Union.

Few would dispute that an integrated market in services is essential if the European Union is to fulfil its promise and integrate markets deeply. Yet the relatively poorer members, with sometimes lower standards of regulation and lower labour costs, create problems for heavily regulated high-cost countries like Germany and France. These countries fiercely opposed the Bolkestein initiative out of concern over massive foreign competition for their domestic service sector. From the perspective of mid-2006, it is clear that nothing in the spirit of the Bolkestein directive will be implemented, and that it is very unlikely that this bold idea to create a pan-European market in services will revive any time soon.

The list of initiatives that have not been brought successfully to a conclusion is long and growing: no efficient connection of national transportation networks, no liberalization of the service sector, no standardization of pension plan regulations, staggeringly low cross-border mobility of labour, a standstill in the creation of an EU-wide patent and very low integration of capital markets. Even for public procurement – one of the main hopes of the Cecchini programme – no agreement on a standard package is in sight. Although the share of public jobs tendered throughout Europe doubled between 1993 and 1998, it was still less than 15 per cent in 2003. In other words, 17 out of 20 projects were offered only to domestic suppliers. The share of bids placed across borders amount to 3 per cent only. Also, even though the total value of European-wide tendered projects rose from 1 per cent of GDP in 1993 to 2.7 per cent in 2004, only 20 per cent of all public tenders are visible for foreign bidders. There were, however, considerable differences between the countries. The share of tenders published EU-wide varied between 7.6 per cent (Germany) and 40 per cent (UK). However, provided that on EU15-average, 80 per cent of tenders are not visible for presumably more efficient foreign bidders, there is small wonder that only a fraction of potential savings are actually achieved (Eurostat, 2004).

Change in trade volumes

The key idea of the 1992 programme was to increase internal European trade volumes by eliminating non-tariff trade barriers and abolishing customs inspections. More specialization was supposed to lead to an increase in the exchange of goods and to gains in productivity. Above all, competition was also supposed to increase as other European companies entered each other's markets. The hope appeared well founded: the economic success of the European Coal and Steel Community, and later of the European Economic Community, was for the most part based on the increase in trade between member countries. In the period from the 1950s to the 1970s, trade volume exploded. Countries specialized in what they did best, producing large gains for consumers and firms.

As recently as 1960, EEC member states such as Germany and France conducted only 40 to 50 per cent of their foreign trade with the countries that now form the European Union. Today that figure has risen to 50 to 70 per cent of a significantly larger trade volume. This basic trend continued up to the 1980s: trade volume within the EU-15 increased at a rate of 8.6 per cent per year, while trade with the rest of the world only grew by 5.9 per cent.

Amazingly, since the introduction of the single market the situation has been reversed, confounding expectations of an acceleration. Between 1991 and 1999, when the SEA should have boosted volumes, intra-EU trade grew more slowly than trade with the rest of the world: 5.2 per cent versus 8.8 per cent. From 1999 to 2003, trade growth slowed down to 4.3 per cent within the EU-15 and 6.4 per cent with the rest of the world. With the exception of Spain, the share of intra-EU trade in the total trade volume decreased between 1991 and 2003 (Figure 5.2).

At first glance, it therefore seems as if the great single market programme has failed to accomplish one of its main goals. Instead of becoming firmer, the economic glue that was intended to bond the European nations has become more brittle during the last 10 years, at least relative to the rest of the world. To be sure, there are many other

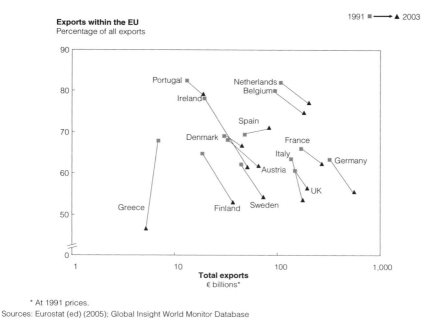

* At 1991 prices.
Sources: Eurostat (ed) (2005); Global Insight World Monitor Database

Figure 5.2 Change in exports of EU member states

factors involved. The fall of the Soviet Union and the opening up of China have created trading opportunities beyond the European Union that did not exist previously. Yet the reversal of relative positions is not just the result of surging trade with the rest of the world. There has also been a marked slowdown of intra-European trade.

Again, other factors may be at play. Since growth slowed compared with its torrential pace in the 1950s and 1960s, trade volumes should also have slowed down. Yet this is not the whole story. The single market has clearly failed when compared with the high aims proclaimed by its progenitors. We believe that Cecchini and his comrades-in-arms created unrealistic expectations, but that the concept itself made perfect sense. Implementation has been the key stumbling block.

It only makes sense to expect further increases in export volumes if the potential for growth is unlimited. From a certain level of existing economic integration, a slowdown must be interpreted not as a sign of trouble, but rather as a consequence of normalization. The other country will no longer be distant and foreign, and the division of labour among nations will not dramatically increase any further because it already exists to a substantial degree. Even in Adam Smith's pin factory, there were natural limits to the productivity gains from specialization.

Why has the SEA failed so conspicuously? To draw conclusions about the inability to boost trade volumes – whether it was the result of poor ideas, inadequate implementation or both – we must first trace the channels through which the miraculous effects of the single market were supposed to work. This will enable us to identify the levers now needed for better progress.

Price differences for consumer goods

The Cecchini programme pinned high hopes on price convergence. Yet today, price differences for durable consumer goods are still amazingly high within the European Union. The same television set can cost up to 60 per cent more in one member state than in another. The differences are even more obvious for household staples; there is not even a tendency toward convergence. Figure 5.3 shows the degree of imbalance in prices for different products in 1992 and in

2002. For some goods, such as batteries, olive oil and Coca-Cola, price differences have decreased. For compact cars, aspirin and tinned tomatoes, they have remained the same, and for a handful of goods, such as Teflon pans and coffee, they have increased dramatically. The law of one price does not prevail universally in other large countries either (in the United States it sometimes pays to buy a car on the East coast and have it shipped out west). Yet it seems relatively clear that the price differences in those regions, almost without exception, are smaller than within the European Union. On average, differences in automobile prices in the United States are only a third of the differences observed in the European Union, and for most other goods the differences are half the EU figure.

If there had been convergence at the lowest price, consumers would have saved a lot of money. But it was always naïve to believe that the implementation of single market rules alone could bring this about. The final price paid by the consumer has three components: the seller's purchase price, the seller's overheads and the seller's

	1992	2002	Change
Batteries	0.45	0.31	−0.14
Olive oil	0.45	0.34	−0.11
Coca-Cola	0.40	0.34	−0.06
Compact cars	0.22	0.21	−0.01
Aspirin	0.38	0.39	0.01
Canned tomatoes	0.35	0.37	0.02
Ground coffee	0.29	0.39	0.10
Teflon pans	0.38	0.48	0.10

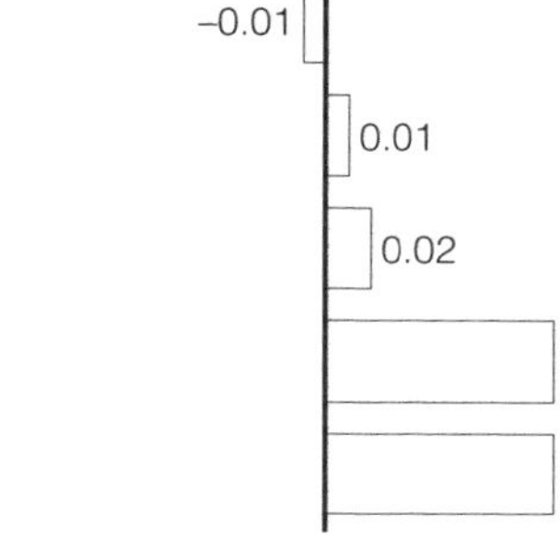

* Incl. taxes.

Sources: Economist Intelligence Unit (2002); own calculations

Figure 5.3   Variation coefficients for prices* within the EU-15, 1992 and 2002

markup, which is determined by the competitive situation. Even if fully implemented, the single market could affect only the first and the last factors. It could harmonize purchase prices and reduce the market power of suppliers that were once dominant nationally.

However, it is not easy for end customers to shop around for most consumer goods, even durables such as cars. The drive from Helsinki to Cadiz takes four to five days by car, no one wants to haul a 28-inch television on the plane, and no Glaswegian is going to travel to Milan to buy shaving foam. For consumers, arbitrage is not a viable mechanism for price equalization. It is conceivable that stronger competition among intermediaries – for instance, through parallel imports from cheaper countries – would have an effect on prices; but the bulkier and heavier the product, the less frequently distributors enter the market to take advantage of any arbitrage opportunity.

Without a fundamental change in wholesale structures, the single market cannot even produce many changes in retailing. Although French retailer Carrefour can now operate supermarkets in Spain, and German operator Aldi has stores in England, the fierceness of local competition is largely determined by building regulations and the like. Brussels cannot influence those at all. People who want to shop, for example, in the city centre of the English university town of Cambridge still have only one choice of supermarket; more are not allowed in the historic town centre.

Even more important are the systematic differences in operating costs. Every supermarket has to pay rent – either imputed or real – for its premises, and the rent varies from country to country depending on real estate prices and the tax situation. The same applies to wages, the cost of electricity, water bills, work safety regulations and many other factors. These costs can make up a significant portion of the end price. And without macroeconomic convergence, the price of television sets is no more likely to converge than the price of haircuts.

It is astonishing that for years the European Commission operated on the assumption that large-scale price convergence would occur even without effective arbitrage and without convergence of macroeconomic fundamentals. On top of that, many barriers to trade persist more than anyone would have thought likely in 1986. For instance, wholesale trading of automobiles in Europe is not completely integrated, partly because the automobile manufacturers want to safeguard their pricing power and branded retail presence.

Until early 2001, Brussels justified this state of affairs by saying that there could be no price convergence as long as there was no single currency. Since the euro has been jingling in consumers' pockets, it is clear even to the last '1992 optimists' that we are unlikely to see uniform prices for consumer goods from mineral water to vacuum cleaners any time soon.

BIGGER, BETTER – RICHER?

The single European market was intended to improve the competitiveness of European business. The creation of more European 'champions' – big companies that could intelligently use their head start in a large, integrated market to compete better on the global market – was an integral part of this. Such large companies were supposed to be able to invest more in research and development, and thus become more productive. In industries with high fixed costs, there was also supposed to be an immediate increase in productivity as a result of increased scale, or so it was hoped. The analysis below shows that it would most probably benefit a region like Europe to have bigger companies in addition to sound medium-sized businesses.

Beyond this first wave of sheer economies of scale and learning at company level, market dynamics were also expected to produce superior European business concepts: better companies, fitter for competition and more capable of driving world-class innovation. The first reason for this improvement is that in a larger market, diffusion of innovation, particularly new technology, travels faster. Not only is the payback of a successful investment in an innovative product or process higher, but also – and very importantly – the sheer number of players thinking and investing in new solutions is greater. If the conditions are such that the successes, but also the failures, of this greater multitude of players can be shared and used as learning experiences for other attempts, then the probability of successful concepts emerging is naturally higher.

The second reason, although often discussed, is not an easy one to grasp. It has to do with the fact that a larger market can accelerate the Schumpeterian process of 'creative destruction', with new and successful companies evolving faster, to eliminate or rationalize inefficient companies faster. From an economic perspective, the Schumpeterian process is in effect equivalent to the diffusion of innovation mentioned above. According to Schumpeter, in a larger market, a newcomer has a higher probability of reaching sufficient strength to threaten a less efficient incumbent. The prize for achieving success is also greater. This 'creative destruction' process is not exclusive to large companies. On the contrary, the role of 'new attacker' is typically played by small and medium-sized companies, the world's true entrepreneurs. The Cecchini report considered that such business rationalization and the elimination of sub-optimal production units would lead to substantial gains.

Let us first examine the importance of scale for European companies. The main advantage of big companies is their ability to do things others cannot, in research, in risk-taking, in rolling out brand and marketing power globally, in setting de facto standards and in attracting people with world-class abilities who want to join the global leaders. Larger companies operating in larger markets have an advantage. In this area, Europe does not stand up too well to international comparison. An analysis of the leading companies according to their industry and origin reveals just how overwhelming the preponderance of US groups often is. The United States has the largest companies in about 75 per cent of the leading industries, while Europe only has about 20 per cent. Even relative to the size of the country, there are far more large US companies than would be expected, particularly in those industries where innovation plays a major role, such as telecommunications, semiconductor and software production, and IT consulting and services (Figure 5.4). European companies' best chance exists only in the less dynamic, more traditional industries.

Almost 14 years after the starting gun for the integrated single market was fired, there is an astonishing lack of truly trans-European companies. Examples of large-scale trans-European mergers such as the Unicredito-HVB Group, the AstraZeneca Group, Dasa-

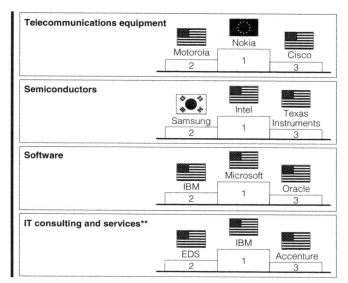

* Measured as a share of sales.
** Excl. Product Support.
Source: Gartner (ed) (2006); iSuppli database (2006); IDC (2006); Gartner (2005); Gartner Inc (2005)

Figure 5.4 Largest* companies in four industries, 2005

Aerospatiale Matra and sanofi-aventis (aventis itself being the result of a Hoechst/Rhône-Poulenc merger) are rare. There are still cultural barriers, considerable state intervention in key industries, language problems, incompatible legal systems and problems with cross-border takeovers, all of which can be explained by a failure of the integration of European capital markets.

Another indication of the lack of large-scale European companies can be seen in *Fortune* magazine's list of the Global 500, the leading companies ranked by revenue. The United States has 176 companies in the Top 500; Europe has 161. However, if Europe were as efficient in the creation of large companies as the United States is, it should, based on its GDP, have 193.

Not only is the absolute number of large companies lower, but as a general rule, Europe's 'champions' also have lower revenues, are more capital intensive, pay more for labour and operate much less profitably. The differences are too great to be explained away by individual distortions such as balance sheet interpretation and option plans that have not been adequately factored in. According to figures from the financial services company GlobalVantage, the return on capital of the top US companies is 60 per cent higher than that of their European counterparts.

The markets take a similar view of the differences between Europe and the United States. Even in 2002, after the bursting of the speculative bubble, the market capitalization of US companies was significantly higher. However, the high total values are also a result of a thoroughgoing consolidation in many industries.

A look at the largest banks and insurance companies worldwide reveals dramatic differences. The market capitalization of the largest financial service providers in the United States (Citigroup, Bank of America, American International Group, JPMorgan Chase & Co, Wells Fargo & Co) was US $884 billion in May 2006, while the market capitalization of similar companies in Europe (HSBC, UBS, Royal Bank of Scotland, UniCredito Italiano, Banco Santander Central Hispano) was only US $586 billion, 66 per cent of the US value. The book value of the European companies mentioned was only 62 per cent of those of the American companies.

Where market size is similar, the extent of the differences in company size is largely the result of industry consolidation. In 2003, the five largest banks in the United States, for example, had a market share of just over 40 per cent; in Europe it was just 16.5 per cent. In retail, the US front-runners had a 40 per cent market share while the Europeans had 26 per cent. In pharmaceuticals, the numbers were 39 to 28 per cent, and the figures were similar in the automobile industry. This shows that, even after the introduction of the European single market, industry consolidation and the resulting increase in company size are far less advanced than in the United States. Lower valuations almost everywhere presumably reflect lower profitability.

Viewed this way, the problem is less the rate of formation of large companies and more their efficiency. The elimination of weaker competitors is still comparatively uncommon. The single market would have been able to contribute to consolidation if the takeover directive had actually been implemented and enforced. Alternatively, increased competitive pressure within the member states – for example with the entry of European rivals into the market – would have led to voluntary mergers. Europe's large-scale companies are therefore comparatively unprofitable: not only are there too few, those that exist are underperforming and are therefore targets for mergers and acquisitions rather than acting as attackers on the global M&A map.

European champions: more than just 'nice to have'?

How problematic is the relative lack of large-scale 'European champions'? It seems that the world's largest companies are greatly increasing their scale and scope, and the resulting institutions are fundamentally changing the competitive landscape. Our projections, based on the experience of the past 20 years, indicate that in 2015, 350 companies will be larger than the smallest company on the list of today's 150 biggest corporations. The largest of them would reach a market value of US $700 billion and earn around US $40 billion a year.

On average, the profits of today's 150 largest companies have risen faster than the diseconomies from increased complexity. In 2004, the 150 largest companies' combined net income of US $650 billion accounted for 46 per cent of the combined net income of the top 2,000 corporations by market capitalization, compared with 39 per cent in 1994. However, as those large companies have increased their share of the top 2,000 companies' total net income, their proportion of total employees has not risen proportionately (Figure 5.5) (Bryan and Zanini, 2005).

One reason that the 150 largest companies have disproportionately high profits is that they use their huge size to create new business models to develop and exploit intangible assets such as employee skills in novel ways. Such business models more than compensate for the diseconomies of increased scale. Also, these companies do not pass on surplus returns to consumers. This, in turn, suggests that they have created unique business models and intangible assets that competitors cannot easily replicate. Consequently, it seems to be attractive for the European Union to facilitate the creation of large-scale companies.

On the other hand, it can be argued that the relative lack of large-scale companies is not too problematic either. On closer examination, it

Top 150 companies**
Companies ranked
151–2,000**

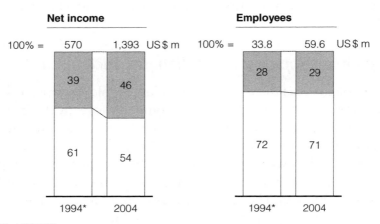

Net income

100% = 570   1,393 US $ m

| 39 | 46 |
| 61 | 54 |

1994*   2004

Employees

100% = 33.8   59.6 US $ m

| 28 | 29 |
| 72 | 71 |

1994*   2004

* Real 2004 US $.
** US and foreign companies with American depository receipts, by market capitalization in 1994 and 2004.
Sources: Global Vantage database; own calculations.

Figure 5.5 Large firms' greater capacity to exploit intangible capital (%)

appears that it is not Europe as a whole that has a different distribution of company sizes, but individual countries. Per trillion US dollars in GDP in 2003, the United States had 26 companies large enough to qualify for *Fortune*'s Global 500. The UK and Switzerland had 30 and 35 respectively. The European countries with the lowest density of big companies were Spain, Italy and Denmark, with six to nine per trillion dollars of GDP. Just a handful of countries that combine a relatively large GDP with a relatively small concentration of above-average-sized companies are responsible for the supposed lack of large-scale companies. Consequently, sweeping generalizations applied to Europe as a whole, such as cultural differences and language problems, do not go very far towards explaining the variations.

If Europe had the 193 mega-companies it should have (assuming it reached the same density ratio as the United States), then there would have to be an additional 34 from Germany, Italy and Spain. Their absence is partially compensated for by Switzerland, the United Kingdom and France, which have more large companies than would be expected based on statistics alone. Countries with an unusually low ratio of large-scale companies, however, are particularly proud of their medium-sized companies, which often operate in highly profitable niches and are leaders acknowledged by a considerable share of the global market.

Where a large, integrated single market can easily be tapped, it is primarily the smaller companies in new industries that quickly grow and benefit from economies of scale. A company in the United States has a single marketing organization, a single marketing campaign and only one tax system to deal with when it wants to sell a new product to the 290 million potential consumers in the United States. By contrast, Germany, the largest individual European market, is made up of only 82 million potential consumers: it is less than a third of the size of the US market in number of customers, and less than a fifth in terms of purchasing power. Theoretically, Europe would therefore have a good chance to boost its growth rate by completing the integrated single market.

The present situation is exacerbated by the fact that the effective size of the individual European national economies is smaller than it could be, as we discussed in Chapter 2. If a similarly high percentage of the population in, say, Germany were to work as much and as productively as in the United States, the size of the German market could increase significantly.

This leads to the second wave of positive stimuli emanating from a large market: the dynamics supporting the creation of highly successful rather than simply big companies. In the following, we shall show that market size correlates with the creation of successful dynamic restructuring processes. More important than the creation of European counterparts to the giants on the other side of the Atlantic – and the higher competitiveness on world markets that comes with it – is more efficiency through economies of scale in a company's own market. If the single market were fully implemented, it should be possible to achieve a high degree of efficiency similar to that in the United States. Yet the smaller the share of the 1992 programme that is implemented successfully, the more likely it is that the effective market size will fall well short of the sum of the individual member states' market sizes.

However, bigger markets could increase the efficiency of production itself and thereby lead to higher profits and greater global competitiveness. To achieve that, there would have to be more evidence of economies of scale, but in reality they are seldom found. In many industries the market size before 1992 was most likely already sufficient to reach minimum efficient scale.

Detailed analyses by economists suggest that, for most industries, the existence of economies of scale largely depends on the size of the magnifying glass used to view the national economy. If the search is begun at the level of the company or of individual, narrowly defined industries, barely any evidence of economies of scale is found. At best, double the work and capital means double the output, but no more. Less than double is rarely found, since the existing degree of efficiency can be achieved anew by repeating what is already practised.

It might appear paradoxical, but the higher the level of aggregation, the larger the effect that is found. If economic activity is examined not in detail, but rather at the level of the national economy as a whole – possibly differentiating between the manufacturing sector and the rest – large increases in efficiency through economies of scale are suddenly visible. Under this lens, and depending upon the analysis and time period examined, a doubling of the inputs can multiply output by as much as 2.5 to 3.4.[1]

How can this contrast be explained? The higher the level of aggregation, the greater the change in the composition of the basic unit of analysis in phases of economic change. New products and processes emerge, some industry segments grow much faster than others, superior companies develop much faster than weaker ones and some competitors are either taken over and restructured or eliminated.

This difficult but ultimately beneficial dynamic process greatly depends on entrepreneurial quality, defined as the discovery and capture of new opportunities for superior products and processes. Entrepreneurial quality can reside in big companies, but also in smaller ones. What counts is that an entrepreneur is able to roll out the new concept – product or process – in a large enough market, on an unfragmented, transparent and level playing field. The bigger the 'home market', the greater the number of companies, the greater the 'incubation space' (more players, greater interaction, faster trial periods), the more room there is to ensure innovation, the more technological development is feasible and the bigger the rewards for winning concepts. In the United States, online brokers like Schwab or E-trade could quickly reach a nationwide customer base of millions (needed for breakeven). In Europe, systems that cost every bit as much need to be built for every member state; few of them can reach profitability as quickly as their US counterparts.

The same logic holds for the Schumpeterian game of creative destruction. The larger the market, the greater a company's ability to grow and replace less efficient competitors: that is, to win. Under the macroeconomic lens, what is measured as 'economies of scale' is also influenced by these changes in composition, and this effect is even stronger when entire industries are considered. Companies with higher efficiency also have a higher demand for the factors of production; their share in the total production increases. The advantages of a large single market therefore essentially stem from a greater weight of superior business concepts, driven by faster, more successful innovation and a Schumpeter-like process of creative destruction.

It is not size, then, that is the key to increasing efficiency, but successful structural change: the rapid replacement of losers with winners. The faster the wrong concept is 'disproved' by the market, and the more frequently superior companies enter the market and grow at above-average rates, the sooner economies of scale can be realized. It is therefore no wonder that Europe has not profited from the single market as hoped. A simple increase in market size was never going to guarantee greater efficiency. Only liberalized product markets, combined with free entry (and exit) by competitors, would allow the advantages of the 1992 programme to become a reality.

There are several reasons that we do not see faster product cycles, higher rates of innovation and more creative destruction in Europe. Neither the structural change – the replacement of old industries with new ones – nor the intensity of competition in individual industries has significantly increased as a result of the single market. Most European governments are quick to come up with a package to save large companies teetering on the brink of failure. Whether it is

Philipp Holzmann in Germany, Crédit Lyonnais in France or Railtrack in England, the protection of jobs and existing structures almost always takes priority. If a company is insolvent, its capital base will quickly be restored with state funds. And the situation is no different in the preservation of old sectors; whether it be basic material industries, agriculture or fisheries, no sector is so unprofitable that the European Union or its national governments will not keep it alive with subsidies.

Corporate weaknesses add another dimension to the problem. European companies are less attractive to the next generation of highly skilled workers, who are becoming more and more important for the success of companies. Students generally prefer employers from their native culture. Typically, 64 per cent of European students are interested in signing on with a European company; in the United States, 83 per cent want a US employer. This suggests that a larger share of Europeans looking for a future employer are open to 'switching' than in the United States. In Chapter 8, we return to ways to solve this critical problem for Europe, the fact that highly qualified people turn their backs on it (or remain here less than enthusiastically).

The surveys in which *Fortune* analyses the most-admired companies show where the weaknesses lie in the eyes of many observers. The 10,000 analysts, managers and directors interviewed chose the 10 best companies in categories such as innovation, quality of management and employee talent. Of the top 10 companies in the employee talent category in 2005, nine were US companies and just one was European. For innovation, eight were US companies and two were European. The situation is even worse for quality of management and financial soundness: nine of the top 10 in these categories were US companies, one Japanese – and not one was European.

The European market does not yet have the characteristics of a large, level playing field that rewards the best entrepreneurial innovations appropriately and quickly enough to allow for a globally superior fitness process. Entrepreneurs need an unfragmented market and an absence of bureaucratic hurdles to develop innovation and increase value creation. In this sense, achieving a qualifying market size matters, not only for the world's biggest, but also for the world's best, be they large or small.

FINANCIAL SERVICES AND CAPITAL MARKETS

One sector that was supposed to lead to especially high growth in Europe is financial services. The Cecchini Report expected an increase of 1.5 percentage points. Approximately 0.2 percentage points of this was supposed to come from a reduction in bank fees to a uniform and overall lower level. The rest was expected to result from the indirect advantages of a more competitive financial services sector. In particular, the creation of a single European capital market was supposed to lower the cost of financing for companies and create diversification benefits for investors. The rationale was simple: the financial services sector was involved in nearly all transactions in the national economy, and therefore it was to work as a multiplier and generally provide for more efficiency.

The central instrument for attaining these goals was the Investment Services Directive (ISD), otherwise known as the 'single European passport' for investment services. Any financial institution regulated in one member state was to be able to offer its services across the whole European Union. Combined with the elimination of capital transaction controls and monetary union, a single European market was supposed to become a reality not just for goods and labour, but for capital as well.

Customers who require financial services across borders have seen few benefits. Despite a directive about fees for money transfers abroad (but in the European Union), and despite the introduction of the single currency, charges often remained sky-high. Some advances have been made, however, and more plans are in the pipeline. Since 2003 the so-called European transfers have brought relief for clients transferring less than €12,500. To facilitate future progress, the European Commission has stepped up pressure for the creation of the Single Euro Payments Area (SEPA). A pan-European system should be in place by 2008 so that people can use payment cards and direct debits and transfer cash across borders as cheaply and quickly as for their domestic transactions. The European system is supposed to replace national systems by 2010. Banks have begun working on how to make SEPA a reality by the two deadlines, but are still a long way from the SEPA goal. This is mainly because of their worries about the cost of creating the infrastructure on the one hand, and forgone revenues due to price cuts on the other.

There are also difficulties surrounding service charges for accounts. Here, too, market entry by foreign competitors and increased competition should have harmonized fees at a lower level. In fact, there has been a tendency for fees in Europe to increase, and there is certainly no question of harmonization. For example, while in many cases there are no charges for personal cheque accounts and cheque transfers in the UK, Italians have to live with average annual fees of around €133 (Figure 5.6). Even the fee models are not converging across Europe. In Portugal most of the account maintenance costs are covered by transaction fees, whereas in Germany non-transactional fees are much more important.

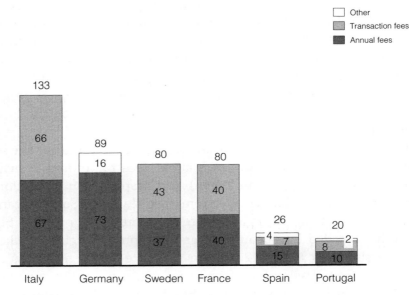

Source: Our estimates based on data from national central banks and consumer organizations.

Figure 5.6 Composition of annual bank account maintenance costs in the European Union 2003 (€)

Market forces can only work where new entry is possible. The September 2004 agreement between the European Union and Germany regards the German state-owned regional banks or the 2005 Unicredito-HVB Group merger as positive examples. Yet in too many member states (often in southern Europe), foreign competitors are kept out by a combination of red tape and carefully orchestrated national ownership. That is why cross-border mergers remain elusive in many EU banking markets. The only acceptable solution is a pan-European takeover code. It would benefit both the financial services industry and all other sectors.

Nationalistic meddling is a fact of life when it comes to bank mergers, yet parish-pump politics can only explain so much of the lack of convergence and cross-border entry. Bank structures and financing models are often part of a complex structure of economic relationships, and are embedded in tradition, the legal system and culture. No one expected a rapid correction of the differences that have been developing since 1850 between universal banking (as practised in much of continental Europe) and group banking, where commercial and investment banks are separate (as in London). Where it is taking place, the single market is not the cause. In the past 10 years commercial and universal banks have also started to put up a good fight in investment banking, in both New York and London.

In his speech at the German stock exchange's New Year Reception in 2001, Deutsche Börse's then CEO Werner G Seifert joked that the 'integrated European capital market' was not integrated or especially European or much of a single market. He was referring in particular to stock markets, and unfortunately his assessment was justified. In a well-functioning single market, Europeans would be just as likely to hold shares from other EU countries as from their own domestic market. The fact is, however, that they still invest most of their money domestically, although this tendency is changing. According to securities account statistics of the German central bank for 2004, almost 80 per cent of the shares in German securities custody accounts were from Germany, while holdings from elsewhere in Europe accounted for just 13.9 per cent in 2003. Germans thus owned nearly six times as many domestic shares as they would if the single market was a reality.

Put another way, controlling for other factors that influence cross-border holdings, such as distance, the European Union's attempts at harmonization have failed to encourage cross-border flows. Most sovereign states are better at facilitating inflows and outflows of capital than the European Union is, even among member states. There would be considerable advantages in more internationally diversified capital investments. Correlations between the European markets are not perfect, and people who invest some of their money abroad usually either increase their return, or reduce their portfolio volatility. Diversification is particularly important when the market is weak. However, the reasons that domestic markets are preferred are not far to seek. At the moment, the only options for private investors are to pay enormous bank fees for purchases on foreign stock exchanges, or unfavourable prices with very high trading margins on their national stock exchanges. Combine this with the absence of a common language or integrated information, and the home bias is not hard to understand.

In stock trading, the highest volumes of a particular stock are usually concentrated on the issuer's domestic stock exchange. Almost no stock is traded at high volumes on two exchanges, as the cost savings from lower trading margins that occur by concentrating on one place are simply too high. For some time it was hoped that European trade would eventually become concentrated. At present, significant volumes of trading in foreign stocks can be found at only two stock exchanges in Europe: London and (much further behind) Frankfurt. However, neither exchange has been in a position to challenge the other's dominance in its domestic blue-chip stocks. Today, experts largely agree that a truly European stock market cannot become a reality without stock exchange mergers or unified pan-European rules and regulations.

This lack of progress is unsatisfactory. It would be far cheaper for companies to raise capital if all European investors had access to domestic and foreign stocks at the same transaction costs. Investors would also be able to diversify their portfolios more effectively, and overall investment could increase.

While an integrated market in equities remains largely elusive, monetary union did improve companies' ability to raise outside capital. Thanks to the EMU, interest rates in Europe have converged at Germany's low level. This has meant a billion euro gift first to the banks, especially in the South European Mediterranean countries, part of which they passed on to customers by lowering interest rates on loans. External funding of investments has therefore become cheaper for many companies. Also, households found that they could suddenly afford much bigger mortgages, bidding up the value of real estate in the process.

While housing investment has grown sharply in the EU member states that received the largest windfall from the low German interest rates, investment spending by firms has not seen a comparable surge. Nor did the single market lead to a breakthrough in direct investments. Volumes did not increase until after the introduction of the euro, although by then the increase was a worldwide trend and therefore should not be attributed to the single market. All in all, the single market has fallen spectacularly short of its potential in European capital markets.[2] The European Union therefore set up a commission under economist Alexandre Lamfalussy in the summer of 2000 to come up with extensive recommendations for reform. It concluded that the existing EU legislative framework for capital markets with its focus on minimum harmonization and mutual recognition was not sufficient to achieve a real single capital market (Committee of Wise Men, 2001). Consequently, the Lamfalussy Committee called for a four-level approach to regulation, based on two new committees, the European Securities Committee (ESC) and the Committee of the European Securities Regulators (CESR). Both were set up by the European Commission in June 2001.

Sooner or later, according to the Lamfalussy Committee, national regulatory authorities will have to align their organizations. At present there are two competing models: the all-in-one model of the Financial Services Authority (FSA), which oversees the regulation of all financial services performed in the United Kingdom, and the separate-parallel model in which special authorities work separately in parallel on regulating banks, stock trading or insurance companies (depending on the country). Both models are relatively efficient in the supervision and enforcement of existing norms.

However, industry experts increasingly feel that the FSA model is more suitable in terms of cost reduction, efficient monitoring of universal banks and those banks that combine banking and insurance (bancassurance) and the hiring of sufficiently highly qualified personnel. The last point in particular underscores one of the key deficits identified by the Lamfalussy Committee: at the EU level, only a few officials possess adequate knowledge of the capital markets.

It is still unclear at this point whether there will be a financial regulator for Europe as a whole. The Lamfalussy Committee sketched out two scenarios in 2000, recommending trial of the four-level regulatory approach (see Chapter 6). If it succeeds, all is well. If not, it might be appropriate to create a single financial regulator for Europe as a whole. Whereas France preferred a centralized solution, the United Kingdom wanted to retain the existing decentralized structure. Experts in Germany were undecided, while the German central bank favoured national regulation. In the end, the Commission's green paper, launched in May 2005, decided to retain the current, largely unsuccessful structures, but with some token concessions to those preferring centralization.

Just as important for the creation of a European capital market is the question of the stock exchange and settlement structure. Although two dominant and internationally leading derivative stock exchanges have been formed over the last 10 years through cross-border mergers (Eurex in Frankfurt and LIFFE in London), the Federation of European Securities Exchanges (FESE) still has 24 members despite the euro and the single market. However, this number is slowly decreasing. Although Euronext, the union of the stock exchanges of Paris, Brussels, Amsterdam and Lisbon, operates more in the form of an alliance than as a completely integrated stock exchange organization, attempts towards further integration will follow. In May 2000, a merger between the Frankfurt and London stock exchanges to form International Exchange (iX) was intended to create the biggest stock exchange in Europe, accounting for 53 per cent of European trading with blue-chip stocks. Expectations ran high, particularly for a general wave of consolidation and easier cross-border trading. Even then – if the present-day structure continued to exist – one prerequisite would still have remained unfulfilled: the maximum possible integration of the clearing and settlement operations. This is an area where Europe significantly underperforms when compared with US markets, and that constitutes a major hindrance to efficient cross-border transactions.

Two questions need to be asked of the European Union's attempts to integrate its financial markets. If progress is so difficult, is it worth the effort? And if so, how can the European Union do better? To answer the first question, we should take a fresh look at the expected economic benefits. More than a decade of thinking about the economics of financial markets and growth has unearthed many pertinent findings. The bottom line is that the Delors Commission may in fact not have been optimistic enough about the likely benefits of deeper financial integration. If a fully integrated European capital market arrived, it would ensure two things. First of all, it would provide access to funding for firms across the EU on equal terms. Second, it would allow Europeans to reap much larger diversification benefits as portfolios are diversified across the EU.

One standard measure of financial development is the ratio of total external financing (private credit and stock market capitalization) to GDP. Where this ratio is high, firms should have access to ample funds. Where it is low, both new and old enterprises will struggle to tap fresh funds. This ratio for the European Union as a whole is markedly lower than in the United States.

Given how well documented the link between finance and growth is, we can predict how much faster Europe could grow if it actually managed to raise the determinants of financial development to the maximum EU standard. The growth effects for the laggards today will be much greater than for the leaders. As Figure 5.7 makes clear, gains for the UK and the Netherlands will be relatively small. Greece, Denmark and Italy will profit much more. Overall, Europe's growth rate for value added could accelerate by almost 1 per cent per year, a tremendously large windfall for a continent where a good year sees a 2 per cent increase.

The diversification benefits are every bit as impressive. Europeans still stay at home with their investments to a surprising extent. If they did not, they could reduce the risk of their portfolios, or make greater

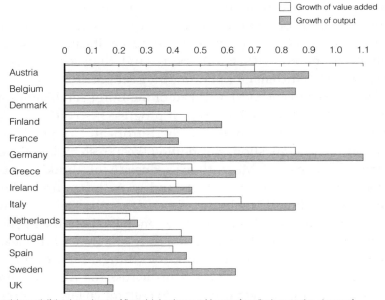

* Potential growth if the determinants of financial development (degree of creditor's protection, degree of shareholders' protection and judicial efficiency) are raised to the maximum EU standard.
Source: Guiso *et al*, 2004.

Figure 5.7 Potential growth of value added and output in the manufacturing industry (%)*

gains while keeping risk constant. Germans, for example, could gain at least €100 billion per year on their investments, keeping risks constant, if they achieved a decent degree of pan-European diversification. Gains in other member states will be just as large. If investors can take greater risks with individual investments, funding start-ups and the like should be easier, generating further gains.

If the benefits are so large, and past initiatives to reap them have failed so conspicuously, how can the European Union do better? Financial market integration is arguably the one area in which subsidiarity should be done away with immediately. It not only gets in the way; it is at the heart of every problem. National regulators preserve their own influence by not implementing EU directives in the spirit in which they were intended, even if they follow the letter of the law. If there were (relatively slim) economic gains from EMU worth the tremendous psychological, logistical and political efforts to make it happen, financial market integration should be feasible. A pan-European regulator, a takeover code, one legal form for all listed EU companies that is binding and not just one option among many – these are, in the greater scheme of things, relatively small steps that the European Union could undertake if it decided that economic dynamism is not just a phrase for the manifestos at the end of summits.

EXPANSION: A BIG STEP TOWARDS THE SINGLE MARKET?

After five rounds of enlargement, the European Union has expanded from a six-member entity into the world's largest single market, with 27 member states and a population of 489 million. Accession negotiations with Croatia and Turkey opened in October 2005.

With the recent joining of 12 mainly Eastern European countries, the European Union gained significantly in inhabitants and variety. The European Union's area increased by 34 per cent, and its population by 27 per cent. Its GDP, however, rose by just 6.5 per cent, far less than in each previous expansion step, with the exception of the expansion to the north and the joining of Austria in 1995.

Including the 12 new member states, the European Union's per capita economic performance fell by about 16 per cent, and wealth disparities in the enlarged European Union are enormous. The new members in central and eastern Europe are significantly poorer than longer-standing members, and in comparison with previously integrated countries (such as Spain and Portugal), their economies are unusually fragile.

What, then, can the eastward expansion contribute to the solution of the European Union's current problems? In the short term, the answer is almost nothing. The continent is not exactly short of workers, market size will barely increase, and Europe will have to struggle with still more difficulties in joint decision making. Large-scale inflows of labour are unlikely, and downward pressures on wages are not going to materialize. Over the longer term, the big expansion eastwards will help the European Union to maintain its role as an economic heavyweight. As the new member states catch up with western productivity levels, they will add more and more to the European Union's GDP; without them, the European Union in 2050 would be a markedly weaker entity.

The central and eastern European countries have high shares of agricultural labour today. Throughout the developed world, reallocating labour from agriculture into industry and services has been a key factor in rapid growth. The EU's Common Agricultural Policy (CAP) threatens this transformation process. Subsidies and other measures intended to preserve farm life, though wasteful and expensive, are accepted in Western Europe and not too costly: they are received by only 2–3 per cent of the population. For the new member states, however, they could easily become a growth trap. This will not show up immediately. After accession, as the spigot of EU agricultural funds is gradually opened, output and productivity will surge. It will take about 5–10 years for the slowdown in structural change to begin to weigh down the performance of the new members.

Viewed this way, it can almost be regarded as a stroke of luck that the European Union is to place restrictions on the agrarian aid it provides to the new members. A similar rule applies to regional and structural funds, which have helped to fund many infrastructure projects in the last 20 years, mainly on the Iberian peninsula, in Greece and southern Italy. Nevertheless, the southern European countries appear determined to ensure that comparable aid will not be available for the new members.

Increases in per capita income, as suggested by the successful examples of Ireland, Portugal and Spain, could be harder to come by for yet another reason. Not every member state gains. When Greece joined the EEC in 1981, it had a per capita income that was equal to 66 per cent of the average of today's European Union, based on purchasing power parities, and it remains at that level today.

If the new member countries adopt the euro as their currency, they will have additional problems. Poor, fast-growing countries often experience relatively high rates of inflation. This makes perfect sense. As the productivity of their traded sector increases, the prices of non-traded goods have to rise. This shows up as inflation. Devaluations are an obvious way to avoid negative effects on the country's competitiveness. If the new countries simply adopt the euro, they will lose this option. To stop inflation, they will have to follow a restrictive fiscal policy – and there is little reason to assume that this would work any better in central and eastern Europe than it did as part of the Stability Pact in Western Europe.

Another cause for worry is the political dimension of enlargement, at least in today's decision-making structures. The voting regulations that the European Union adopted in Nice in December 2000 will allow more and more blockades after expansion. Even if the new members prove to be 'good Europeans', with 27 or more states represented in the European Parliament, the European Commission and the Council of Ministers, it will become harder and harder to pass new initiatives. Without extensive reform of the decision-making processes, eastward expansion could prove to be more a curse than a blessing.

When the single market was launched, hopes were high. And for good reasons: a single market should undeniably confer the economic advantages Europe will need even more in the future. Instead of throwing in the towel, therefore, Europe needs to focus on critical implementation efforts. In three key areas – economies of scale through structural changes, an integrated capital market and the freedom of workforce mobility – considerable potential remains to be tapped.

Pure economies of scale cannot exist where markets remain highly fragmented. Achieving higher efficiency through economies of scale in Europe requires a Darwinist takeover process in labour markets. Regulatory hurdles seem to be most important here, although language and cultural differences still feature largely.

Doing the unfinished homework from the 1992 single market programme will continue to be a frustrating and slow process. It might become less so when a clear focus on the main levers is achieved.

There is, however, another game that Europe can play, with similarly high economic stakes. It has largely operated away from the eyes of the public, but the old continent has already played it well in the past, and it may be able to generate more dynamism than the SEA ever did if it continues to do well. The new game is 'smart regulation', and we turn to it in the next chapter.

6

What comes after deregulation? Smart regulation!

Few business leaders these days advocate giving more decision-making power to governments. 'The less state involvement the better' seems to be the consensus in many parts of the business world as well as in academia, since the days of Thatcher and Reagan at least. This shift in the overall intellectual climate has left its mark on a number of industries once thought to be natural monopolies. In these sectors, particularly utilities, it was common for the state to set prices, capacities, the return on capital and the number of competitors. Advances in information technology and diminishing faith in the ability of the state to control the economy following the stagflation of the 1970s created a vision that deregulation – the liberation of the economic process from state intervention – would drive growth, generate higher profits and improve service. And in many cases deregulation has been a huge success.

Yet the call to 'let the market rip' is too simple if Europe is to increase its productivity in key areas of the economy. What should come after deregulation in Europe in our view is not a downsized, passive 'night watchman' state. What Europe needs is a state that performs its core tasks actively with intelligence, good judgement and professionalism. There is much to be done, but, as we shall see, regulation and market forces need not be at odds, provided the state pursues smart regulation.

To describe how smart regulation might work, we illustrate the necessary paradigm shift with examples of successful and less successful regulatory choices in recent years, from simple deregulation to the regulation of new industries. We then suggest systematically adopting four principles critical to smart regulation: applying cost–benefit analyses, giving preference to general frameworks over prescriptive rules, measuring the effects of regulation, and setting fixed expiration dates to ensure that regulation does not outlive its usefulness.

CATCHING UP THROUGH DEREGULATION: TWO EXAMPLES

Deregulation has boosted productivity considerably by abolishing rules and regulations that directly interfere with business and simplifying market access for new competitors. The telecommunications industry offers a prime example of how market deregulation in conjunction with new technologies can be managed to good effect. Yet it does not always have to be high tech. As our second example – the productivity growth unleashed by the deregulation of road freight services – shows, even sectors with little or no innovation in the basic technology also benefit from the liberation of market forces.

Telecommunications

Not so long ago, Europe's telecommunications industry trailed far behind that of the United States. Long-distance calls were expensive and many countries offered no choice of phone besides the standard-issue rotary-dial model with a coiled cord. Today, most of Europe has a higher proportion of mobile phone users than the United States, the range of kit on offer is astonishing, and the cost of both national and international calls has fallen to among the lowest levels in the world.

Deregulation made a major contribution to unleashing rapid productivity improvements in telecommunications – but it was not just deregulation in the traditional sense. Following the deregulation of fixed-line telephony, Europe initially made the right choices in designing the regulatory framework for mobile communications, and these choices proved to be even more important for unlocking productivity reserves than simple deregulation alone.

With deregulation and keener competition in fixed-line telephone services from the mid-1990s onwards, productivity soared. As demand for fixed-line services did not increase at nearly the same pace as prices fell, the resulting drop in income spurred European telephone companies to improve productivity. While French and German productivity in 1992 was still only around half that of the United States, both countries managed to close a good part of the gap, especially after 1998. Today, labour productivity in the fixed-line network segment still lags behind the United States, but the gap is much smaller: 13 per cent in Germany and 38 per cent in France (McKinsey Global Institute, 2002). These figures are particularly impressive considering that productivity growth per worker in the United States nearly doubled in the same period. Key contributors to the gains on the European side were investments in modern technology such as ISDN and labour-saving infrastructure (for instance underground cables, which are less susceptible to damage).

The other side of the coin is capital productivity, which was at about half the US level in both France and Germany, in part thanks to the thousands of kilometres of buried cable and the related infrastructure in the exchanges. On balance, however, the improvements outweigh the setbacks; Europe has significantly boosted its overall productivity in fixed-line telecommunications for all factors of production. European regulations after 1990 were crucial in opening up telecoms markets. Without a push from Brussels, competition would probably have taken much longer in arriving.

The Commission also kept its foot on the accelerator. In the mid-1990s, the Information Society Forum, a committee of experts engaged by the European Union, reported that Europe was trailing far behind the United States and Japan. In early 1996, the European Union approved a timetable for the liberalization of all telecommunications markets to begin on 1 January 1998, with special regulations for smaller countries and those with an underdeveloped infrastructure. It stipulated that the telecommunications markets in all member states should be completely deregulated by 2003 at the very latest.

The arrival of new market entrants and the resulting increase in competitive intensity helped to raise productivity. Layoffs were an unavoidable consequence. Between 1994 and 2005, more than 100,000 employees had to leave Deutsche Telekom AG, which is responsible for Germany's fixed-line network,[1] while France Télécom reduced its headcount in its fixed-line divisions by 30,000. Further cuts are generally expected in the near future.[2] The good news is that the deregulated telecoms industry has so far created more jobs than have been lost.

Road freight

In terms of technology, the road freight industry is a traditional or even stagnating sector, but its deregulation brought forth another success story of reinvigorated productivity growth. In the United States, market entry was liberalized in 1980, and mandatory price lists abolished. Labour productivity, which had fallen between 1976 and 1980, then began to rise – by 1 per cent a year over the next 10 years – at a time when productivity in the United States was otherwise largely stalled. Today, the sector handles 40 per cent more ton-kilometres per working hour than in 1980. Deregulation has also meant much higher pressure of work, however. Truck drivers spend up to 90 hours a week behind the wheel, and their wages are much lower than before liberalization.

Before 1988, European trucking was still subject to traditional regulation. Truck size classes were specified and monitored in detail, official prices were set for national and international shipments, and only domestic companies could supply the respective domestic market. Danish shipping agents, for example, could not arrange shipments between two cities within Germany. Cross-border transport was regulated by bilateral agreements, which meant that an Italian company sending a consignment to Paris had to comply with different regulations than for a shipment to Munich. Cross-border traffic within the European Union has been liberalized since 1989, and fixed price lists are a thing of the past. In 1993, restrictions on shipments between destinations in other European countries were lifted, and rules for truck sizes and weights were liberalized.

As in the United States, the increasing role of market forces in road freight in the European Union has boosted productivity. In 1992, road freight productivity in Germany and France lagged behind the United States by 35 to 40 per cent, a gap that has since shrunk to around 15 per cent (Figure 6.1). Economic output per working hour in road freight increased by 5 per cent per year in Europe, approximately three times faster than for the economy as a whole. Part of the remaining difference versus the United States is attributable to that country's geographical advantages and higher total economic

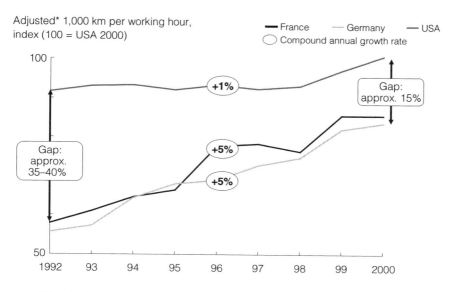

* Price-related adjustments for express and defined date deliveries.
Source: McKinsey Global Institute, 2002.

Figure 6.1 Labour productivity in road freight: France, Germany and the United States

output. An average truck run in the United States covers almost twice the distance of the average run in Europe, and the United States also permits larger and heavier trucks. The combination of greater distance, size and weight substantially increases the number of ton-kilometres per driver hour in the United States.

However, in both economies the effect of deregulation has been the same: lower prices. In Europe, road freight prices dropped by as much as 25 to 50 per cent between 1993 and 1997 alone (McKinsey Global Institute, 2002). The productivity gains unleashed by deregulation thus mainly flowed to customers rather than to the industry.

The elimination of regulated prices for road freight offers a particularly clear example of the link between deregulation and productivity gains. Before 1994, price competition in European road freight was restricted by the government, which enforced industry-wide price lists. After liberalization, price competition shot up, putting pressure on trucking companies to increase their productivity by reducing the number of empty runs, building networks and lowering administrative expenses.

Market concentration in Europe is still low. While the six leading suppliers in the United States boast market shares of 15 to 46 per cent (depending on the segment), the six largest European road freight companies account for a mere 9 per cent of total market sales. Market share and company size affect a company's ability to realize productivity gains. The lack of integration of the European capital markets when it comes to takeovers hampers consolidation of the road freight industry in Europe. We can therefore assume that the initial progress towards closing the Europe–US productivity gap will slow down considerably. In any case, provided Europe continues to promote the use of IT in road freight, it is expected to nearly close the productivity gap with the United States. In many ways this sector is a perfect example of the benefits that EU-wide deregulation can bring.

LIMITATIONS AND RISKS OF DEREGULATION

Simply lifting price controls and removing barriers to market entry is not the solution to all economic ills. It will not always work as well as it did for road freight or long-distance phone calls. Yet in these cases and others, specific decisions made by regulators were clearly critical to the transformation from government administrative structures to a functioning market. Issuing predefined access regulations for fixed-line telecommunications networks, for instance, proved to be a much smarter choice than the pricing formulas imposed in the United States and the United Kingdom.

Widespread deregulation and the privatization of utilities such as telecommunications have also brought about a more fundamental change. The role of the state has clearly shifted from that of a business owner to that of a regulator. In an ideal world, the state should act not as a key player, but as an impartial referee, umpire or arbitrator in the competitive process.

To fulfil this new role, however, regulators have to acquire and develop a deep understanding of the industry as well additional technical and economic skills. After all, the traditional notion that certain industries were natural monopolies arose because of their technical features, with a network structure being a notable common denominator. It was advances in information technology in the 1960s that first made it technically possible to separate the production of utility services such as electricity and telecommunications from their distribution, paving the way for deregulation.

If regulators today are to determine what framework or even what charges are appropriate when granting third-party suppliers access to the end customer via the distribution network of an incumbent monopoly, they need suitable cost models and evaluation processes. The need for industry-specific expertise holds true for many regulatory decisions, from gas and electric power distribution, the pricing of ADSL lines, the use of the last mile and the issuing of mobile communications licences to the purchasing of landing rights at airports. Where this expertise is lacking, both regulation and deregulation can have disastrous results.

Although reducing the state's influence through privatization was undoubtedly the right approach, continuing to pursue deregulation – simply ending state involvement in the economic process – is not the answer. What is needed instead is smart regulation: principles and processes for determining the best way to reach goals and set policies that will promote competitive markets. The regulator should ensure that competition works wherever it is technically feasible and makes sense ethically; it can also play a role by insisting that companies agree on technical standards that cannot be left up to the invisible hand of the market.

Smart regulation as we understand it currently exists only in piecemeal form. To encourage it to take root and spread in Europe, we believe it is instructive to examine the limitations and risks of regulatory decisions in more detail. In the following we take a closer look at mobile phone regulation in the United States and Europe.

One of the most striking examples of regulations providing only poor guidance, almost ruining a promising industry, is mobile telephony in the United States. In late 1999, the *Economist* described the case of Anne Schrader, a Denver journalist who was sent to Columbine High School to report on the tragic school shooting incident. Instead of driving straight to the scene of the crime and maintaining crucial contact with the editorial office by mobile phone, Schrader had to try to borrow one of the office's six cell phones, as she did not have one of her own. But all had already been lent out. So away she drove with her pager. When it beeped soon afterwards, she had to stop to call the office from a pay phone at the nearest drugstore. This happened several times on her way to the school. At the crime scene, she managed to borrow a phone from a colleague, but by then the local network was so overloaded that she could not get a connection (*Economist*, 7 October 1999).

In short, at a time when teenagers all over Europe were beginning to treat mobile phones as a fashion accessory, middle-class adults in the United States around 1999 commonly went without. At the end of the 1990s, the United States was far behind Europe in mobile telephony. A variety of factors were responsible.

First, licences were issued for astonishingly small cells. Providers had to buy access rights for several small areas in the same state simultaneously to be able to provide comprehensive coverage. In the 50 federal states, the Federal Communications Commission (FCC) granted a total of 734 area-based licences in the first round alone. This type of regulation was aimed at bringing as many competitors onto the scene as possible, and small basic units for the issue of licences initially facilitated market entry at local level. As a consequence, however, instead of several national mobile phone networks, a motley assortment of more than 300 providers emerged, each covering small, specific markets.

Second, there was a raft of different technical standards: European GSM, TDMA, CDMA. It took a long time for digital technology to replace analogue telephones with their disturbing crackling and noise, and the systems were frequently incompatible with one another. A telephone bought for Sprint PCS, for example, often did not work in a GTE system. Even more importantly, because of the incompatibilities and the fragmentation of the markets, business travellers from the US East Coast were unable to use their own phones when visiting the West Coast. At a time when a Spaniard had no trouble calling home from Finland on his mobile, a New Yorker in LA found it no easy matter to do the same.

Third, in retrospect, the rate structure often seemed difficult to grasp. Not only was it hard to get a connection outside one's home state, but the cost of calling home was prohibitive. A cartoon in the *New Yorker* in 1998 reflected widespread opinion. It pictured a buffalo in the middle of the prairie expressing his woes on his cell phone: 'I love the convenience, but the roaming charges are killing me.' To top it off, the person receiving the call had to pay a large share of the charges without knowing where the call had originated or what it would cost. One result of the regulatory choices in the United States was that people tended to use their cell phones only occasionally, as portable telephone booths, not as constantly activated links and accessories, as in Europe. According to a 1999 study by the Yankee Group, almost a third of all US cell phone owners used their phone only for outgoing calls, and a further 20 per cent never switched their phones on for more than two hours a day.

Europe got it right in the 1990s and became the world leader in mobile phones. No other continent has such a high concentration of users, most calls are inexpensive, transmission quality is excellent, and usage across borders is amazingly simple.

This success story is mainly attributable to the Global System for Mobile Communications or GSM, the high-tech digital standard that served as the basis for nearly all licences issued to mobile communications providers in Europe in the 1990s. The right to operate a network was granted at the appropriate economic level for that time: the national level.[3] As a result, each European market saw the emergence of a few companies that were able to combine national coverage with relatively high volumes of calls and customers, and that competed intensely with one another.[4] Thanks to economies of scale in the processing of customer data, invoices and the like, providers in Europe were able to become very efficient very quickly – and had to.

Intelligent price models were a further plus. There were no charges for inbound calls. Mobile phone customers had no reason to leave their phones switched off all the time. Anyone who called a mobile phone number knew from the code that it would cost more than a call to a fixed line. European mobile communications providers also pioneered prepaid rates: their customers could easily use their mobile phones at a fixed price per minute (thanks to prepaid telephone cards) with no set monthly charges. They could also include their children at affordable prices. These new price structures sent subscriber numbers through the roof. In Germany and France, the number of mobile phone users per 100 inhabitants rose from less than 20 in 1998 to between 74 and 86 in 2004, despite the fact that income per subscriber fell slightly (Figure 6.2). In the late 1990s, these three advantages – easy nationwide roaming, portability across borders and intelligent pricing – drove a nearly 200 per cent increase in the income of the mobile companies within two years.

The launch of GSM across Europe created outstanding call quality with broad coverage. This, and economies of scale conferred by high-volume production of telephones and base stations, allowed rapid expansion of communication networks. The introduction of GSM can be regarded as an all-round success throughout Europe. Apart from the technical standards and the basic rules of competition, implementation was left up to the national regulators. Depending on the size of the market and its degree of development, regulators could, for example, restrict the number of competitors and determine the procedure for the issue of licences. Uniformity where necessary, flexibility and adaptation to local conditions where possible, combined with the decision to rely on the best technology: all these features give

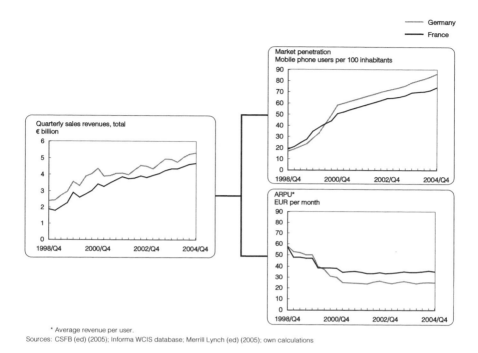

* Average revenue per user.
Sources: CSFB (ed) (2005); Informa WCIS database; Merrill Lynch (ed) (2005); own calculations

Figure 6.2 Sales per customer and market penetration, mobile phones: France and Germany, 1998–2004

Europe every reason to be proud of how its mobile phone market has developed since 1990.

The regulatory structure also had severe consequences for productivity. In France, labour productivity in the mobile communications sector was more than double that in the United States in 2000, and Germany's lead was 45 per cent (McKinsey Global Institute, 2002). Almost two-thirds of the French lead is attributable to the right regulatory structure. An employee in the mobile phone industry in France supports over twice as many customers in an hour as his or her US counterpart. Half of the difference is because of the sub-optimal size of US companies, while another fifth can be put down to the technology used. To be fair, in Germany, there are indications that high output per employee in the mobile phone industry was also achieved in part by the use of a high level of capital. The output of German mobile phone companies per unit of capital is likely to have been lower than that of US competitors. This was not the case in France, where capital productivity is thought to have been relatively high and at par with the US level at the time. If we combine both indicators – labour and capital productivity – Germany is behind the United States, while France is ahead.

This performance is not bad considering that Europe otherwise lags significantly behind the United States. It is also worth noting that the capital productivity figures for the United States are artificially high because of the lack of investment in base stations. While this raises US capital productivity on paper, the resulting poor service – as experienced by the unlucky reporter at Columbine High School – really ought to be factored in as reducing the value of actual output.

Rapid productivity growth in European mobile communications is a recent phenomenon. Until 1995, the United States led the way in labour productivity, and it is only since 1998 that France and Germany have taken the lead. In all three countries, economic output per employee rose considerably. In the United States it has more than doubled since 1992. For an economy as a whole, productivity gains in a sub-market are especially beneficial when the corresponding product or service accounts for a large share of overall demand or when this share can increase rapidly. This is what happened in the mobile communications sector.

The United States lost its lead to Europe in mobile phones in the 1990s solely because of poor regulation: no guidance from the regulator on setting a nationwide phone standard, excessively small units for which licences were parcelled out, a misguided belief that the market alone would fix things. Where new technologies are concerned, more than a nudge from intelligent government regulators is required. The US example shows how quickly a lead can be squandered.

SMART REGULATION INSTEAD OF SIMPLE DEREGULATION

The list of more or less failed attempts at deregulation is now fairly long. If we add the cases that did not go quite so badly wrong but which fell far short of expectations, such as mobile communications in the United States, an analogy comes to mind: deregulation is like nitroglycerine. It is an explosive compound and highly effective for demolition, but only in the hands of experts. And, like demolition, deregulation alone is no panacea.

As noted initially, what is needed is not so much less state intervention as better types of interaction between business and the state. Much of what the state does in the regulatory arena can and should be done much better. We believe smart regulation can be applied effectively across the regulatory spectrum to contribute to increasing Europe's productivity.

The regulation of economic activity is pursued for three widely accepted reasons, all of which can benefit from smart regulation. First, in a number of sectors, perhaps most notably utilities, competition is possible only with the help of regulatory intervention. This applies not only to industries with high fixed costs that were once regarded as natural monopolies, but also to goods such as radio frequencies and networks that are public, but not available in an unlimited supply.

Second, the state may intervene when economic activity by individuals or companies would have unacceptable disadvantages for others. Here, the state must often try to anticipate future events and intervene with appropriate regulation: for example, prohibiting industrial plants from dumping untreated waste in the nearest river. Broadly speaking, the work of competition watchdogs (the cartel office in the European Union, the anti-trust authority in the United States) also belongs to this category.

Third, the state may be called upon to set technical and legal standards as frameworks in the bounds of which private enterprise retains its freedom of action. Setting standards should not automatically be the task of the state, however. Ideally, standards should be adopted by a number of companies acting in mutual agreement. At times, the state can simply play a helpful role by requiring companies to reach consensus. More broadly, this third category also covers the removal of information asymmetries: the intention of accounting and financial reporting standards, for example.

To start on the road to smart regulation, the European Union and European member state governments should work towards developing measures not in isolation, but as part of a comprehensive process. The process should encompass not only the design of individual measures, but also their implementation, effects, and ultimately retirement. In other words, for smart regulation, four questions need to be answered: why, what, how and how long. 'Why' probes the purpose of the proposed regulation and the cost–benefit ratio. 'What' looks at the choice of design options, ranging from establishing frameworks to prescribing explicit targets. 'How' relates to the type of implementation: the exact incentives, the controls put in place, and the mechanisms installed to trigger corrective action when things go wrong. Finally, 'how long' ensures that the lifetime of a regulation is commensurate with its purpose and that it does not remain in force indefinitely. In the following, we discuss each of these principles of smart regulation in turn.

Objectives and results, costs and benefits

The transition from heavy-handed state intervention to smart regulation can take various paths, depending on which of the three reasons for regulation is the motive. While regulation abounds, what is almost entirely lacking is information on whether the objectives of individual regulations are relevant and attainable, and whether the cost–benefit ratio is acceptable. Is a given regulation really generating sufficient benefits to justify potentially reduced levels of innovation and growth?

The first step towards improved regulation is obvious enough. Cost–benefit calculations and the resulting implementation milestones to gauge the success of a regulation over its lifetime would benefit nearly every sector of the economy, from foreign trade statistics and work safety regulations to store opening hours and truck weight limits.

Assessing the costs and benefits of regulation has to start on day one. When a draft regulation appears on the horizon, the groups affected often paint alarming pictures of impending economic doom or exaggerate the technical problems in parliamentary hearings or in the media. For some time, certain European car manufacturers maintained that it was impossible to install catalytic converters in European cars (although they were already installing them in the cars they sold in California). Currently, government bodies are not always in a position to counter such objections with technical knowledge and expertise. More importantly, the ministries of EU member states often lack centres of competence able to evaluate economic and other consequences of new regulations.

The benchmark for skill and independence is set by the Congressional Budget Office (CBO) in the United States. Although part of the legislative branch of the United States government, the CBO operates largely independently. For important forecasts and estimates (such as the development of national debt), experts tend to trust the figures of the CBO rather than those of the government department in question. Europe would benefit from having such an institution, impartial and highly skilled in assessing the direct and indirect costs of new regulations from the start.[5]

Evaluating the costs and benefits of regulatory intervention systematically and constructively is already a step forward towards smart regulation. The second step has to come from regulators themselves: away from rules towards broader principles.

Frameworks rather than rules

In general, economic results improve when rigid rules are replaced with broad principles that leave market forces intact. For example, while it is true that pollutants can be eliminated easily by outlawing individual products or processes, an outright ban often jeopardizes the existence of companies (putting jobs at risk) that create important, useful products, the production of which necessarily creates a certain level of emissions. Who would want to ban aluminium, for example?

In such cases, the purpose of regulation is better served by general principles that allow economic agents to come up with their own solutions. Emissions trading is a brilliant example of this. Governments specify permitted pollution levels for a sector as a whole, and companies trade 'pollution rights' among themselves.

This is useful when the optimum volume of the output to be regulated is not zero (which excludes asbestos, for example). Technical progress can also change the best parameters for meaningful regulation from rigid rules to flexible frameworks. For many years, for example, a regulation referred to as the Delaney clause prohibited food sold in the United States from having any trace of pesticides or insecticides. With advances in measurement techniques, however, even infinitesimal traces became detectable. Very soon, almost all foodstuffs would have become illegal.

The setting of standards and norms is an area in which government intervention is traditionally considered essential. For example, the decision to use a uniform alternating current of 235 volts with a standard plug simply makes life easier for everyone. However, in the majority of cases, it is actually unclear whether government bodies should set standards. The decisions to use VHS or MP3 as video and audio formats were taken by the respective industries, sometimes after fierce competition. Despite some debate, economists have yet to prove that this has led to significant inefficiencies.

Industry associations and voluntary organizations often create new standards that are then accepted or approved by government bodies, one example being the standardization of derivative contracts by the International Swaps and Derivatives Association. An industry can set the technical and legal standards that it needs. Sometimes, governments endorse these after the fact.

Generally, officially mandated standards should be confined to those cases in which they are technically inevitable and are either unable to evolve in the market or will develop only at a very late stage. An example is the choice of the colour television standard in Germany in the 1960s. It was not until after PAL was chosen (over SECAM or NTSC) that broadcasting corporations and television manufacturers could plan reliably.

The choice of criteria for measuring success can make or break the efficiency of a regulation. Rigid specifications such as the number of competitors in a sector or a price reduction of x per cent are not suitable targets. When these parameters are specified or are an integral part of the regulatory process, inefficiencies are inevitable.

While increasing competitive intensity is a worthy goal, the number of companies in an industry is not necessarily the right benchmark. Mergers need not pose a problem even when they result in greater concentration among providers, provided that market entry remains possible. As the theory of 'contestable monopoly' implies, as long as new competitors have a fair chance, monopolists behave as companies in a market with atomistic competition do. The regulation of telecommunications bears this out: productivity gains were greatest where regulators emphasized ease of entry instead of imposing price caps.

In this context, Europe can turn its diversity into an advantage: it can experiment with new forms of regulation in more than two dozen test tubes, so to speak. The United States is already using its large number of federal states to test new solutions. Since 1998, the United States has handled some aspects of environmental regulation by allowing the individual states to experiment, albeit within relatively narrow limits. If a phase of experimental regulation was introduced across Europe, the uniformity of regulations in Europe would initially be reduced, at least in part. French companies would be allowed to pollute under different laws than Greek ones, for example. After a predetermined period of several years, however, the results could be reviewed and uniform solutions imposed. From creative chaos, Europe could choose the best approach to regulation.

Good regulation changes economic incentives without directly prescribing or prohibiting forms of behaviour. As with any rule, there are exceptions. Regulation by command and control is useful where the state has access to easily verifiable information or where the cost of controlling or enforcing new rules is low. Such cases are rare. The valid instances involve the use of public goods or issues relating to the rules of competition. For example, one area in which prescribing explicit safety measures is the right approach is nuclear power generation. No one would dream of setting general guidelines on the basis of the number of deaths from a nuclear power plant disaster, no matter how this figure was calculated. It would be irresponsible and cynical to allow trading in life-endangering credits for a little more or a little less reactor safety. A less dramatic example of the wrong use of the framework approach would be the attempt to impose a tax or fine based on a 'shadow' market price on companies found to be preventing market entry by new competitors. This would be inferior to the strict command-and-control approach. Cartel offices have to be able to enforce compliance with anti-trust regulation, even if it means resorting to draconian measures. However, this should be done on a European level.

After the costs and benefits have been thoroughly weighed and a suitable form of regulation with sensible targets and incentives is found, it then has to be implemented, the next step on the journey towards smart regulation.

Implementation and controlling results

These days, Western countries increasingly transfer regulatory tasks from the general civil service to independent authorities. At its most extreme, very high degrees of independence are tolerated, as in the case of central banks. This trend allows experts to be paid better and to practise their art far from the influence of politicians. In this way, it corrects for the decline of the old civil service model. Independence of civil servants from political influence was once thought crucial. Today, dependence is widespread and has often been institutionalized through politically appointed permanent secretaries or the introduction of a 'political civil servant' category, as well as the proliferation and growing influence of spin doctors. However, even if the supervisory bodies for telecommunications and the securities markets are not as independent as the Bundesbank used to be, they are organized along similar lines. Independent regulators are the best way to curb the market power of existing players

There is, of course, much more to implementing smart regulation than setting up an authority and announcing the ground rules. A large share of 'implementation' should consist of regular reviews to assess whether regulations are doing what they are intended to achieve.

How can the interested public know whether the Portuguese telecommunications market or the German financial services market is well or badly regulated? The size of the purse does not necessarily determine the quality of regulation. Each bundle of measures and each draft law in the regulatory arena should therefore include explicit metrics for evaluating its success or failure. Such a metric might take the following form, for example: 'charges for long-distance phone calls in Spain should not exceed the cheapest rate in Europe by more than 10 per cent within a period of two years'. This would not be the target for the competing companies, but rather the explicit, measurable target for Spain's regulatory efforts.

More review and public criticism of regulation, similar to the approach taken by the Federal Auditors Office in Germany, would be a step in the right direction. Europe could borrow and build on the example of the Office of Management and Budget (OMB) in the United States, which reports to the president's office. In particular, it has a separate department called 'The Wastebasket,' which is responsible for identifying and reforming wasteful programmes.

Giving regulation a fixed expiration date

Many rules, regulations, taxes and bans have survived far longer than their originators ever imagined. Although the arms race with the Royal Navy is history, Germany's excise tax on sparkling wine, introduced in 1902 to finance the building of the High Seas Fleet, remains in place. Currency convertibility remained a distant dream for a decade and a half after 1945. It took twice as long to get rid of currency restrictions as it took to fight the Second World War. It was not until 2001 that Germany overturned the Price Rebate Act, introduced in 1933 by the National Socialists, which banned retailers from offering discounts. The restrictions on pub opening hours, originally introduced in the United Kingdom in a bid to reduce beer consumption during the First World War, remained in force until 2005.

Regulations can develop a life of their own. 'Sunset clauses' can be an elegant solution. These stipulate that a regulation will expire automatically unless renewed. US legislation now makes extensive use of such clauses. Economic efficiency is also boosted when regulations are generally regarded as temporary. The US Congress requires regular reports from the Federal Telecommunications Commission, for example, on the regulations it has terminated.

Institutionalizing review pushes almost forgotten regulations onto the agenda. Does Massachusetts really want to continue to ban individuals from importing California wine? Should bakers in some parts of Europe actually have to learn their trade for longer than paramedics? In financial markets, for example, the limitations and opportunities of government intervention are constantly shifting because of technical and economic reforms and – for this reason – many regulations need to be returned to the test lab practically as soon as they are implemented. In contrast, some regulations, such as those governing environmental protection, may be in force for a very long time before the need for review arises.

The right institution for abolishing obsolete regulations would be an organization structured along the lines of the Office of Management and Budget described above. A regulation awaiting extension would have to pass through a two-level filter: first, recommendation by the OMB, then approval by parliament or the authority in question.

NEW GROUND RULES FOR THE OLD CONTINENT?

Bad regulation can quickly cost billions of euros. No one knows the exact amount, of course, but the OECD has estimates. Experts on Europe's larger countries estimate that the direct and indirect costs of regulation amount to about 3 to 6 per cent of GDP. For the EU-15, that would be €290–590 billion a year (OECD, 2001).

Even minor, gradual improvements are worthwhile. The OECD estimates that the total savings generated from the prevention of poor regulation correspond to the total gains expected from the single market project.[6] This may be an underestimate. In the few cases where Europe has been able to catch up with or even overtake the United States in terms of productivity, smart regulation has been one of the main contributing factors.

Tackled the right way, regulation can create considerable value. Substantial improvements are often seen in externalities such as air and water quality, security and health. For example, in 1997, US environmental protection, work safety and health programmes together generated direct and indirect costs of US $198 billion, but created benefits of at least US $298 billion, with the highest estimates reaching US $3.55 trillion.[7]

Does smart regulation represent a special opportunity for Europe to increase its competitiveness and productivity? Or is it just 'nice to have'? What are the most important steps Europe must take to reach this goal? And if smart regulation offers Europe the chance of a lifetime, should Brussels be at the wheel?

Europe's chance

The quality of regulation in many European countries is much lower than elsewhere, including the United States. The OECD documented this clearly in a study that examined regulatory improvement and awarded points to each country (OECD, 1999b). Criteria included the extent to which countries took an integrated view on regulatory requirements, used transparent standards in the regulatory process and established accountability at a high level. The United States received 97 of a possible 100 points, and the European Union 66. In terms of transparency, the gap was even wider. And there are many further shortcomings at the industry level. This is in line with the findings of the McKinsey Global Institute (MGI). MGI analysts compared Germany, France and the United States and concluded that regulatory problems were the main cause of Europe's productivity shortfall (MGI, 2002).

Once the shortcomings were identified and eliminated, however, Europe would be able not only to catch up with the United States but actually surpass it in smart regulation and corresponding performance rankings such as the one mentioned above. Unlike Europe, the United States is hobbled by a range of structural problems in its regulatory processes. The main problems in the United States lie in the highly legalistic approach taken to regulation and the adversarial nature of legal proceedings. Moreover, a bureaucratic mindset and highly complex organizations are not found only on this side of the Atlantic. When Bill Clinton and Al Gore came to power, the improvement of regulations and the removal of red tape were high on their agenda. Vice President Gore demonstrated the need for reform particularly vividly by tracing the decision-making process in a federal office on a 6-metre-long organizational chart with 373 sections.

Despite fine achievements, the United States also has its share of poor regulations. Two of the most striking examples are the maximum consumption levels set for car producers' fleets and the regulations governing the 'Superfund', created to finance the clean-up of production sites contaminated with toxic waste. Many regulations in the United States are much more detailed than is economically useful in order to guarantee legal certainty, a necessity in the litigious United States. For example, rights and obligations relating to care for the elderly are governed by over 500 federal regulations, partly to make the limits of liability as clear as possible. On top of this come the regulations in the individual states. The result of all these provisions is not impressive. Geriatric care in Australia, by contrast, is governed by just 31 relatively sweeping, results-oriented provisions and regulations. According to the OECD, its quality of care (per dollar spent) is far superior to that in the United States.

The proliferation of regulations in the United States is accelerated by a constant barrage of lawsuits and the often chaotic initiatives of individual members of congress. According to the OECD, the coherence of regulation in the United States is also greatly impaired by competing legislation and the unsystematic nature of case law, which sometimes weaves a web of chaotic, case-by-case rules.

Europe is protected against many of these problems: it has a Napoleonic (codified) legal system, houses of parliament with strong national political parties (a curb on maverick legislative initiatives), few lawsuits decided by jury, moderate regulations governing damages and a strong judiciary. If Europeans apply best practice and implement it systematically while making extensive use of performance standards, cost–benefit analyses, sunset clauses and so on, the quality of European regulation could become world class.

Example of capital markets: reversing subsidiarity

Alexandre Lamfalussy's 'Committee of Wise Men' and their work on the reform of capital market regulation, discussed in Chapter 5 in connection with the single market, was also pioneering in the context of smart regulation and the right allocation of decision-making authority within Europe. The committee's programme was not just an ambitious list of directives; it also entailed an intelligent modification of the subsidiarity principle.

The average legislative process at EU level (without its implementation into national law) takes over two years, and the implementation of capital market directives can take even longer (Committee of Wise Men, 2001). However, the basis for regulation relating to the capital markets often changes at much shorter intervals, often as a result of advances in technology. Furthermore, EU directives contain too much technical detail (resulting from the lack of expertise in the EU Commission, as the Lamfalussy Committee argues) but are very superficial in areas that require attention to detail.

Even after the latest reforms, most of the initiatives in Europe go through what is known as the co-decision procedure. This is an often time-consuming process of harmonization, tit-for-tat blocking manoeuvres and negotiation of details, accompanied by the usual political haggling in the Conciliation Committee between the Commission and the Parliament.

To speed up regulatory and legislative processes, the Lamfalussy Committee proposed to limit the influence of the European Parliament on technical issues and to treat the Parliament only as a consulting body on issues relating to the capital markets. Specifically, the Lamfalussy approach would break up regulatory work into four levels. Level 1 is to consist of legislative acts, namely directives or regulations, proposed by the European Commission following consultation with all interested parties. In adopting each enactment, the Council and the Parliament agree, on the basis of a European Commission proposal, on the nature and extent of detailed technical implementing measures to be decided at Level 2. At Level 2, the European Securities Committee (ESC) assists the Commission in adopting the relevant measures. Level 3 measures aim to improve Level 1 and 2 acts in the member states. The Committee of European Securities Regulators has particular responsibility for this. At Level 4, the European Commission strengthens the enforcement of acts.

In essence, this approach treats the Parliament only as a consulting body on issues relating to the capital markets. For Level 2 questions, adoption of the Lamfalussy Committee's proposal would abolish the complex rights to invoke mediation between the Council of Ministers and the European Parliament in the case of a rejection. Parliament would be listened to, as are the representatives of issuers and investors, but it could no longer stop legislation on financial market issues.

What many observers regard as the disempowerment of Parliament is rather a move closer to the normal roles of the legislative and the executive branches of government. In nearly all countries, the setting of the legal framework is the task of parliament, while the elaboration of regulatory statutes is traditionally the responsibility of the executive. Previously, the lack of differentiation between laws and regulations – directives usually contain elements of both – has contributed to the excessively 'technical' nature of European legislation in international comparison. Meanwhile, there have been increasing calls to extend the four-level reform to other areas, beyond financial market regulation.

While it is too early for a final assessment of the Lamfalussy process, it does appear that the bold reform proposed by the Committee has been largely accepted. Public discussion of the Lamfalussy reform focused on the role of Parliament. However, much more interesting in our view is the recognition that Europe needs to change its basic approach to the single market. In some areas, the subsidiarity principle has to go, and quick implementation has to take precedence over elaborate consultations with Parliament.

Implications for Europe: efficiency, Brussels style

Many people associate Brussels with bureaucratic inertia. The Acquis Communautaire, the corpus of all EU regulations and resolutions that new members have to implement into national law, for example, has over 80,000 pages. Yet Brussels is often the source of liberalization initiatives.

Telecommunications is a case in point. As mentioned in our initial discussion of deregulation in Chapter 5, the Information Society

Forum, a committee of experts engaged by the European Union, reported in the mid-1990s that Europe was trailing behind the United States and Japan. In early 1996, the European Union approved a timetable for the liberalization of all telecommunications markets, throwing them open to competition from new entrants, national or foreign, by 2003 at the latest.

In light of the concrete benefits of liberalization in this sector, which are visible everywhere, an observer can only wonder why it didn't happen sooner. Why did Europeans have to wait for more than 10 years after the breakup of the AT&T monopoly in the United States? Why did they have to put up with overpriced services for so long? When the European Union did act, it was clearly instrumental in improving performance in the telecommunications industry. Why is Brussels often successful in liberalizing markets? Interest groups are often stronger at the national level than at the European one. They find it difficult to speak with a single European voice; their interests cannot be brought under the same umbrella. The interests of incumbents in the telecommunications market, for instance, vary considerably given that this group still includes state-owned monopolies as well as highly competitive firms in liberalized national markets. The same holds true for road freight companies, airlines, rail and airport operators and postal services. The situation is radically different only for the agricultural sector, an area in which all EU farmers have more or less the same interest: maintaining their subsidies.

While the European Union is often popularly criticized for its 'planned economy' approach, it has also in many areas actually enabled and enforced the implementation of free market enterprise that generates benefits for customers and creates corporate value. Road freight and telecommunications are perfect examples; deregulation of the parcel service industry also belongs in this category.

However, much remains to be done. In many sectors, the European Union could and should create more fair competition, especially to establish parallel deregulation paths and speeds in all EU member countries, which is not the case for example in the mail sector. As we have argued, this does not require less state influence, but rather a more competent and more impartial regulator acting as a referee, and not subject to 'regulatory capture' – excessive influence by the regulated parties on the regulator – as in the past. There is another good reason to establish decision-making authority in Brussels for the regulation of many industries with a high level of state involvement and/or high fixed costs. Today, the subsidiarity principle in Europe works in a way that might be described with a quip about the United States usually attributed to Winston Churchill: 'Americans can always be counted upon to do the right thing, after all other possibilities have been exhausted.' In Europe, authority for regulatory decision making is eventually established at the right level, in Brussels, but only after all other levels have been exhausted or have failed. We advocate giving Brussels decision-making authority in the appropriate areas in advance for the following three reasons:

- First, where regulation is necessary, an institution operating away from the influence of the interest groups would presumably enact better regulations. Lobbying in Brussels will continue, but the heterogeneity of the lobbies' interests neutralizes their impact.
- Second, most of the factors triggering regulatory intervention are already of a pan-European nature. Whether for a nuclear power plant near the border of two countries or sodium dioxide (SO_2) emissions that know no borders, shifting regulatory expertise to a higher authority is almost automatically a good idea.
- Third, as the problems in implementing the single market show, the subsidiarity principle creates such huge differences in the implementation of EU regulations for many individual issues that it is currently impossible to speak of uniform regulation across Europe. Whether peer reviews or the actual shifting of authority to Brussels is the better approach to homogenizing, the implementation of these regulations is of less importance.

Smart regulation is perfect for Europe. It conforms to the continent's legal tradition of codified law (as distinct from case law in the United States). Codified law tends to avoid overly detailed and extensive regulations, and helps to rein in the tendency for regulations and authorities to take on a life of their own. Smart regulation fits with a Europe that is gradually growing and changing. It offers the opportunity to decide on the best form of regulation for economic purposes on a 'greenfield' basis. And, finally, smart regulation can use Europe's diversity to its advantage, by employing it as a laboratory for systematically testing different approaches in the member states in individual cases prior to implementing EU-wide regulation.

Key elements of smart regulation

Governance: regulatory authority assigned to Brussels

In regulatory matters, the European Union should turn the subsidiarity principle on its head. For new communication frequencies, postal services, electric power or air traffic, Brussels should have the authority it needs, not the member states.

Purpose: clear objectives and cost–benefit ratios

New regulation should include a clear statement of purpose and get a hearing only after cost–benefit analysis shows that state intervention will be beneficial in achieving the objective. To conduct these analyses, Europe needs expert, independent institutions, modelled on the US Congressional Budget Office.

Design: frameworks and incentives instead of prescriptive rules

Smart regulation is not only about fewer rules but also, and primarily, about replacing rules with frameworks that create the right incentives to steer behaviour in the direction desired. Efficiency is typically boosted both by harnessing market forces and by leaving room for further optimization by competing companies. Design also includes specifying performance criteria to measure the success or failure of a regulation once it goes into effect.

Implementation: independent authorities and effective controlling

In addition to shifting decision-making authority to Brussels, in most cases it is desirable to create an independent Europe-wide regulatory authority and assign it responsibility for the consequences of regulation in the given industry. An independent authority is the best means to curb the market power of existing companies. A large share of the authority's work should consist of regular reviews to assess whether regulations are meeting their intended objectives in line with defined performance criteria. These functions also benefit from greater credibility and acceptance when handled by a neutral agency.

Expiration: independent monitoring and 'sunset clauses'

Regulations, even smart ones, should not develop a life of their own. They should be audited to ensure they are still 'fit for purpose' and that their benefits outweigh the cost they incur. This requires an institution, perhaps modelled on the US Office of Management and Budget, to review regulations and abolish them as needed, and sunset clauses that terminate regulations automatically after a set period unless they are explicitly extended (by parliamentary vote, for example). Regulation is not forever.

7

The concept of category definition

How does a society become successful, economically, technologically and ecologically? And how does an economic area become an object of admiration and a magnet for funds and talent from other countries? Illuminating as international comparisons of productivity and best-practice analyses can be, the most they can do is to enable catch-up with the productivity leader. They cannot show Europe how to take the lead. This requires fundamental innovation. Existing ideas can inspire and instruct, but to put the economy into high gear Europe has to come up with something new and original. It needs to reinvent the rules of the game, set unique standards for new products and processes, and transform them into economic success.

We call this concept 'category definition'. Some of the world's top companies owe their success to category definition, and we believe the concept can be extended to other enterprises, to entire industries and to the whole of Europe. It could provide guidance for setting management and government priorities. In particular, management could pursue more deliberate value strategies based on specific European advantages. Governments could consider using category definition as a criterion for funding basic research and investing in education. We explain this in more detail later in this and the next chapter. We see category definition as a way for Europe to achieve economic success by deliberately and systematically playing to its specific strengths and values in many more areas than it does today.

Kleenex, Nescafé, Scotch tape and Walkman are all well-known trademarks used colloquially to refer to the product in general. These are extreme and iconic examples of successful category definition. It is the dream of every marketing strategist: the new brand or product becomes synonymous with an entire product category. Not only innovative and radically superior products but also new or refined processes can establish entirely new categories or make existing categories obsolete. In both cases, the ability to define a category embraces not only the theoretical ability to define a product or process, but also the ability to translate it into lasting economic success. Those who successfully define categories often set new standards. The standards can be technological, but are as likely to be psychological, or a blend of both.

Applied to Europe, category definition has to mean that it becomes associated automatically in people's minds with a consistent set of specific values and experiences. A hotel guest in Sydney or Tokyo might, for example, find the design of the furnishing 'delightfully European': chic, modern, of high quality and with subtle charm.

To describe category definition in more detail, we look first at a number of successful examples. We then turn to potential opportunities for European category definition. Europe has natural strengths in a wide range of areas, and distinct values giving it a positioning advantage that it should systematically translate into economic success.

CATEGORY DEFINITION AND REDEFINITION

Category definition can take two different forms: category creation or category redefinition. Category creators either establish a new type of product, as Nestlé did with Nescafé, or they radically change an established manufacturing process for an existing product, as was the case with Henry Ford's first assembly-line cars. Although Ford's automobile was not as technically sophisticated as many of its rivals, Ford made cars suddenly affordable for many people. This is the classic form of category definition: if you introduce a completely new product or process to the market (in Ford's case the assembly line), your name will often become synonymous with your innovation.

Sony's Walkman is another example. It became the popular name for an entire generation of pocket cassette players. Although the tape recorder and the headphone had been around for a while, it was Sony's excellent miniaturization capabilities, a headphone weighing only half as much as the one offered by its fiercest competitor and a passionate belief in the concept that enabled Sony to create and dominate a new product category that generated excellent profit margins for many years. The Walkman established Sony's reputation as a master of miniaturization and the source of extremely desirable consumer electronics.

Category redefiners, as the term indicates, do not produce an entirely new product. But they do succeed in changing the rules of the game in a long-established market to such an extent that other competitors have to adapt or exit. For example, by employing several teams working in parallel, chip manufacturer Intel found a way to speed up innovation in microprocessor design to a pace that forced many other manufacturers to give up. Wal-Mart's innovative approach to sales management and logistics redefined the retail industry in the United States, driving established competitors like K-Mart into bankruptcy and creating new opportunities for imitators like Target.

It is far from easy to define or redefine a category, and even harder to ensure that the new definition lasts. Some individual companies and industries have succeeded in defining a category, only to lose their hegemony soon after. In addition, if we advocate transferring lessons learnt at the corporate level to a regional level and to Europe as a whole, we will also have to consider the economic implications. We intend to show that defining a category need not be restricted to products and processes, but can also include generic characteristics, such as reliability, quality, innovativeness and technological leadership, superior design, cultural depth or even *savoir vivre* entirely in the tradition of phrases such as the German saying 'Living like God in France'.

CREATING AND SUSTAINING CATEGORY DEFINITION

There are various ways to define a category and change the rules of the game for entire classes of products or processes. What they all have in common is a visionary element, a new product or a new process that breaks existing norms, often entailing a high degree of risk and pursued with an almost missionary zeal.

New product categories are frequently created by highly motivated and enthusiastic inventors and tinkerers who not only improve existing ideas but also create something entirely new. This group of inventors includes Richard Arkwright, who in 1769 developed a machine-operated spinning frame and was thus among the first to introduce mass production in the textile industry; Karl Benz, who in 1886, after many years of dedicated research, succeeded in inventing the world's first automobile with a gasoline-powered internal combustion engine; and Oskar Barnack, who first made photography truly portable with the 35mm film and the first Leica camera, introduced in 1925. Where new processes define the category, we find that definition is often triggered by economic motives – as with Ford's first assembly line, or lean production and just-in-time delivery as developed by Toyota.

However, remarkable as innovation and the pioneering spirit may be, the acid test for category definition is commercial success. The fax machine was invented in Europe and successfully used around the world; office life became unimaginable without it. However, as an economic opportunity, it was not exploited by European firms. No company seized the opportunity to define the category of fax machine (Frühwald, 1996; Marples, 2004).

Critically, category definition shows up as increased productivity. The automobile industry is a case in point. The margins that Mercedes automobiles are able to command at the upper end of the market are based to a large extent on the company's skill in defining its category: these are the cars that define what a state-of-the-art limousine is, in some cases a way to communicate the success one has achieved in life while at the same time moving at the cutting-edge of technological development. This margin effect is applicable not only to individual companies, but also to entire industries. Thus the success of German mechanical engineers in the 1950s and 1960s encouraged other companies in this sector to relocate to the south-west of the Federal Republic of Germany around Stuttgart. The category of German mechanical engineering was defined in matters of precision and quality, and then reinforced by the region's infrastructure and well-qualified, motivated staff.

Silicon Valley to the south of San Francisco is another example of the economic impact of category definition. About half of the 70 or so semiconductor firms located there (including Intel and Advanced Micro Devices) sprang directly or indirectly from Fairchild Semiconductors, the nucleus established in the valley in the 1950s. The existing infrastructure required to do business, including crucial services and skills like dedicated investment banking, coupled with close cooperation with universities, contributed to the unparalleled success of this region even if much of the production is also done elsewhere.

Category definition is not a trophy won for all time, but a challenge cup that must be defended time and again. Defending it normally requires a very different culture from the one with which it was attained. The passion for taking a gamble, vision and sometimes haphazard experimenting in the early years as well as the complacency of the 'fat years' of seemingly incontestable market leadership can interfere with a company's ability to continue steering a profitable course.

Henry Ford's empire started to wobble as early as the 1920s. By then, the market had grown accustomed to low-priced automobiles from the assembly line, so Ford started to look into an intelligent combination of mass production at low cost and an ability to customize his cars. Even from a cost perspective, the volume of sales in the market as a whole was by then large enough to allow him to turn his back on the radical standardization of the famous Model T: 'available in any colour, as long as it was black'.

What can Europe learn from the concept of category definition? Just as Richard Arkwright, Karl Benz, Oskar Barnack and Henry Ford were not content with simply eliminating the faults and weaknesses of existing products, a genuine European strategy must start with something fundamentally different, and not be merely a mad dash to catch up with the US paradigm. The right approach for Europe is not tagging along, but setting the direction.

This applies first and foremost to European companies. Thanks to Europe's lifestyle and *joie de vivre*, its sophisticated consumers, highly qualified labour force and sheer diversity, Europeans have a good chance of defining categories in a number of industries where the specific European 'touch' is in high global demand. We are convinced that the list of industries in which Europe should be able to succeed at category definition is fairly long. It includes obvious candidates such as automotive and mechanical engineering, fashion and luxury goods, and high-end home appliances. Europeans should surely also be able to achieve category definition or redefinition in other industries where genuinely European values coincide with European strengths. The possibilities here include areas such as caring for the elderly and maintaining quality of life for older people, tourism and wellness, architecture and the construction industry, environmental engineering and 'functional food' for healthy nutrition. These sectors are large and employment intensive, and could thus make a significant contribution to European prosperity in the coming decades.

Europe needs to pursue category definition systematically because it raises productivity, which can then help to pay for social transfers and growing cohorts of the elderly. Moreover, category definition also creates high levels of aspiration and emphasizes specifically European strengths. Europe still has a lot to do to raise its game: the rate of innovation, quality standards, pioneering spirit and the infrastructure need to improve for Europe to succeed at category definition in a way that becomes noticeable. If it fails to do so, however, it may be downgraded to the status of a low-margin subcontractor in the international specialization of labour.

The concept of category definition is best illustrated by a series of examples. We start with success stories of European companies that have achieved category definition, and then look at some missed opportunities before concluding with some implications for European industry and government authorities.

EXAMPLES OF EUROPEAN CATEGORY DEFINITION

There are two sides to category definition: on the one hand, an exciting idea for a product or process that is resolutely implemented, and on the other the creation of commercial success based on this innovation. Both aspects have been successfully demonstrated with power saws from Stihl and cars like Mercedes in Germany, with luxury goods made by Swarovski in Austria and Gucci in Italy / France, in Spain with fashion by Zara, or in Britain with vacuum cleaners from Dyson as well as in a host of other comparatively small niche markets.

The world's Number One chain saw: Stihl

More often than not, when a tree is felled in the woods, you'll find a Stihl power saw on the scene. Stihl, a medium-sized German company based in Waiblingen near Stuttgart, produces (as its advertising claims) 'the world's Number One chain saw'. The company has been the world market leader since 1971, selling 17 out of every 20 saws outside Germany.

Andreas Stihl, who founded the company in the 1920s, invented the first tree-felling machine and the first power saw, the legendary Stihl Contra, built in 1957. Ever since, the undisputed world market leader has remained a step ahead of competitors. In 1995 Stihl built the 023L, the world's quietest power saw. As far back as 1989, on its own initiative and without the threat of impending regulation, the company introduced a chain saw with a catalytic converter. Stihl developed a special fuel mixture for its power saws to reduce harmful emissions further. From the start, the company attached a high degree of importance to improving safety features. There is also Stihl's characteristic attention to detail: for example, the product range includes a chain saw with a heated handle. This allows lumberjacks in the north of Lapland to work more comfortably at minus 30 degrees Celsius.

However, the buzz isn't all about power saws. The company's business results are also headline-grabbers. Sales of around €600 million in 1989 rose to over €1.8 billion by 2005, while sales per employee shot up by more than 100 per cent.[1] At the same time, the number of employees rose by more than a third, a gain of about 2,700 jobs. Stihl illustrates that high profits and rapidly rising productivity need not be the result of job cutting, as critics of 'turbo capitalism' are wont to claim. On the contrary, growing profitability went hand in hand with rising capital investment (€80 million in 2001, €133 million in 2005), higher sales and significant job creation.

Top design and engineering, strong implementation, clear positioning and a consistent message to the market, all combined with continuous product development: these are the ingredients needed to define a category. In Stihl's case yet another factor comes into play: an in-depth understanding of the company's own strengths. One of the reasons that Stihl was able to expand so rapidly was that management realized it had an advantage in portable power equipment, and went on to apply this knowledge to equipment other than power saws. In the 1980s, the company was still manufacturing almost exclusively the same product that Andreas Stihl had sold: chain saws. Since then, however, it has diversified: mobile garden recyclers and gasoline-driven drills were added, along with brushcutters, high-pressure cleaners and gasoline-driven tillers.

What was good for the power saw – high performance, low fuel consumption, environmental friendliness, low noise – also turned out to be good for Stihl's other gardening and forestry equipment. Thanks to its reputation for top-quality products, Stihl rapidly gained market share, increasing the efficiency of its own investment in research and development and boosting the growth of the company. Today, the group also enjoys healthy sales of its so-called 'timber-sports collection' – clothing and fashion accessories for the woodlanders of today, from checked shirts and fleece jackets to winter caps and the original Stihl penknife.

Stihl's successes illustrate how traditional European strengths such as excellent engineering and continuous innovation can help to define a category and create wealth and jobs.

Cars: the 'Mercedes' of an industry

Few other products are as much of a status symbol, an ego booster for their owners and an object of desire as the 1,500 kilos of steel, glass and plastic commonly known as cars. Small wonder that many users claim their four-wheeled chariots have almost magic powers. In the film *Local Hero*, the protagonist claims that he used to get migraine headaches 'when I was still driving a Chevy!' When he traded it in for a Porsche 930, he explains, the turbo blew away the pain in his head. In the 1950s and 1960s, automotive assembly lines were marked by enormous differences in engineering and quality-assurance capabilities. Breakdowns were much more frequent with some products than others. Today, these differences have become small. Where significant performance differences exist, they are often hard to appreciate in practice. Often drivers all sit in the same traffic jams, with few chances to test acceleration or top speed.

And yet some customers spend much more on their automobiles than the average person earns in several years. You could buy a small freehold flat in many countries for the price of a Mercedes SL. It would be easy to draw up a long list of product features to justify the price: the retractable roof, the silky smooth engine, the intelligent gear shift, the electronic driving aids, the exceptional build quality, the high resale value and all the rest. But all this only partly explains the car's success.

The remainder is explained by the concept of category definition. The Mercedes brand stands for more than just an automobile, more than just a safe, comfortable and swift means of travel from A to B. Mercedes is a visible synonym for safety and reliability. The larger classes of Mercedes communicate the status of their owners as having made it to the top – of a company, a profession or even a country: no other company produces more government limousines than the Stuttgart firm. The name Mercedes, or that of the elegant cars from the high end of its range, is even routinely invoked to extol products in other categories ('the Mercedes of ...', or 'the 'S-class of ...') – from electric shavers and iPod headphones to high-end computer notebooks and turboprop planes.

As the Mercedes example shows, defining a category means far more than just slightly extending the application of marketing and branding. Detroit in many ways has been at the forefront of marketing for the last 50 years, without ever getting close to defining the category of automobiles anywhere but in the United States. The decisive factor is the substance behind the spin: the coherence of the message communicated is based on genuine strength of product development, manufacturing and distribution. Without that strength, people would just yawn at the slogan 'The future of the automobile' used in Mercedes' advertising. Mercedes has repeatedly adapted this message to the sprit of the times, defining (together with a handful of other manufacturers) the category for premium automobiles. Although the German automotive industry makes only about 10 per cent of the automobiles sold worldwide, what makes a premium automobile is almost entirely defined for the whole world in Stuttgart (Mercedes and Porsche), Munich (BMW) and Ingolstadt (Audi).

When reliability and safety were the most important product features, because of frequent breakdowns and an alarming rise in the number of fatal accidents, Mercedes-Benz more than held its own by being more reliable than virtually any other manufacturer. The 200D model of the 1970s and 1980s was affectionately referred to as 'the Ferrari that runs on heating oil'. It has been widely used in Europe as a taxi, and often clocked up 500,000 kilometres and more without much more maintenance than the occasional oil change. At a time when reliability was enough to differentiate a company, this made a huge difference, and was extremely useful in achieving category definition, as reflected in higher prices.

However, there came a time in the early 1990s when this traditional strength was no longer enough to maintain Mercedes' lead. So the company invested heavily in product development. Innovative products such as the SLK, with its revolutionary retractable roof, established a new category of automobile: the coupé-convertible. For years, this breakthrough remained a unique selling proposition for Mercedes. The first successful imitations did not come on the market until four years after the SLK was first launched. No other car kept its value as well as the Mercedes with the retractable roof, because even people who could only just afford one second-hand bought it.

In an industry where new product ideas are generally reflected in acronyms comprehensible only to engineers, the SLK achieved a real breakthrough: the 'sporty, light, compact' convertible is completely winterproof, so can be used for 12 months of the year instead of just three or four. The glamour of such technical breakthroughs also adds lustre to other products from the House of Mercedes. From its elegant S-Class models and the A-Class aimed at young families to the sportier handling of the C-Class, Mercedes did a lot to translate category definition for robust, safe vehicles into a similar edge in innovative, sleek, dynamic and intelligent automobiles, like the CLS nowadays for example.

What looks like a lucky strike holds some wider lessons. Many companies in Europe have succeeded in similar fashion. Where intelligent management and long-term product development go hand-in-hand with engineering excellence and stylish design, the products often start to sell like proverbial hot cakes.

Category definition is, of course, not confined to the automotive industry. The fashion and luxury goods industries – with their polished leather, fine fabrics and sensuous fragrances – have long since proved that they can also define categories, provided the right concepts are well implemented.

Luxury goods: Gucci, Swarovski and the tradition of refined European craftsmanship

Consumerism and fashion are not inventions of the 20th century. With the onset of the industrial revolution, the manufacture and consumption of clothing and accessories, particularly as an expression of personal taste and individuality, ceased to be a privilege of the aristocracy. From the 18th century onwards, cotton goods became much cheaper. A confident and increasingly prosperous middle class took an interest in dressing for every occasion. What had until then lasted for a generation was now discarded within a few years, for reasons more of looks and style than of utility. Fashion took off in a big way.

The market for luxuries is attractive. Even narrowly defined without luxury cars, housing and first-class services, customers worldwide spent about US $70 billion on luxury goods in 2003, with year-on-year growth of 6 to 10 per cent during good times. The total – more or less equivalent to Hungary's gross domestic product – is spent on jewellery, expensive watches, haute couture, fine shoes and accessories.[2] The demand for luxury goods is increasing rather than decreasing, and creates many follow-up service opportunities. Over the last 20 years, prices of luxury products have risen much faster than the prices of ordinary goods in a department store. The US price index more than trebled between 1976 and 2004, but the price index for the 'cost of living extremely well' (as calculated by Forbes) rose to eight times its 1976 value. The price of a Steinway grand piano was seven times higher than it was 28 years earlier, a Harvard degree became seven times as expensive, and Beluga caviar was nearly 12 times the price it was in 1976.

It is therefore not surprising that there is also a lot of money to be made from well-off customers. According to estimates by industry experts, companies in the luxury goods and fashion industries earn margins of between 10 and 25 per cent, depending on the product group. At the same time, there is scarcely another industry in which Europe is as successful. In other sectors, Europe rarely makes it to the winners' podium of the biggest and the best, which one would otherwise expect given its population and economic output. Yet the old continent's lead in the luxury goods and fashion industries is indisputable.

The majority of the world's largest companies in this sector are European (Figure 7.1). The situation is similar in the individual segments: in watches or perfumes, haute couture or jewellery, Europe is well ahead. A total of seven European companies are among the top firms.

What makes Europe so successful in this sector? The refined taste of consumers in the majority of European countries gives the continent an important head start. In markets such as Italy and Spain, it is mainly domestic companies that are successful in producing the right colour for the season or an elegant cut for summer fashion with apparently effortless ease. In addition, Europe's discerning customers are served in this sector by a labour force with superior skills, often supported by a long tradition of outstanding craftsman-

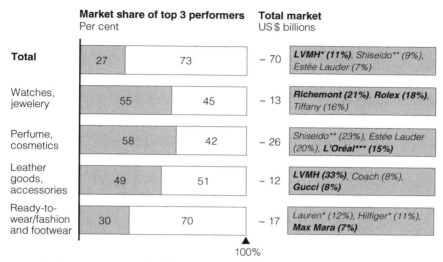

Figure 7.1 Market share of the top three competitors in luxury goods by industry segment, 2003

ship. Luxury labels like Prada and Gucci started with shoe making. Louis Vuitton started out as a trunk maker, Hermès as saddlers. Combine this with an excellent infrastructure, a rapid exchange of information and a flexible production structure, often based on small units, and the key ingredients for success in the fashion industry are in place.

At first sight, this list of reasons for success seems so long that one wonders how European companies could ever fail to be successful. However, on closer inspection we see that these companies have worked hard for their sales and profits.

Just over 10 years ago, Italian fashion label Gucci was on the verge of takeover – or bankruptcy. The family was quarrelling, the products flopped on the market and the brand was suffering from an inflationary licensing policy: the Gucci brand could be found on a whole hotchpotch of products, from tennis shoes to playing cards. Moreover, these products were often of inferior quality and sold in outlets over which Gucci had hardly any influence. Slowly but surely the magic of the brand name was disappearing. Hardly anything was invested in the brand: just 2.9 per cent of sales was being spent on advertising. In 1992 the group made a loss of US $40 million, and in 1993 it turned in a loss of US $22 million.

However, the fashion company was able to fight its way back to the top thanks to a radical restructuring. By the mid-1990s the designer Tom Ford had succeeded in catapulting the brand back to the centre of the fashion world with his exciting collections. In the years that followed, he was put in charge of the group's communications strategy, down to the design of the annual report and the fittings in the shops. At the same time, CEO Domenico de Sole closed outlets that didn't reinforce the brand. Thanks to improved pricing and his skilled handling of suppliers and producers, profitability rose quickly. The advertising budget was dramatically increased and in 2000 accounted for over 10 per cent of sales. The number of products was reduced by more than three-quarters and cheap junk was no longer permitted to sail under the Gucci flag. The same idea led to a restructuring of the sales channels. Instead of allowing licensees and department stores to sell this exclusive Italian brand's product to the end customer, the company now has a large number of its own shops to ensure that the brand name is not associated with bad service or second-rate shopping areas.

The company controlled the design of its own shops itself – and controlled its advertising to an even greater extent – and has placed all these responsibilities in Ford's hands. As he put it: 'Anything visual, anything that tells you about the company, is my area. In a sense, every single person in the company ... reports creatively to me' (Harvard Business School, 2001: 8).

The attractive new products very quickly produced attractive results. Gucci's sales soared from US $203 million in 1993 to US $3,227 million in 2004. In that year, French Pinault-Printemps-Redoute (PPR) acquired Gucci for US $7.2 billion to create a new force in luxury goods. PPR owns brands such as Brylane and Yves Saint Laurent, high-end department store chain Printemps, FNAC book and music stores and Christie's, the renowned English auction house. The two companies believed they were ideally suited to build a leading luxury goods group together. Gucci was thought to provide a substantial platform for future growth, having the management capability to replicate with other brands the success it had achieved with its own.

Speaking of luxury goods and auction houses, we must not forget that two Europeans defined the latter category: James Christie, who held his first art auction in London in 1766, and Samuel Baker, founder of Sotheby's, who started his bookselling business in 1744. Whether they are selling old masters, modern paintings, antique furniture or precious jewellery, art auctions are major attractions on the world's social agenda, and both Christie's and Sotheby's are still relevant in the market.

If it sparkles and is not a diamond, it's probably made by Swarovski. Since the 1970s, Swarovski has become a brand name for crystal jewellery stones used in fashion, jewellery, lighting and interior design, for gift items, collectibles and decorative objects. The world's leading manufacturer of cut crystal, headquartered in Wattens, Austria, it has 17,000 employees worldwide and group revenues of €2.1 billion (2005). As with many other category-defining companies, Swarovski's success story begins with a technical invention. In 1892 Daniel Swarovski thought up a machine for cutting crystal and thus revolutionized the jewellery and fashion industry. Until then, the cutting of crystal was a traditional craft, and painstakingly slow. With his new machine, Daniel Swarovski laid the foundation on which the success of the world's largest crystal manufacturer still rests. More than 100 years later, research and development are still very important to Swarovski, with more than 600 people employed in that field. As the company founder put it: 'Every new era offers new possibilities for action and development. Development never stands still. Innovations in one field inevitably lead to innovations in others. One must remain alert at all times, always ready to make the very best use of what emerges.'

In the mid-1970s, in order to increase its influence on the retail side, the family-owned company established the first Swarovski shops in Singapore, the United States, Hong Kong and Germany. The quality and craftsmanship of Swarovski products played their part in setting a psychological or aesthetic standard, enhancing the fashion acceptability of once-disdained 'paste' crystal. By 1999 new boutiques had opened in London, Paris, Amsterdam and Buenos Aires, all with an internationally standardized shop design. Swarovski has conquered the world with sparkling success.

Fashion: Zara in Spain redefines supply chain excellence

Diamonds may be a girl's best friend. Disposable chic probably comes a close second: here today, gone tomorrow, affordable to many, and often bought from Zara. Inditex, owner of the Zara apparel chain, is a prime example of a European company that has succeeded at category redefinition. As an errand boy for a Spanish shirtmaker, Armancio Ortega Gaona developed a keen interest in analysing how costs build up in the apparel supply chain. He put this knowledge to good use by creating one of Europe's most successful and fashionable apparel companies.

Ortega started a housecoat manufacturing company in 1963 and decided to integrate forward into retailing in 1975 when he opened his first Zara clothing store in La Coruña, Spain. The value proposition was 'mid-range fashion clothing at affordable prices'. By 1980, a dozen stores were in operation within Spain. In 1990, every city in Spain with over 100,000 inhabitants had its Zara store. As Zara expanded, other apparel brands were added to Inditex's portfolio to help facilitate international growth.

We can see a parallel with Ford's innovative manufacturing process at work in Zara. Ortega and Inditex redefined the fashion retail category by adopting and integrating new information technologies into the apparel value chain at a time when competitors were still doing business the old-fashioned way. This enabled Zara to be highly responsive to changing market conditions, whether supply or demand driven.

In 1976 Ortega, an enthusiastic gadgeteer, was one of the 10,000 people on earth who owned his own functioning computer. In 1985 he sought the help of IT and business professional Jose Maria Castellano, who helped leverage significant investments in IT and logistics into Inditex's expanding supply chain. Jose would go on to work at Inditex for 20 years.

Starting in the early 1990s, Inditex created a successful just-in-time (JIT) manufacturing facility near its Arteixo headquarters. JIT allowed rapidly changing fashion trends to be incorporated into new designs in the facility and then quickly moved through the production and retail processes to meet demand. The more sensitive a product is to changing trends the more critical it is to have internal production, and speed in the retail process. Here, too, Inditex displayed remarkable flexibility, contracting sensitive items out to European apparel manufacturers close by. Logistically, all products whether internally or externally manufactured are shipped through a central distribution facility to well-positioned stores every two weeks, keeping inventory low. The resulting vertical integration reduces the 'bullwhip effect' where expectations of final consumer demand across the supply chain are exaggerated by each supply chain member (economic actors from different parts of the supply chain each overcompensate for what they expect to be higher consumer demand, resulting in oversupply for most intermediate products/goods). The total lead time for new or modified apparel products is five and three weeks respectively, while competitors need nearly nine months. Despite an abundance of available apparel logistics programmes, Inditex developed its software internally in order to meet the demands of the interrelationship between flexibility and customization.

Customization is a second way in which Inditex redefined the apparel category. The stress on customization and customer focus evolved out of Ortega's realization in the 1970s that other retailers who ordered clothing from his manufacturing facilities did not have a clear sense of the variations in customer demand and preferences. Zara's designers, for instance, relentlessly tracked customer preferences to incorporate changing demand into the production process in real time while producing in small batches. Apparel products were also further customized by country, rather than just for the overall European market. Sales information (quantitative and qualitative) was gathered through a state-of-the-art IT sales system. Products were tested in key stores before being rolled out across each brand, resulting in a 1 per cent 'failure' rate for apparel products versus the industry's 10 per cent. In one year, 11,000 distinct apparel items were produced under the Zara brand, in various colours, sizes and fabrics – far outpacing the 2,000 to 4,000 items for relevant competitors. Zara earned 10 per cent margins. By 2005, Inditex business lines (including Zara) had nearly 2,250 stores, sales of €5.7 billion, and a market capitalization of €18 billion.

Overall, Inditex changed the rules of the game through innovative changes in the apparel supply chain, through its closeness to customers logistically and through a keener fashion sense. This has allowed Inditex to command higher margins than the industry for business lines like Zara, and to enjoy sustained commercial success (Harvard Business School, 2003).

Thus, the fashion and luxury goods industry is one in which Europe traditionally defines the categories, due to the exacting demands of European consumers, and the old continent's heritage of superb design skills and flair for fashion innovation. Our objective can and must be not only to maintain this established realm of European category definition, but also to extend it into other sectors.

Integrated shopping and leisure centres: Sonae Sierra sets new standards for retail ambience

A school of tropical fish swims at a distance, displaying extraordinary colours and shapes; crystal-clear waters filter the blazing sun from above, creating a tantalizing view. On the floor, there are corals and seashells – and we are not taking a dive in the Caribbean seas. It is just a visit to the Vasco da Gama Shopping Centre in Lisbon, one of 16 owned and operated in Portugal by Sonae Sierra. The centre consists of more than 160 shops in a carefully designed ocean-themed setting, eloquently illustrating the changes that have occurred in Portugal's retail sector.

From the 1980s onwards, rising purchasing power and increased exposure to international markets whetted consumer desires for greater diversity, innovation and convenience than Portugal's traditional retailers seemed able to offer. This pent-up demand touched off an eruption in shopping centre development. As the format matured, it became clear that financial success required professional, innovative management of spaces designed to convey a special effect. This was the context of the founding of Sonae Sierra (re-named in 2005, formerly Sonae Imobiliária). In May 1991 it opened its first shopping and leisure centre – CascaiShopping – expanding from there to achieve clear leadership in Portugal and beyond. By the end of 2005, Sonae Sierra owned more than 1.5 million square metres of gross lettable area in 38 shopping and leisure centres in Portugal, Spain, Italy, Greece and Brazil, providing retail space to more than 6,900 tenants.

The basic concept driving the growth of Sonae Sierra is the integrated management of shopping and leisure centre development, investment and operation. Sonae Sierra pays special attention to finding innovative solutions that make its spaces more attractive, not only to the families that visit them and shop there, but also to the established business community.

Fifteen years after its founding, Sonae Sierra has an enviable track record and enjoys international recognition for its innovative high-quality solutions, including 'firsts' in format innovation (first multi-regional shopping centre, Centro Colombo, in 1997; first retail park, Sintra Retail Park, 2000) and concept innovation (such as shop lease agreements as a function of use levels, and themed shopping centres). To date, Sonae Sierra has won more international awards than any other company in the sector.

In order to ensure the creative freedom deemed essential to apply its management and innovation skills to other shopping centres, Sonae Sierra developed further skills in investment and real estate. The resulting combination of skills seems to be the company's 'recipe' for success. Its involvement begins at a very early stage in the development of every project; its influence has been described as shaping the very configuration of the market.

The company's financial investment management is backed up by its SIERRA real-estate fund. SIERRA is a Europe-wide fund with share capital of €1.08 billion (2004) and owns 23 shopping and leisure centres operated by Sonae Sierra. As the fund is 49.9 per cent owned by institutional investors, it ensures that Sonae Sierra can exercise its preference for controlling the assets it operates while considerably leveraging on its financial capacity in order to pursue continued expansion.

After consolidating its position in Portugal, Sonae Sierra expanded its operations in a select group of markets including Spain, Italy,

Greece and Brazil. Its objective is to achieve a leading position in each market by choosing local partners who provide insight into each market's specificities and help capture market share by introducing and developing new concepts. In markets such as Italy, Greece and even Germany, Sonae Sierra has actively identified and exploited investment opportunities.

The careful strategy makes use of the company's special management skills in introducing new formats and concepts, following the strategy adopted in Portugal 15 years ago, when the company started its operations.

In Greece and Italy – countries with complex bureaucracies, where the shopping and leisure centre formats developed by Sonae Sierra are not yet part of consumers' daily habits – the company is currently developing several projects. Mediterranean Cosmos in Thessalonica, opened in 2005, is the first large shopping centre in Greece. In Germany, where shopping centres account for less than 10 per cent of retail sales, Sonae Sierra is planning to create a new shopping centre concept, thus contributing to the sector's modernization. Alexa (at Berlin's Alexander Platz) and 3DO (in Dortmund) are currently under development and scheduled to open in 2007 and 2009, respectively.

As a developer of highly specialized real-estate opportunities, Sonae Sierra is a good example of a company that has defined a category in a market niche that nevertheless gives the company more than enough room to grow profitably. It also shows how some traditional Portuguese strengths – the merchant tradition and entrepreneurship – enabled a company to define an internationally successful category in a previously eminently local market, thereby creating wealth and jobs with a high value added.

Vacuum cleaners: Dyson delivers dream machines

One of the finest examples of category definition for Europe in the 1990s is Dyson Appliances. Today the phrase, 'doing a Dyson' is part of the British business vocabulary. It means taking a standard chore and working out a way of doing it better. There are few recent examples of a sole entrepreneur armed just with persistence and an innovative idea creating a furore in a complacently mature market controlled by large manufacturers, and becoming one of the dominant forces in the industry, economically and technologically. James Dyson did just that. And unlike many of the major innovations of the 1980s and 1990s, Dyson's technological breakthrough was not associated with software or computing. It was the product of plain engineering ingenuity at its finest.

An inventor at heart, James Dyson constantly looked for ways to improve products. After struggling to renovate an old farmhouse in 1974, Dyson thought up a new and improved wheelbarrow, one which rolled on a plastic sphere instead of two wheels. Manufacturers dismissed the idea, but Dyson pressed forward to get his invention into people's hands. He succeeded, and just four years later he was assigned the Building Design Innovation Award. But as investors poured more money into the company that commercialized the new 'Ballbarrows', Dyson soon became a minority shareholder and lost control of the future direction of the invention. Dyson was later to use the lessons of this experience with his future vacuum cleaner company, one where he would retain nearly full ownership.

In 1978, Dyson started developing a better vacuum cleaner. He was frustrated by the reluctance of major vacuum cleaner manufacturers to address the core problem of their products, the clogging of the bag. His basic observation was this: no matter how powerful a machine was, suction dwindled quickly and the cleaner lost power. Suction was reduced because the pores of the vacuum bag were only designed to have air pass through them, so that when they became clogged with dust, power diminished. Paradoxically, one would never get full power out of a vacuum so long as it was doing its job (and picking up dust). Dyson reacted with a cyclone-type vacuum where multiple cyclones would pick up dirt without the need for a bag, and thus ensured constant suction. He enthusiastically approached the major vacuum manufacturers such as Electrolux and Siemens with the intention of partnership, but most never bothered to reply. One reason for their reluctance was that selling replacement bags is a big business.

After more than 5,000 prototypes, several near bankruptcies, 100 patent filings and multiple lawsuits, Dyson Appliances was founded in 1993 and brought forth the first Dual Cyclone vacuum. Less than two years later, this was the best-selling vacuum cleaner in Britain and in foreign markets (including the seemingly impenetrable Japan). Revenues jumped from £2.4 million in the first year to £426 million in 2004, making Dyson Appliances one of the UK's fastest growing companies, and its owner James Dyson Britain's 39th richest person, according to the *Sunday Times* 'Rich List 2005'.

Appliance manufacturers around the world worried that Dyson had not finished improving household appliances – and they were right. In 2000, Dyson released the Contrarotator. This was the first multi-drum washing machine. The objective was to make a washing machine that could wash clothes as well as if they were washed by hand, releasing dirt quicker. The Contrarotator is able to wash larger loads faster and better than conventional washing machines. Research and development again proved to be a key factor for Dyson's success. In 2004, the company invested 12 per cent of its turnover in R&D, a fortune by British standards, where the average R&D investment is a meagre 2.1 per cent.

Dyson's products are able to command higher markups than traditional products because they are perceived by many customers as better in almost every sense. In the sense that 'form follows function', Dyson admits that aesthetics were never a priority in the design process. Still, commenting on Dyson's autobiography, the well-known British designer Terence Conran said: 'James Dyson's brilliant design skills, entrepreneurial flair and dogged persistence have made his company one of the most successful UK businesses in recent years. His story is a lesson in how companies who overlook the value of design do so at their peril.'

Dyson defined a category and revolutionized the way engineers think about household appliances. His initial objective was neither to gain fame nor amass a vast personal fortune, but simply to create a product that would ease the burden of common household chores. The level of craftsmanship Dyson insisted on and his extraordinary dedication allowed him to experience the fruits of successful commercialization and, in the process, become one of the UK's entrepreneurial role models in the 20th century (Imperial College, 1999).

MISSED OPPORTUNITIES FOR CATEGORY DEFINITION

Category definition is the exception, not the rule. Companies that produce superior products may fail to convert their lead into category definition. Xerox invented the graphical user interface so admired on today's PCs and Apple computers. Apple developed the Macintosh computer, which was years ahead of its time and the competition. For all their success, Xerox and Apple were missing the ingredient that still enables Mercedes, Gucci, Zara and Dyson to translate category definition into market share.

Xerox 'simply' missed the potential in the market for PCs; and the Apple Mac had a user interface with most of the characteristics of today's versions of Windows as early as 1984, yet it did not become the commercial standard. Although Microsoft took six years to bring out a product with some comparable features (Windows 3.0), it ended up dominating the industry.

Despite repeatedly bringing in outside managers, Apple did not exactly start out producing commercial successes. At the beginning of 1995, the company had more than US $1 billion worth of orders on its books, which it was unable to fill. Michael Spindler decided not to let Apple computers be produced under licence and to go for a premium-price policy. The company neglected however that high sales figures give the right incentives to software developers to create new applications, which in turn makes the computers more attractive, although Steve Jobs in 1984 had taken advantage of precisely this mechanism when he introduced the first Mac and put a huge effort into granting developers early access to any important information.

Apple in that instance had failed to 'earn the right to grow' by putting the prerequisites in place for growth. This is critical for successful category definition, and technical product leadership will not compensate for its absence. A few years later, Apple returned to the cutting edge, delivering an example of 'category definition regained'. The launch of the iPod was the start of a new Apple success story that looks set to continue. In 2005, responding to 42 million players sold and more than a billion paid downloads from the firm-owned download portal since 2001, the stock market responded to the iPod by more than doubling Apple's share price. Thanks to the enormous growth in iPod sales, the first quarter of 2006 was the most successful in the firm's history, marked by US $565 million in net quarterly profits (Apple Computers, 2006). The high market share in the music player business has also had a positive 'halo effect' for sales of Apple's 'traditional' desktop computers.

Whereas Apple managed to integrate its product into the lifestyle of young people all around the world and to turn that competitive advantage into sustainable profit, the history of the MP3 standard itself is another example of missed opportunities: Since the 1980s, researchers at the University of Erlangen-Nuremberg and the Fraunhofer Institute for Integrated Circuits in Germany had worked on algorithms for audio compression. From 1992 on, the standard was available and accepted by the ISO (International Organization for Standardization). In 1995 it was named MP3, but it was not until 1998 that it was used for the first time in a portable music player. The technique had already been presented to large companies in Europe, but none of them had been able to foresee the immense potential that a standard for miniaturized portable music players could have. In the end, two medium-sized companies, in the United States and in South Korea, launched the first headphones that used solid-state flash memory to store and play compressed MP3 music files (Fraunhofer Institut Integrierte Schaltungen, 2006). European high-tech companies had missed a great opportunity for innovation and category definition, as a result of being too risk averse and too inflexible in imagining future market development.

Missed opportunities for category definition do not always take the form of spectacular flops. Germany is famous throughout the world for its beer. However, a lead in terms of product does not necessarily bring about any substantial productivity. Germans will not readily give up their favourite microbrands in favour of Budweiser, Amstel or Corona, and only a handful of domestic brands are sold nationwide. Customers mainly stick to their local brews, which means that German brewers are far removed from conquering the global market with huge market shares, rapid growth in employment and high profits.

BEYOND THE COMPANY: 'MADE IN GERMANY'

These three words are well known. Less familiar is their origin as a gift of British protectionism. German manufactured goods have had to bear the 'Made in Germany' mark in the United Kingdom since 1887 when the British Merchandise Marks Act came into force. At the time, British industry was complaining about competition from the continent.

German products back then had the same reputation as Japanese products did in the 1950s and South Korean ones in the 1980s: cheap and of inferior quality. At the 1876 World Exhibition in Philadelphia, the newly founded German Empire did not have much to be proud of. All reports about the German exhibits at the fair were unanimous. Workmanship was poor, reliability low and design atrocious. The shock of the World Exhibition left a deep impression. In his influential letters home from Philadelphia, the German mechanical engineer Franz Reuleaux called for continuous improvements to products and processes, while maintaining prices and enhancing quality. It was suddenly and patently clear to the business community in the age of Kaiser Wilhelm that this should be more than just a business strategy for a handful of German firms. Scholar and politician Friedrich Naumann argued that the largely agricultural, backward Germany of his day had to transform itself into an industrial nation. By this, he meant not just more production. Rather, he hoped for a transfer of specific German skills and 'virtues' to the new world of mass production. This would foster integration within the new nation and help to conquer a big slice of the world market.

Germany then set about transferring the traditional system of apprenticeships and master craftsmen from old-style workshops to new, gigantic firms. Human capital was upgraded quickly. This aided the production of products with higher value added. No longer did industrial production have to be synonymous with 'dumbing down', as it had been for much of the 19th century. Development was reinforced by massive investments in research and development, particularly in the chemicals industry. Between 1886 and 1900, the six largest German companies patented 948 inventions in Britain; the six largest British companies managed a total of just 86 (Cipolla and

Borchardt, 1985). At the turn of the century, these German companies had over 500 scientifically qualified chemists; their British competitors often employed only 30 or 40. German success quickly followed. Although Britain had dominated the production of dyes until 1870, by 1900 Germany had overtaken it. The former 'workshop of the world' now supplied only primary products such as coal tar, and purchased high-quality chemical end products from Germany. The systematic use of scientific findings by industry became a hallmark of the German approach.

Germany's share of world trade rose rapidly between 1870 and 1913. Britain, on the other hand, having commanded about a quarter of world trade in 1870, fell back to the level of its competitors across the North Sea (Figure 7.2). 'Made in Germany' began to take on the ring that it has to our ears today: a symbol of quality workmanship, technical innovation, reliability and modern design. At the 1893 World's Fair in Chicago, just 17 years after the embarrassment of Philadelphia, the situation had changed radically for the better. Almost 80 per cent of the German machinery exhibited won prizes.

As early as the end of the 19th century, British manufacturers started to forge the 'Made in Germany' mark and apply it to their products. The German strategy of investing in research and upgrading the skills of the workforce had transformed it into a seal of quality. In just two decades, a backward, poor, initially fragmented economy secured a leading role for itself in the high-tech industries of the 19th century. Interestingly, imitation was not important to this success. Germany deliberately chose its own, culturally compatible path, and reinvented itself as a modern industrial nation. The passion for craftsmanship and attention to detail that had produced the Gothic cathedrals and Mittenwald violins now brought forth Blohm & Voss ships and Borsig locomotives.

The story of Germany and the healthy jolt from the 1876 World Exhibition is not that unusual. Other countries have similar 'rags to riches' stories to tell. Switzerland, Denmark and Italy transformed themselves from agricultural backwaters to wealthy, highly productive economies. Will Europe be able to achieve a transformation similar to theirs in the early 21st century? Will the old continent

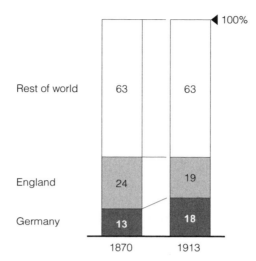

Source: Maddison, 2001.

Figure 7.2 Shares of world trade: Germany, England and the rest of the world (% of total exported goods)

manage to leapfrog the formerly leading economy, as Germany eventually did? What is the package that will make 'Made in Europe' a success story along the same lines?

CATEGORY DEFINITION FOR EUROPE

Sophisticated engineering and highly skilled workers producing top-quality products are no longer enough. Many developing countries are rapidly closing the quality gap to the current leaders. What, then, is to be done?

The concept of category definition provides a lens for seeking out the industries in which Europeans can play to their natural strengths and identify key factors for success. This can work if individual European regions and industries identify their respective talents and what is unique to them, regardless of national borders, and consciously build on these strengths. This will make it easier to define categories successfully.

As we have seen, some companies and industries in Europe are already world class. But there are too few of them. If far-sighted entrepreneurs could be similarly successful in another 5 to 10 industries, a large share of the productivity and employment problem would be solved. If furniture from Italy and Finland, sparkling wines not only from the vineyards around Reims, but also from, say, Catalonian vineyards (Penedes Cava) and time in mountain spas in the Alps were produced and marketed in the same holistic sense of category definition as products by Armani, Nokia and Audi, Europe would have more regions that are rich in wealth and jobs.

Category definition arises wherever people implement a vision with more in mind than earning a fast buck (or euro). Europeans tend to think that they know more about *savoir vivre* and culture than people in other places. It does not matter whether this is really true or not: the world accepts it. So why not go a step further: take *savoir vivre*, culture, sophisticated, demanding consumers, skilled workers and innovators with a vision, build on category definition wherever it can be attained, and exploit the opportunities it offers? This would include an intelligent combination of product and process innovation and, crucially, managing the surrounding image.

Europe could, for instance, attempt to define all those categories of products that are in any way connected to status and luxury. Europe is sitting on a host of luxurious secrets. If high tech is now as likely to come from East Asia as from the United States, and the South Koreans are building reliable cars, what products are going to generate the income needed in Europe with its high wages and generous social services?

As Porsche boss Wiedeking said at the launch of the Boxster: 'Eroticism comes at a price. We are not in the business of building tin-can cars' (Winter, 2000: 59). The good life in Europe, already a watchword, could be the source of real competitive advantages, if Europe built consistently on high-end, 'high-affinity' consumer goods. Premium-priced products such as Pommery, Moët & Chandon and other well-known French champagne brands, sold by virtue of category definition into selected, attractive market segments, may provide part of the answer. Custom-made luxury yachts from

Benetti, haute couture from Milan and private jets from Dassault can equip the world's wealthy.

The market for luxury goods is set to grow in the future. While it is true that most of the billions spent in east Asia and Latin America over the next 20 years of growth are likely to go on people's first washing machines or their first cars, the fact is that income inequality is substantial in areas with high growth rates, and this means that the demand for luxury products ought to outpace other growth. Demand for luxury often follows quickly on the heels of industrial development. In 18th-century England, Henry Fielding wrote about the 'torrent of luxury which of late years hath poured itself into this nation' (Voth, 2000: 193).

These days, luxury labels earn a significant portion of their sales in Asia; on top of this are the purchases made by tourists from Japan and other Asian countries who buy heaps of designer goods from Louis Vuitton, Gucci and Hermès when they are on vacation in France and Italy. If, after overcoming the current economic crisis, growth rates in Asia were to revert to the 6–10 per cent that prevailed before the start of the new millennium, it would take only 10 years for the global market in luxury goods in the narrower sense of the term to reach US $130–160 billion, and that does not even include cars, wine or chocolates. Add to this all the areas where a luxury or premium category has only just been invented. What used to be called roller skates have turned into inline skates, and the good old tea kettle is now a design icon in brushed aluminium, manufactured by Siemens and designed by F.A. Porsche.[3] What used to be a coffee filter is now a technologically advanced, self-cleaning, electronically controlled €1,000 espresso machine by Jura or Krups. Wherever it is possible with the aid of design talent and engineering know-how to turn a well-known, simple product into something completely or nearly new, Europe has a good chance to be out in front.

Dealing responsibly with the environment is another area in which Europe should be well on the way to defining a category. Where else should it arise, if not in heavily populated and prosperous Europe, blessed as it is with so many people thinking ecologically? A number of hopeful starts can already be detected in the production of alternative energy by solar and wind power, the purification of industrial exhaust gases and recycling. Waste paper is a useful raw material for the paper industry around the world, even shipped from Europe to China. Europeans already collect 55 per cent of their used paper, with some countries such as Germany or the Netherlands serving as role-models with recycling rates of over 70 per cent (Verband deutscher Papierfabriken, 2006). Regulation has encouraged the growth of the European wind power industry. Power-generating windmills come, for example, from Vestas in Denmark. It started with 60 workers in 1987. Today, it is a market leader with more than 10,500 employees. Europe as a whole holds 73 per cent of the world capacity, way ahead of the American continent (15 per cent) and Asia (10 per cent) in 2004. In the future, many more countries will rely on wind power as an alternative to fossil fuels. European industry, having already defined the category, is likely to profit from this worldwide trend.

The health care industry is yet another area in which Europe should define a category. The continent will be in the forefront of population ageing, with many negative economic consequences. Yet the same ageing of most European societies can be turned into an advantage for the health care industry. Reliably growing demand for health care services will stimulate the medical care industry. Diabetes is one of many diseases that become much more common with old age and changes in lifestyle. Novo Nordisk, Denmark's largest pharmaceutical company, has the broadest diabetes product portfolio in the industry, including the most advanced products within the area of insulin delivery systems. It is the global market leader in diabetes care with an overall market share of 20 per cent, expanding its global leadership position in the insulin market, where it has a total share of more than 50 per cent.

Other European companies should seize the opportunity and anticipate future industry evolutions in order to be among the definers of new categories. Heart disease is the single biggest cause of death. Hence, pacemakers are big business. Biotronik, headquartered in Berlin, is an example of a European category definer in the field of electrotherapy of the heart (cardiac pacemakers and defibrillators).

Its founder, Professor Max Schaldach, developed the first German-made pacemaker in 1963.

Another potential area of future strength could be in functional food and neutraceuticals, particularly healthy forms of foods, often containing special ('active') ingredients. These include the special lactic acids in yoghurt, and there are also food and drinks that are prepared with vitamins and minerals to suit particular age and requirement profiles. The scope for category definition in neutraceuticals could conceivably extend to dispensing doses of pharmaceuticals in food.

The same applies to high-quality capital goods. This is where Europe needs to follow the path advocated by mechanical engineer Franz Reuleaux in the light of Germany's embarrassing showing at the 1876 World's Fair: supply products and services that fetch premium prices (without which high wages and even more expensive environmental protection would be unaffordable) and offer exceptional customer value. 'Functional differentiation' is key, that is, concentrating on those parts of the value chain where Europe can really exploit its advantages. Pure production is an ever decreasing component of this. When low-wage countries can make practically flawless products, including technologically highly complex ones, Europe is bound to lose global market share in production. This does not have to be a problem, as long as the activities with the highest value added, the creative design, architectural, engineering and product development elements in the big multinationals, stay in the old continent. Engineering skill, craftwork and design savvy join the desire for luxury in the building of high-quality boats, for example.

There is no doubt that Europe is capable of advancing as a leader with well-designed products in the future. In a number of technological sectors, Europe is already a world leader or at least up with the front runners. OMX and Deutsche Börse Systems build world-class trading systems for futures and equities; Nokia leads the market for mobile phones; in medical technology, Siemens, Philips and B Braun Melsungen are leaders in their field; and in enterprise resource planning software, SAP with its NetWeaver technology is well positioned globally. There are others, possibly less well known: Bosch in automotive electronics, Schlumberger in oilfield services technology, ST Microelectronics and Philips in the budding chip card industry, Trumpf in laser cutting technology, and Merck in chemicals for flat screen liquid crystals.

These sectors are well established, they are in a well-defined market and, apart from a certain amount of basic research, firmly in the hands of engineers. Equally important to category definition in Europe, however, are those industries where applications are still on the drawing board or just leaving the basic researchers' laboratories. Two sectors deserve more attention: nanotechnology and composite materials.

K Eric Drexler's book *Engine of Creation* first awakened public interest in nanotechnology in 1986. Many of the ideas in it still sound like science fiction, but some products based on this technology are already reality. Future developments could be breathtaking. Nanotechnology uses structures of up to 100 nanometres in size, about a thousand times thinner than a human hair (100 nanometres are approximately equivalent to the linear extent of 35 gold atoms). At this scale, quantum effects play a significant role, and this is what makes this field so exciting: materials and mechanisms of this size can take on all kinds of completely new characteristics. Non-adhesive, highly reflective or dirt-resistant colours; extremely precise processes for turning, welding and polishing in the production of silicon wafers; and processes for measuring to within an atom, such as scanning tunnelling microscopy (STM), exemplify some of the solid results that have emerged from this field already. The giant magnetoresistive effect has revolutionized the storage density of computer hard drives and the lamination of surfaces, and using nanotechnology makes plastic lenses in eyeglasses scratch resistant.

The range of the products mentioned gives an idea of the way nanotechnology can be deployed across the board. It brings together the basics of physics and chemistry with applications in all kinds of sectors, from basic chemicals through drugs to electronics. Conservative estimates give a figure of at least €100 billion for the global market in 2005.

The leading industrial nations have been quick to recognize nanotechnology's potential and have subsidized it accordingly.

Development grants in the European Union amounted to €740 million in 2004. Figures on research development grants are difficult to compare internationally because different criteria are applied to define the boundary lines. That said, the figures for the United States and Japan are approximately €850 million and €800 million respectively, suggesting that Europe should devote more funds to nanotech research.

In Germany, there are currently approximately 300 research groups and about 250 German companies, including 40 large ones, working on nanotech projects. These include Audi, BMW, DaimlerChrysler, Porsche and Volkswagen in the automobile industry and Bosch, Infineon and Siemens in electronics and IT. As far as the results of all this research are concerned, Germany is level with the United States and Japan, followed by France and China. Europe has to stay on top and cannot afford to fall behind.

Another area where Europe has an opportunity to achieve lasting category definition is composite material technology. Its growing importance may be gauged from a glance at aircraft construction. In a Boeing 767 built at the beginning of the 1980s, composite materials accounted for 3 per cent of the structural weight. In an Airbus A320 (the first of which flew in 1987), this proportion already stood at 15 per cent, and in the forthcoming A380, 20 per cent of the structures will be made of carbon fibre composites and other new metallic materials.

There is a €40 billion global market for composite materials. North America has a share of 47 per cent, while 28 per cent is made in Europe. There is no reason why a Europe that invests in its future should not reverse these ratios and become a world leader.

There is no lack of areas with opportunities for category definition, even though Europe still allows itself to be weak in many of them. In a Europe that defines design categories, Nokia should no longer be having its cell phones designed in Los Angeles. No appeal to European patriotism (which is practically non-existent at present anyway) will help. Instead, we need to roll up our sleeves and create the prerequisites for defining categories in Europe.

Category definition cannot be achieved in a vacuum: competition is everywhere. If there is a place on earth where efforts are 'well coordinated', it is Singapore rather than Europe. Europe can define categories successfully only where it genuinely possesses strengths of its own and links up with its traditions. Europe's tremendous tradition in education should be used to start the return to its own strengths: the concept of scientific objectivity, scientific discovery as an open process the results of which are made accessible to the public, the modern research university incorporating teaching, as first conceived by Alexander von Humboldt – the list could be continued.

Germany in the late 19th century was able to build its industrial strength and economic power using a niche strategy with a focus on chemical research and engineering know-how. Today there are hardly any attractive sectors left that are not heavily dependent on highly qualified graduates (from every discipline) and contacts with excellent research universities. Europe should set itself the goal of having many universities by the end of the decade that can hold their own with publicly funded US institutions such as the University of California at Berkeley, and sooner rather than later, with the prestigious private universities such as Stanford, Chicago and Princeton as well. The costs would be relatively low, and any estimate of the direct and indirect benefits suggests that investing more in higher education would offer a really economical path to achieving category definition.

The various strategies for category definition in Europe – whether financial services in the UK, engineering products from Germany, or fashion and design from France, Italy and Spain – all require specific skills and therefore depend on an educated labour force. Only the rapid and smooth transfer of knowledge will give Europe a chance of keeping up with the growing number of countries targeting the same segments of global demand. This requires a change in our mindset, which brings us to another point, closely related to the issue of education: the significance of culture in general.

Top cultural achievements should form part of the concept of category definition. In the era of Queen Victoria and Kaiser Wilhelm, European countries impressed the world not only with textile engineering and chemical products, but also with operas by Verdi and Wagner, novels by Charles Dickens and Victor Hugo, and the philosophies of John Stuart Mill, Schopenhauer and Kierkegaard. Nowadays, Europe is still a region rich in culture. The lively art scene in London, successful art fairs in Cologne, Madrid or Basel (Art Basel was even successfully exported to Miami Beach), France's post-modern philosophers, modern British historians, Gerhard Richter's or Georg Baselitz's art, the Venice Bienniale, the numerous festivals like those of Avignon, Cannes, Glyndebourne and Salzburg: they are all in the top league and show that European culture still has what it takes to be the best, even if Hollywood dominates what we watch at the movies.

Culture is conceived as ubiquitous in Europe. The continent is dotted with castles, palaces, art museums, theatres, opera houses and the like. Many cities with 100,000 inhabitants or fewer have superb museums and host classical concerts of outstanding quality, not to mention having well-preserved and cared-for architectural monuments dating back hundreds of years. Cultural institutions are regarded as educational and are mainly state funded. Europeans are proud of their history and cherish its remnants. Out of 628 cultural sites of the UNESCO's world heritage list, 274 are to be found in EU-25 countries. Thus, with only 7 per cent of the world's population, Europe represents 44 per cent of the world's cultural sites. For many regions in Europe their museums, castles and picturesque villages are a huge asset, attracting tourists from all over the world.

Europe also has plenty to offer outside the established cultural scene and higher-brow entertainment. In September 2002, in an article in the *Frankfurter Allgemeine Zeitung*, correspondent Dirk Schümer wrote jokingly about 'Italy's dominant culture'. Despite all the complaints about the dominance of US culture, in fact Italy is at least as successful today in exporting its lifestyle, eg fashion, food and product design as the United States. The country demonstrates how, despite many structural disadvantages but thanks to category definition in a number of key areas, a successful business concept can develop. Italian food has become the global standard for light and tasty meals, ending with an espresso. Around the world, more kids want spaghetti than hot dogs, and they meet in the Italian ice-cream parlour while their parents go round the corner to shop for prosecco, balsamic vinegar, gnocchi, Parma ham and parmesan cheese. People in Silicon Valley start their day with a latte. Add to this a good portion of the global fashion industry, from Brioni suits to Benetton and haute couture from Milan – anything sold on aesthetic appeal frequently comes out of Italy.

What today is synonymous with an easy-going and slightly luxurious lifestyle is actually due to the countless Italian émigrés who fled miserable economic conditions back home, and introduced the world to pasta and pizza. The images of vacations in Tuscany, sunglasses, cabriolets, smart clothes, light cuisine and good wine were shaped only after the Second World War. 'A journey to Italy' was for a long time a northern European dream that only few experienced: sons of English aristocrats on the Grand Tour and fortunate artists sponsored by their patrons. Eventually, by virtue of category definition for everything beautiful and good, success followed for la dolce vita. A country that was desperately poor in 1945 now has, in its north, one of the most dynamic growth areas in Europe and in the world, underpinned by thousands of small and medium-sized companies that, thanks to the appeal of the *stilo italiano*, enjoy record sales on global markets.

Europe as a whole can be similarly successful, not by inventing an artificial Euro-identity but by intelligently bringing together existing tradition with the value of potentially high-prestige products coming from Europe. There are certainly examples of how to do this. In the 1980s, Audi realized that its brand was perceived outside Germany as belonging to a company that was vaguely foreign, but not specifically German – not good, given that the country has a reputation for the attention to detail, reliability and cutting-edge engineering which at the same time characterized Audi cars. An international advertising campaign memorably set the record straight with the slogan *'Vorsprung durch Technik'* featuring the high tech product content 'Made in Germany'. The claim was backed once again in 2005 with a successful remake of the advertisement showing the gravity-defying ascent of an Audi up the 80 per cent gradient of the timber-framed Pit-kävuori ski jump, first filmed in the early 1980s.

HOW THE PUBLIC SECTOR CAN SUPPORT THE CATEGORY DEFINITION PROCESS

Growing a company – in particular a small one – is a delicate process that bears fruit only in certain environments. This process has four key drivers: systematic access to sources of new technologies and ideas, availability of capital, entrepreneurship, and an environment that nurtures excellence and a single-mindedness of purpose.

Two decades ago, management theorist Michael Porter analysed the interplay between these drivers, trying to explain where dynamic, competitive companies come from. Clusters of firms producing similar products can be hotbeds of innovation. Some economies produce vertically deep clusters involving many levels of the value chain and also expanding to suppliers of equipment and other specialized inputs. Other economies may also configure horizontal clusters of interrelated industries with independent value chains. In this case, the dynamics are largely supported by the existence of opportunities for cross-fertilization of knowledge and resources (Porter, 1998).

Can these processes of company growth and the development of new category players be stimulated? Considering international benchmarks, the answer is yes. Such an effort involves six main stages. Stage one requires the creation of competitive knowledge and technology cores. University or corporate technology centres (for example, in the automotive industry) are typical back-up 'infrastructures' for stage one. The next two stages consist in strengthening individual start-ups and establishing back-up services for them (such services include access to venture capital and incubator services). Two key elements at this stage are energizing entrepreneurship and mobilizing local business communities. Initiatives such as business plan awards can be critical instruments in supporting mobilization, as the coaching and exchange elements of such contests help overcome barriers and encourage convergence among the interests of different stakeholders. In the United States, the Massachusetts Institute of Technology (MIT) has frequently supported this kind of initiative, and in Europe there are also several similar experiments with positive results (in London, Munich, Cologne, Stockholm, Gothenburg, Helsinki and elsewhere). The remaining three stages have a more specific (and often more political) nature and are mainly aimed at ensuring the medium- to long-term competitiveness and sustainability of the companies developed – for example, promoting 'reference cases' and developing international marketing activities, as well as giving incentives to foreign investors and phasing out structural restrictions.

Correctly handled, the pursuit of category definition can go a long way towards revitalizing European business. Governments can support this effort by putting money into cluster strategies, the supporting infrastructure and human skills. Where this money should go, and where it should come from, is the topic of our next chapter.

8

Reinventing the state

George Orwell's *Road to Wigan Pier* (1936/2001) eloquently describes the depths of the Great Depression. It also contains an example of shocking waste. It shows how, at the height of the crisis, unemployed English coal miners had to dig for scraps of coal in the rubble near their old mine shafts, which stood idle. The waste was one of human and industrial resources: miners spent hours collecting a few bits of coal when they could have produced tons under ground.

Europe today is a long way from Wigan Pier, yet some of the problems are eerily familiar. The continent has many gleaming factories full of high-tech machinery; many of them operate at far less than full capacity. A large part of the workforce sits idle. At the same time, people would like to consume more goods and services. Europe produces many brilliantly creative minds, yet fails to educate them to their full potential or to retain the largest possible number. In many ways, some parts of the old continent seem to be suffering a sad waste of potential.

Other parts of it, however, show how Europe can escape this impasse. By changing the way it uses scarce resources, Europe can lay the foundations for a resurgence of growth. Governments need to play a pivotal role if Europe is to turn itself into an economic power-house. The state at all levels, from Brussels to municipal councils, is crucial as an enabler of productivity improvements in private indus-try, as we highlighted in Chapter 6 on smart regulation. The scope and focus of those government activities that consume resources and affect the fiscal budget also need to change. Political leaders must be convinced and then convince a sceptical populace of the need for change, and implement far-reaching changes in the way the state taxes and spends. The purpose is threefold. First, in order to insulate Europe from the coming demographic shock, people must save more and set aside a larger part of existing savings to fund their pensions. At the same time, Europe must find ways of using its production capacity to the full. Therefore demand should increase, not decrease. Finally, Europe must invest more in its human capital as a source of category definition (described in Chapter 7). Otherwise, it will be unable to achieve the suggested 'high value-added' strategy that is needed to finance its social goals. We present a solution that addresses precisely these challenges.

Completing the single market, smart regulation and category defi-nition are key initiatives to strengthen Europe's economy. However, their success depends on a fourth element: Europe also needs to reinvent its welfare state and to change the way it delivers public services generally. This requires far-reaching alterations in the member states' mode of operation and the European Union's organ-ization. Europe should aim to reform its way of doing things from top to bottom: from its administrative processes down to the regions and the municipalities. This is a more far-reaching objective than a new European constitution.

To reach its objectives, Europe must invest more in its future, but how can this be funded? There is a simple reason that savings have to be found in government budgets: it is the only source of room for manoeuvre. Increasing taxes would be a bad idea, given how large the economic role of governments has become. In many European states, the government allocates close to half of all economic resources. This is a stunning amount. A mere century ago, many states made do with 5 to 10 per cent of total output. Not all of this money is spent on actual government services. On average, European states take around 22 per cent of GDP in order to provide government services: policing, defence, foreign affairs, and in many European countries schools, universities and (in part) health (Figure 8.1). Much of the rest is spent on social transfers and government-run insurance schemes (such as health care and pension schemes).

Producing wholesale change in large organizations is often an extremely difficult undertaking. McKinsey's experience in transforming major corporations suggests that many stumbling blocks can be avoided if a coherent, holistic approach is applied intelligently. One method, the 'V concept', has often proved effective (Figure 8.2). It is called the 'V' concept because it consists of two closely connected steps, like the two strokes forming the letter but timewise not necessarily subsequent. First, inefficiencies are reduced and responsibilities redefined. The second step aims at consolidation and development, using the freed-up resources to strengthen sectors with

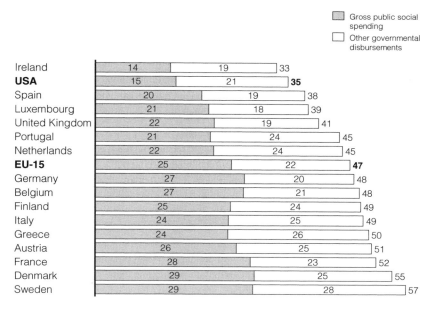

Sources: OECD (ed) (2005) *Society at a Glance*; OECD Economic Outlook database

Figure 8.1 Total governmental disbursements and gross public spending, EU-15 and United States, 2001 (as % of GDP)

potential. The idea here is to avoid simple cost-cutting programmes, which have produced mixed results in the past. Instead, improving the efficiency of current operations is an integral element in an over-arching plan that also incorporates major increases in investment for the future. This facilitates the acceptance of change and produces fewer difficulties, especially if staff can be reassigned to new tasks. In this way, major productivity increases have gone hand-in-hand with successful plans for capturing future growth opportunities.

Many of these corporations are faced with challenges every bit as radical as the ones confronting the European Union. Corporations can implement change within a few years. Entire states will have a harder time, but a change process taking place within 5 to 10 years would be as long as Europe can afford to take. The faster Europe acts – on the national and Union levels – the sooner it will be prop-erly equipped to face the challenges of competing in a globalizing world economy.

Figure 8.2 shows the essentials of what the V concept for Europe entails; these are explained in more detail in the next section. The state will have to cut back drastically on some of the things it does, and do others much more efficiently. Crucially, the focus of the welfare state also needs to change to provide more help for those living in poverty. Some of the gains generated by these steps will then be used to reduce the state's role in the economy. They will also be reinvested by governments to provide superior government serv-ices that are vital to protect Europe's future.

We first look at what Europe must invest to safeguard its future, and then discuss how to finance these investments.

INVESTING IN EUROPE'S FUTURE

Europe needs to spend more in a number of key areas. Fresh spend-ing is necessary to combat the coming demographic challenge and to produce world-class research and education. Europe also needs to do more to boost private consumption in order to reduce waste in the form of idle capacity (and unemployed workers).

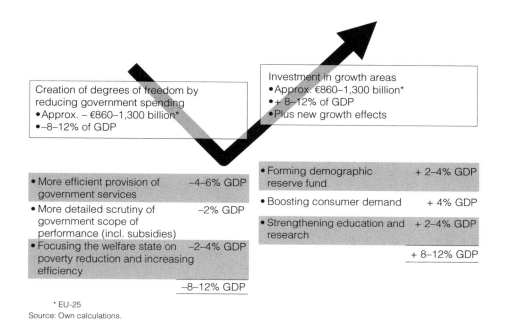

Creation of degrees of freedom by reducing government spending
- Approx. – €860–1,300 billion*
- –8–12% of GDP

Investment in growth areas
- Approx. €860–1,300 billion*
- + 8–12% of GDP
- Plus new growth effects

- More efficient provision of government services   –4–6% GDP
- More detailed scrutiny of government scope of performance (incl. subsidies)   –2% GDP
- Focusing the welfare state on poverty reduction and increasing efficiency   –2–4% GDP

–8–12% GDP

- Forming demographic reserve fund   + 2–4% GDP
- Boosting consumer demand   + 4% GDP
- Strengthening education and research   + 2–4% GDP

+ 8–12% GDP

* EU-25
Source: Own calculations.

Figure 8.2 The 'V concept' for government reform in Europe

Demographic reserve

Saving more for retirement is an obvious way to confront the coming demographic squeeze on Europe's pension systems. At the moment, citizens realize that the old pay-as-you-go pension systems will not provide for them, and that they have to save more. Yet they are doing so in an unstructured, unsystematic way. While the public pension system swallows huge resources, Europeans still save massively: much more than Americans, say.

An important part of the solution has to come from a reduction in uncertainty. Some of the existing savings should be clearly earmarked for pension purposes, possibly with some tax incentives. Europe will also need to put a bit more aside to cope with the deterioration of the age structure. We recommend that 2–4 per cent of GDP overall (including tax incentives) should be dedicated to additional retirement savings, and that some of the existing private savings be transferred to a pension 'lock box'. Additional funds must be used to make this switch more attractive, and to combat the mounting costs of health care and long-term care.

Some of the savings detailed in the first half of this chapter will therefore be earmarked for return to taxpayers in a different shape, as compulsory savings for retirement. It doesn't matter a great deal if these are provided on an individual retirement account basis, or via a general fund for the pension system as a whole (as is the case in the United States at the moment). There are European examples showing how effective this can be. In 1998, the Netherlands installed a public pension savings fund to address the foreseeable need arising from the ageing of its population, financed by public pension debt reduction. It also gives ample incentives for companies to provide occupational pension funds and for households to build up their own nest eggs for retirement. As a result, approximately half of all pensions drawn today come from various forms of pension funds, and not from PAYE contributions by the working population (Natali, 2004).

Private consumption and investment

Europe's workers, entrepreneurs and employees have long seen many of their productivity gains go to the government. Private consumption has not grown at anything like the pace seen in the United States. We believe that some of the resources freed by a leaner, more efficient state should be handed back to taxpayers. There is more potential here in countries with a higher government share in GDP, such as the United Kingdom. Higher levels of private spending would boost demand for housing, for restaurant meals and clothes, for cars and vacations. Much of this spending would be in Europe, creating profits for shopkeepers, jobs for workers and VAT revenues for governments.

After years of disappointing growth, capacity utilization in the EU is not very high. There is plenty of potential for inflation-free growth. We will later explain how both goals – more savings for pensions and more private spending – can be achieved at the same time. More and more people are becoming confused by requests from politicians both to save more and to consume more, with no explanation of how both can be done. We shall argue later that the state has to consume less and increase available private income. We shall also argue that transforming state into private consumption is growth-creating. If 4 percentage points of Europe's GDP were returned to taxpayers' pockets, this would represent an increase of approximately 7 per cent in private consumption. This could produce a veritable boom in some sectors of the economy.

Education and research

Today, Europe invests shamefully little in research and education. What it spends, it often spends badly. Although the educational systems of some European countries regularly lead international rankings, many European schools and universities are mediocre, and there is a dearth of top-flight institutions.[1] Across Europe, there is no real coordination of research policies. The EU spends directly on research programmes, but few would argue that it does a particularly good job. Nor are European countries good at learning from each other.

We recommend that Europe spends another 2–4 per cent of GDP on education and research. Today, in the EU-15, governments spend 5.9 per cent of GDP on research and education; the United States spends 6.2 per cent. Assuming the ratio to national output holds, such a boost would allow Europe to become world class.

Yet because output is so much lower, the current gap is much more impressive in absolute numbers: Public spending on research and education is equivalent to about US $1,456 per capita in the EU-25, but about US $2,338 per capita in the United States. This means that the European Union would only close the gap in absolute numbers if it spent 9.5 per cent of GDP, and the absolute numbers matter when it comes to attracting top talent and buying expensive research tools.

The mix of expenditure is similar on both sides of the Atlantic. The EU-25 member states spend 0.7 per cent of GDP on research and 5.2 per cent on education, while the US government spends 0.8 per cent of GDP on research and 5.4 per cent on education (Figure 8.3).

In the United States, private sector funding is markedly more generous than in the European Union. European firms devote 1.0 per cent of GDP to research, while in the United States this figure is 1.7

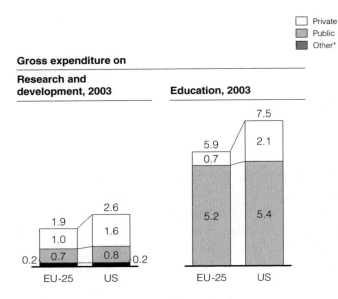

Figure 8.3 Private and public expenditure on research and education in the EU-25 and the United States (as % of GDP)

per cent. The situation is similar in education. Private individuals add 0.7 per cent of GDP to educational funds in Europe, and 2.1 per cent in the United States. Doubling government research funds would cost Europe only a further 0.7 per cent of GDP, and doubling the money spent on early childhood and top-tier college education would require 1.3 per cent of GDP.[2] We believe that, if savings are large enough, a quadrupling of funding should be seriously considered. Relative to government spending today, these are still small numbers.

The efficiency of Europe's research funding today is actually surprisingly high. Figure 8.4 shows that, per dollar spent, Europe generates more patents and publications than the United States.

High efficiency is one reason that more spending is likely to yield big returns. With just a small increase in funds, Europe could again become world leader in terms of education and research. True, Europe's proudest traditions in education are far back in a distant

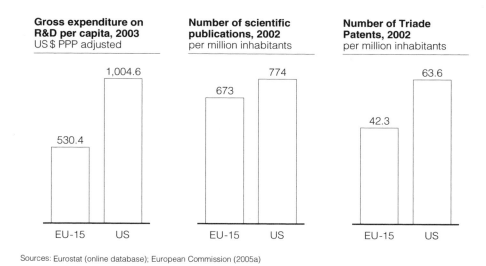

Gross expenditure on R&D per capita, 2003 US$ PPP adjusted	Number of scientific publications, 2002 per million inhabitants	Number of Triade Patents, 2002 per million inhabitants

Sources: Eurostat (online database); European Commission (2005a)

Figure 8.4   Research in the United States and the European Union

and glorious past. Padua, Heidelberg, Berlin and the Sorbonne were once known and admired all over the world for the quality of their education and research. Today, bright young scholars flock to the other side of the Atlantic. Top universities without European equals such as MIT and Stanford are genuine centres of excellence, and they produce millions of jobs indirectly, through the technologies they pioneer and the firms they spawn. Such elite centres of education are the envy of the world. Yet with only a bit of additional money, Europe could replicate many advantages, and even think of doing better.

Current problems are not solely financial. Europe builds even less on its natural advantages and opportunities in education than it does in economic matters. Europe's secondary education with its emphasis on languages and mathematics often ranks very favourably in international comparisons. Finnish pupils perform outstandingly in the OECD Programme for International Student Assessment. Europeans graduating from good sixth-form colleges in the UK or a good Gymnasium in Germany or Switzerland often speak more languages, know more maths and have much better writing skills than their American peers.

In large parts of Europe (with the United Kingdom a notable exception), the public sector still has a quasi-monopoly on providing education. This, for once, is a good thing. In education, private sector 'competition' is not likely to be very effective, because its scale is so small and because it may create consequences in the political economy. A society where parental income determines whether a child becomes well educated is in general incompatible with European values. Also, it is a waste of scarce talent and – because of poor incentives for private investments – threatens the funding of education in the first years of life. That is one of the reasons that the United States (and the United Kingdom) with their mix of private and public schools struggle to maintain high average education levels: public funding for good public schools (state schools in the UK, where 'public schools' are fee-paying establishments) garners little support when some middle-class parents already pay €10,000 or more for private schools. Going back to a monopoly state-run education system is hard, since one generation would effectively have to pay twice, for fixing the public (state) schools and for their children's fee-paying schools. Europe has the advantage that its public school system is not (yet) in ruins.

Europe's public school system is still fairly sound for the moment. If Europe invests more heavily in its public schools, adds funding for better pre-school education, provides more offerings for highly gifted students in secondary schools and learns to adopt best-practice solutions from the most successful systems, it can turn a current weakness into a real strength. We shall not discuss the private school system here, since it is very much the minority in most of Europe.

At the university level, circumstances are different. In this case, too, additional funding is urgently necessary. However, as incentives for private investment are much bigger whereas public funding is scarce, the former will have to play a more important role than in the school system. In any case, the state has to keep an eye here on the danger of selective mechanisms that are other than academic. Both privately and publicly funded systems are in danger of reinforcing social differences rather than offering equal chances to all gifted students. We believe that the European tradition of state-funded universities and new ways of private investment and engagement in the sector of academic education – reasonably balanced – could prepare the ground for a truly meritocratic system that offers an outstanding education to every student with the intellectual capacity.

Such a system could become world class in turning out top-quality graduates. Admissions with a focus on academic ability only could quickly create institutions in Europe that are every bit as selective as the best US universities, and more focused on academic excellence.

Better structures for the universities and some additional money for education and research could make a world of difference. In addition, research spending should be reorganized. There should also be a single, pan-European funding body for research, modelled on the US National Science Foundation. All European universities should be able to compete for funds. Europe already has a good track record in some of its large-scale research initiatives, such as CERN, the Southern Observatory and the Molecular Biology Laboratory. CERN in particular shows what can be achieved if Europe puts money where its heart should be. Two Nobel prizes underscore the fact that consistently bundling funds and bringing together the best and the brightest researchers in a given field in a single location can lead to world-class results.[3] Twenty European countries joined CERN to finance top-flight research that does not shy away from taking risks. Funding is roughly proportional to the countries' national products. The focus is on elementary particle physics, and the primary goal is basic research. Nonetheless, scientists there often cooperate with industry.

Europe's research efforts should aim not only to define categories in higher education and research, but also to target investments in technologies that use the skills of the European population particularly well. In many fields, Europe can boast a particularly broad base of comparatively well-educated workers (Figure 8.5).[4]

In most countries, Europe has relatively few functional illiterates, and a large number of people with average abilities. In the Netherlands, for example, a good 44 per cent of the population are in the middle group, with 20 per cent in the top category. The large middle category of relatively well-educated citizens is one of the reasons for Europe's strengths in culture and art, for its egalitarian values and also for its political stability. Europe should do more with

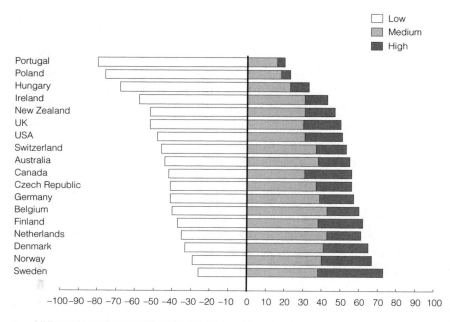

* Ability to read and understand instructions, forms, timetables, maps, tables, and graphs.
Source: OECD, 2000.

Figure 8.5   Document literacy* in OECD countries, 1994–98

this comparative advantage. In addition to high-tech clusters such as are seen on Boston's Route 128 or in Silicon Valley, it should push 'mid-tech', such as investments in engineering, or in design and architecture schools that could enable Europe to define categories in more traditional industries. This would not be an alternative to top-quality research in important new fields such as biotechnology, but would supplement these efforts. Scientific culture is ultimately indivisible: no country can be a world leader in the applied sciences without also massively investing in basic research.

Investments in education and research must be linked closely to initiatives that aim to achieve category definition. There is a need for an integrated programme to identify sectors that are in a position to push ahead to become the best in the world and to support these sectors via applied research. Matching grants for venture capital funds that recruit university researchers in high-priority research fields are a possibility, as are Institutes for Enology in Tuscany, Penedes and Bordeaux directly funded by the European Union with appropriate training programmes. Similar efforts could focus on professional schools for design, architecture and medicine.

Such initiatives could become engines for economic development in the surrounding areas. The leap to joining the world's best can come astonishingly quickly in regions that discover the logic of clusters for themselves and share the newest procedures in research, applications and marketing among the cluster participants. A generation ago, California's Napa Valley, for example, was mildly scoffed at as a wine-growing region. True connoisseurs were confident that French wines would remain the 'real thing' for the foreseeable future. Today, many experts believe that French vintners have a hard time keeping up with the US competition. The network logic of companies exchanging employees and ideas while simultaneously competing, borrowed from Silicon Valley (150 miles further south), helped them to challenge Bordeaux at its own game. We believe that Europe can do the same in a number of industries, creating a wealth of economic dynamism as a result.

There are already promising examples of this in Europe, although they are still rare. An example of the regional promotion of technology companies is the Technologiezentrum Dortmund (TZDO), which has existed since 1985. It is positioned as a pioneer in innovative ideas with the goal of enabling young companies to launch their technological products on the market. It is home to around 225 companies providing more than 8,000 jobs. The companies that have moved into the TZDO can take advantage of a package of services, as well as space and an industry-specific infrastructure that allows them to avoid capital-intensive investments.

TRIMMING STATE SPENDING TO INVEST IN THE FUTURE

We have presented a long shopping list: more money for consumption, for research and education, for pensions. Where is it going to come from? We argue that government budgets are not only the best place to look. They are the only place to generate the right kind of savings: big, achievable and without a major negative impact on the economy as a whole.

In many – but not all – European countries, this kind of thinking is considered heresy, or pure fantasy. Personnel costs must not be touched, the argument goes. Talk about reducing spending on government services, and someone will point out that teachers, the police and firefighters need to be paid. When they look at the rest, the argument is often that roads, courts and schools need more money, not less. Talk about reducing welfare expenditure will invariably bring down controversy on the speaker's head. Politicians are reluctant to take bold action for fear of career consequences. Yet, as we shall show, there are a large number of examples of how gridlock, stagnation and continued high spending by the government can be overcome. Case studies also show how much money can be saved by boosting public sector productivity and by focusing money for social causes on where it should go – to the poorest. There is much government spending that can and should be cut, without a decline in the quality of services. In what follows, we look at both sides of public spending: government services themselves and social transfers.

What the pressure of the market is to businesses, a political and economic crisis can be to many countries. When municipalities run into difficulties funding their expenditures, they often take a hard and fresh look at priorities and the way that things get done. Countries in Europe and elsewhere have already made major efforts to reform their public services. Not all of these encouraging starts actually yielded tangible results: improving the efficiency of public services is a tough job. Nonetheless, governments in many EU member states today are already smaller in terms of GDP share than they used to be at the height of their post-war expansion. The most successful examples show how much can be done, and how big the scope for future savings is in those member states where the reform process has only barely started.

Since 1991, lower social spending has shaved some 3.2 percentage points off the government quota. Another 4.5 percentage points were saved from a reduction in expenditures on government services. In many OECD countries, government employment has actually declined by several per cent from its peak: by 10 per cent in Australia between the mid-1980s and early 1990s, 3 per cent in Belgium and 1.2 per cent in Italy (Clayton and Pontusson 1998: 82, Table 7). Yet some countries have done much better than others. Figure 8.6 gives an overview.

Sweden, Finland, Ireland and Spain have been particularly successful in paring back the government sector. There, total government disbursements have declined by more than 9 per cent of GDP over the span of a decade. Less impressive figures were achieved in Germany and France, where the total decline was less than 4 per cent. Yet even there, the size of the state has been shrinking, no doubt aided by the incipient economic tail wind that accompanied the end of the recession in the early 1990s. While public debate in the 'reform laggards' such as Germany and France makes it seem as if major improvements are near impossible, the experience of the Scandinavian countries, of Ireland and – to a lesser extent – Spain suggest that significant reductions are possible and politically feasible.

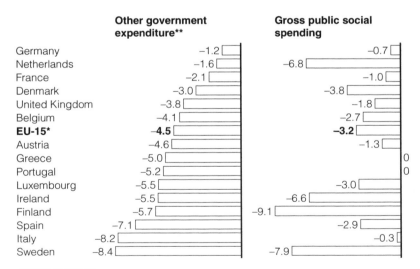

* Uweighted average.
** Total governmental disbursements minus gross public social spending.

Source: OECD (ed) (2005f)

Figure 8.6 Change in government expenditure, latest figures minus maximum during 1991–2002 (as % of GDP)

To finance the 8–12 per cent of fresh spending that forms an integral part of the V concept for Europe, the same process of retrenchment and more focused, disciplined spending that is already under way in some countries should be accelerated. Successful reform examples from around the globe illustrate that savings of this order of magnitude can be achieved.

In the early 1980s, the Irish economy was in trouble. Growth slumped, and unemployment shot up. The government reacted with a set of classic austerity measures, cutting expenditure in a bid to balance the budget. The unusual side of the Irish story is that these efforts continued as the country recovered. In 1987, the Irish government launched its 'Programme for National Recovery'. It provided for further sweeping reforms and spending cuts. Total public employment declined by 14 per cent between 1982 and 1989. Public sector wages were frozen, and the value of subsidies was slashed (by two-thirds). The combined effect of these measures has reduced the size of the government sector by 15 percentage points of total output, from 49 per cent in 1982 to 34 per cent in 2004. No part of overall spending was safe from cuts. The value of social support payments was frozen in real terms, and spending on old-age pensions and health declined. Today, Ireland is one of Europe's fastest growing economies, not least because of the effects of this decisive reform programme.

Sweden provides another instructive example not only of how the government sector can be shrunk, but of how such a roll-back can also be implemented in a way that stimulates growth. Between 1990 and 1994, the size of the government workforce was cut by a staggering 12 per cent: some 170,000 fewer out of a total of 1.42 million government employees (Clayton and Pontusson, 1998). Entitlements to social transfers were similarly reduced and combined with tough means testing and retraining/work requirements in social programmes. Finland went through a similarly wrenching adjustment in the 1990s. It turned its fortunes around with a set of measures that were broadly comparable to the ones instituted by Sweden and Ireland.

Successful reform examples show that Europe can save a great deal of money by wringing savings from government services and from increasing the focus of its social spending. Sceptics may object that it is not clear how this can be done in actual practice. Where are the inefficient procedures that could be performed so much better? Where are the unneeded bureaucrats whose jobs could be lost without a decline in service quality? We discuss possible ways to improve efficiency below.

Reforming government services

Productivity growth in the private sector is a fact of life. In most countries, productivity rises by 1.5 to 2 per cent per year on average in the long term. Be it in the auto industry, computer production, stock trading or beverage sales, each worker today produces significantly more than 20 years ago. Some industries and countries register faster growth than others, but stagnation is very rare.

How much more efficient has the state become? No one seriously believes that governments increased service productivity that much. In actual fact, when some statisticians attempted to measure the productivity of government services, the findings were disheartening. For a quarter of a century, from 1967 to 1994, the US Bureau of Labor Statistics made a heroic effort to measure government output. It went beyond simply measuring inputs like people and wages, and focused on – in a library, say – the number of items issued to borrowers, the number of fines processed and the like. Between 1967 and 1983, the productivity of government services increased at the same rate as those in non-farm businesses in the United States: 1.5 per cent per year. Over the period 1983–94, productivity increases in the government sector slowed to a dismal 0.6 per cent, while private sector output per head stood at 1.3 per cent.

Unfortunately, the BLS discontinued data collection in 1994 (Fiske and Forte, 1997). Therefore, we do not know if the government has continued to lag behind or not. Yet data from an exercise in the United Kingdom strongly suggest that things have not improved. There, government services actually became less efficient between 1995 and 2001, with efficiency falling by 0.4 per cent per year. Elsewhere in the economy, the productivity of services increased by 1.4 per cent per year (Dohrmann and Mendonca, 2004). Even if getting the numbers exactly right is a tough job, the overwhelming weight of the evidence strongly suggests that governments have failed to improve the efficiency of their services at the same rate as private firms.

Nor should this be a surprise. All bureaucracies – those running companies as well as nations – are in danger of becoming inflexible. In politics, special interest groups and the like add particular impetus to these tendencies. Competitive forces are not strong enough to punish bad policies immediately in the way that a company is punished immediately by its customers for a bad product.

The view from up close, of the nitty-gritty detail of how government services are delivered, shows that there is another way. The small successes here and savings there show what can be done, and actually amount to half of the 2 per cent reduction mentioned in Figure 8.2. They thus reinforce the overall picture that we gathered from the examples of successful government reform and pruning of state spending in Europe during the last two decades.

The first element in any strategy to improve government efficiency is to decide on 'make or buy'. Many of the services paid for by governments need not be delivered by them. Outsourcing is a convenient way of overcoming typical restrictions in the public sector. This is not some utopian ideal; there are already impressive examples, such as the British Passport Agency, which outsourced the processing of new passports to SBS, a private company. SBS was also asked to create new back-end and front-end systems in the form of an internet platform and a call centre. Governments could be much more aggressive in exploiting opportunities like this.

Buying can also be handled much more intelligently. Instead of producing long, detailed specifications for how a certain job needs to be done, authorities should ask for tender offers that leave lots of freedom for creative thought, and focus on measurable targets. For example, one German municipality managed to cut the cost of a water-treatment plant by half compared with its neighbour. It did so by simply specifying the expected water purity levels, instead of insisting on specific methods and processes.

Even where a government has to continue providing services itself, it can do much better. It can sharpen its act by applying better management techniques, including pushing for more IT adoption, centralizing functions like purchasing and pooling common infrastructure tasks. Simpler and better management, for example, allowed the tax offices in one European country to significantly improve the speed with which tax returns were handled. Measures such as establishing co-located working groups created more effective supervision of workers and facilitated the pooling of expertise, and resulted in greater throughput without a decline in quality. IT can produce similarly large – or larger – productivity breakthroughs. The Arizona Department of Transport, for example, cut the cost of processing a driver's licence by 75 per cent as a result of an e-government initiative. The US tax office IRS achieved a similar figure.

Also, the scope for pooling back-office staff and functions is very substantial, and has often remained unexploited. The German Länder of Hamburg, Bremen, Schleswig-Holstein and Mecklenburg-Western Pommerania provide an excellent example: by merging their IT departments into the common public service provider, Dataport, they established a basis not only for efficiency gains by centralizing and standardizing IT services, but also for a long-term process of transferring at least some of the responsibility for public IT infrastructure to private companies. In its first business year, Dataport effectively achieved savings of €1 million, without increasing costs for the public purse. These savings could have been bigger if layoffs had been an option.

Centralized purchasing can also help to cut the bills. Currently, many government departments buy services and goods from the private sector. The volume is often impressive. Illinois's various agencies, departments and commissions, for example, spend US $50 billion per year on purchases – the equivalent of a top-100 firm in the United States. Pooling these purchases allows the state to cut much better deals with suppliers, who can then offer volume discounts. Repeat invoicing and the like is cut, and the state can flex its muscles as a bigger buyer. This saves the taxpayer real money, without any change in the quality of goods and services bought: in the Illinois programme US $110 million in the first year, and US $200 million (expected) in the future.

Finally, the easiest recipe: privatization. As we already mentioned, productivity often surges when state-run enterprises and municipal services are transferred to the private sector. In the United Kingdom in the 1980s, gains ranged from 70 to 180 per cent (Coats, 2004). Much has already been achieved, especially in the telecoms sector. Yet many European countries continue to control local water and energy suppliers. Even where privatization has taken place in legal terms, 'golden share' agreements and the like protect some firms from the fresh winds of genuine competition (and the threat of takeovers).

The V concept, applied to companies, suggests that savings of 20–30 per cent are possible. Reaping its benefits in the public sector may take longer, but is certainly possible; when the political will is there, there tends to be a way. If savings on a par with private-sector efficiency programmes were realized, this would produce a reduction in spending of about 4–6 per cent of GDP. This is certainly an ambitious target. However, given that the EU-15 have already managed a decline of 5 per cent of GDP in government consumption over the last decade and a half, it is certainly not impossible.[5]

One additional factor can help in getting there: a reduction in subsidies. They appear at the top of lists of intended cuts time and again. Yet they are hardly ever touched. What some see as payments that can be dispensed with, others see as intelligent adjustment assistance, a bonus for technological innovation, or national energy reinsurance. Yet there is no good reason for European subsidies to be much higher than those the United States. Countries with successful government spending reforms such as Ireland have been ruthless in curtailing spending on those transfers that harm productivity, slow down structural change, and distort incentives and the allocation of capital. Conservatively, savings of 1 per cent of GDP appear realistic.

Better management, including more timely performance measurement and control, is also part of the solution for some government inefficiency. Every year, the Audit Offices throughout the European Union bring examples of public-sector waste to light. Many offices of the German Federal Office for Migration and Refugees were equipped with the latest IT systems immediately before being shut down. The European Court of Auditors regularly criticizes the lack of effective control systems to prevent fraud and mismanagement in subsidiary spending, especially in the agricultural sector, where 47 per cent of the European Union's budget is spent. Between 1971 and 2002, subsidies worth €3 billion were paid contrary to regulations as a result of fraud and mistakes; €300 million have been written off, and recovery of €2.1 billion is uncertain. The European Commission is working on the implementation of auditing systems to better control the money it spends, but there is still a long way to go (Court of Auditors, 2003: 136). Given the scale of regularly reported government waste, it should be possible to save another percentage point here.

Overall, our calculations and examples can only indicate a range of possible savings on government consumption: services, subsidies and waste put together. We believe that saving 6–8 per cent overall (4–6 from efficiency savings, and 1 per cent each from subsidies and waste) is an attainable medium-term goal.

Savings do not stop with government services and subsidies. The welfare state is high on the agenda of those who want to roll back the state now, and more importantly over the next decade when demographic change starts to pinch. Important savings must and probably can be made. The next section looks at them in some more detail.

Reinventing the European welfare state

When we look at genuine welfare payments,[6] we find that European countries spend a sum equivalent to between 4 and 14 per cent of GDP: about 8 per cent on average. The simple number has two important implications. First, the 24 per cent of 'social expenditure' that shows up in the government statistics is a vast overestimate of pure social transfers. The greater part consists of payments to pensioners through government-sponsored insurance schemes as well as health expenditure. Some of these insurance schemes contain redistributive elements. Their growth has been driven in part by political decisions, such as the infamous pension package that German Chancellor Adenauer used to secure an absolute majority in 1958.[7] Yet only one out of three euros spent on social matters is, strictly speaking, a transfer outside government-run insurance schemes. Reforming pensions and health care may yield benefits, but the overall scope for savings is probably not big. Europe already delivers health care services much more efficiently than the United States, for example.

The second striking thing about genuine transfers is that, at 8 per cent of GDP, they are still big. What do Europeans get for them? And what is the scope for increasing the efficiency of this spending?

At first glance, Figure 8.7 suggests a simple and somewhat depressing answer. It is only by using vast resources that European welfare states get their main job done: they reduce poverty rates. This seems to imply that there are few savings that can be squeezed out of the welfare budget without missing the social goals. Transfers have been successful in reducing the number of citizens who are poor in relative terms. The fact that the points in Figure 8.7 are close to the line tracing out the average seems to suggest that there are no quick and simple efficiency gains to be had. On the whole, those who want less poverty seem faced with the simple fact that high transfers are necessary. Truly re-engineering the welfare state would require a downward tilting of the curve in Figure 8.7 to reduce poverty by a greater percentage for every unit of spending. That said, some states do a somewhat better job at reducing poverty than others. Switzerland and the Czech

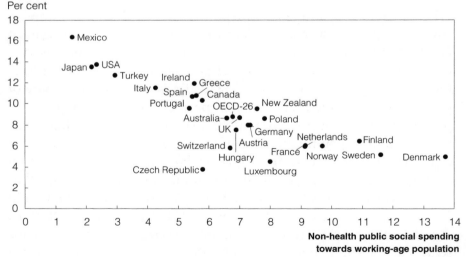

Source: Förster and Mira d'Ercole, 2005.

Figure 8.7   Relative poverty after transfer among the working-age population and social spending, 2000

Republic have lower poverty rates than we would expect, given their spending on social security. Yet the overall picture suggests that if Europeans believe in reducing poverty rates, they have to spend substantially. This they do, devoting almost 1 euro out of every 10 to the purpose (see Figure 8.7).

First impressions can be deceiving. We believe that substantial improvements are possible. To show how this might work, we need to take a closer look at where poverty comes from, and what systems today do to reduce it.

Poverty rates are the result of two factors, market outcomes and transfers. France and Italy, for example, would have relatively high rates of poverty without transfers (Figure 8.8). Norway and Switzerland have less of a problem. Welfare spending reduces these poverty rates greatly in most European countries. France, despite its high pre-transfer poverty rates, ends up with modest ones as a result

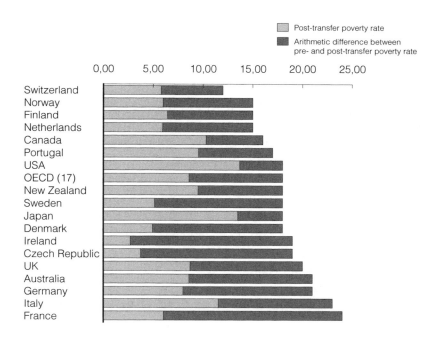

Source: Förster and Mira d'Ercole, 2005.

Figure 8.8 Effects of taxes and transfers in reducing relative income poverty, 2000 (%)

of generous transfers. The United States, on the other hand, has average rates of market-driven poverty, but barely makes a dent in these levels through taxes and transfers (see Figure 8.8).

Per unit of GDP spent, some European countries achieve much greater reductions in poverty than others. This may simply reflect differences in income distribution: where many citizens are only marginally below the poverty line, lifting everyone out of poverty will be cheap. Elsewhere, where there are deep pockets of abject misery, even massive expenditure can hardly make a dent in poverty rates (see Figure 8.9).

To get around these problems, we examine detailed data based on Europe-wide microcensus information that gives incomes (pre-transfer) of different groups of the income distribution.[8] We then ask: how much would it cost to lift everybody out of relative poverty, that is, above 50 per cent of the nationwide median per capita income? In France, for example, everybody below the 25th income percentile would need to receive some kind of transfer. Of course, the amount differs according to market income. Overall, US $39 billion would be necessary to lift everybody to the poverty line: 2.6 per cent of GDP in a US $1.5 billion economy. In some countries like Portugal, this would be relatively cheap, costing merely 1.3 per cent of GDP. Elsewhere (the United Kingdom and Sweden) it would require up to 3.6 per cent. For the European Union as a whole, the total spending required would be 2.6 per cent of GDP: a surprisingly low figure, given how much money is allocated by governments. Eliminating relative poverty, in other words adding to everybody's pre-tax, pre-transfer income until they reached 50 per cent of median incomes, would require less than half of the non-health, non-pension public transfers spent today. The rest, some 4.6 per cent of GDP, could be allocated to other purposes. To put it another way, between 49 (United Kingdom) and 76 per cent (Portugal) of current social transfers could be saved while simultaneously gaining much larger victories in the war on poverty.

Cutting social spending fully by these 4.6 percentage points of GDP would however impose hardships. Some who would lose benefits would be relatively close to the poverty line, and their case for support may be almost as good as that of the neediest. That is why we believe that total savings of at least 2 percentage points are more realistic. An ambitious target would be 4 percentage points.

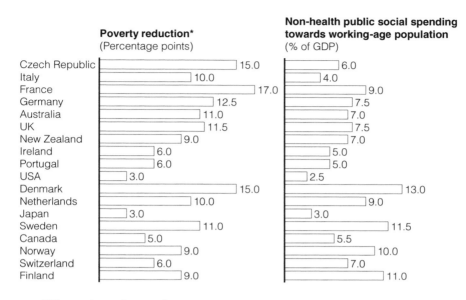

Figure 8.9   Poverty reduction and social spending

To succeed in generating these savings, politicians will have to show genuine leadership by explaining that the neediest have to come first. Indeed, it is surprising that Europe tolerates poverty on its current scale (and at current incomes for the poor) given how much money is devoted to transfers. The measures to capture the efficiency gains from refocusing welfare transfers on poverty reduction may not be popular, but they are easy to defend as 'social' in the European sense. Again, this is not a titanic task that requires unimaginable hardships and a complete change in the political context; social spending in the average EU-15 country has already fallen by 3.2 per cent from its peak over the last decade and a half.

SECONDARY EFFECTS: WHY 'LESS GOVERNMENT CAN BE MORE'

A key feature of the V concept is that change occurs simultaneously: expenditures are not merely cut, but the savings are redirected straight away. This makes the change process more palatable. Nonetheless, some readers will be concerned that reducing government spending will be contractionary, and the substitution by private consumption will be neutral at best. This is, after all, what Keynes taught us. Because of the multiplier effect, government spending can boost growth, especially when capacity utilization is low. Cut government consumption and the multiplier goes into reverse.

We show that all the empirical evidence points the other way. What was good for the Great Depression is not necessarily good for Europe in the 21st century. Reducing government consumption can be growth-enhancing if it is done correctly. The evidence is twofold. A group of Harvard economists have crunched the numbers. Their results confirm what the country case studies suggest. If we look at Europe today, the countries with the most vigorous growth are the ones that curtailed government spending the most. The serious cuts in Ireland and Sweden apparently did something to stimulate growth. Ireland transformed itself from a sorry backwater of Europe (in economic terms) into a veritable showcase. Moreover, Sweden's growth after 1994 beat even that of the United States.

A team around Harvard economics professor Alberto Alesina concluded that fiscal adjustments generally are good for growth, if and

Table 8.1 Fiscal adjustments and the macroeconomy

Measure	Expansionary*			Contractionary		
	Before	After	After-before	Before	After	After-before
Primary spending**	42.96	41.36	-1.60	40.32	40.15	-0.17
GDP growth rate	1.31	3.41	2.10	3.73	1.91	-1.82
Private consumption growth rate	1.16	3.03	1.87	3.76	1.84	-1.93
Business investment growth rate	-0.36	5.24	5.60	4.59	0.29	-4.30

* An episode of fiscal adjustment is expansionary (contractionary) if the primary cyclically adjusted balance as a share of trend GDP improves by at least 2% in one year or by 1.25% in two consecutive years and the average real GDP growth in each adjustment year and in the two years after is greater (lower) than the average real GDP growth in the 2 years before.
** Share of trend GDP, cyclically adjusted. Primary spending is all government spending without interest charges and repayments.

Source: Alesina *et al* (2002a).

when expenditures are cut. In 18 large countries where state spending was reduced, GDP growth accelerated by 2.1 per cent. It fell by 1.8 per cent where deficits were reduced by higher taxes. Some countries achieved startling reductions in government expenditure: Ireland reduced it by 7 per cent of GDP in 1986–89 (Alesina *et al*, 2002a).

The reasons for the growth stimulus (Table 8.1) are surprising, too. The main channel through which lower government spending helps is business profits and investment. Where governments reduce their role, they reduce pressure on the labour market. Wages are more likely to stagnate while productivity, investment and profits surge. Eventually, this produces greater private consumption and higher wages, too. Where the state cuts back, the growth rate of private consumption accelerates to 3 per cent and that of business investment even to 5 per cent. Where it increases taxes, there is a slowdown to 1.8 per cent for consumption and almost zero for investment.

This suggests that cutting back on government services (within reason) is close to a 'free lunch'. It frees resources, and it actually accelerates growth, investment and private consumption. Of all the things that a government can do to 'stimulate the economy', this is the most effective: simply do less, and do the rest more efficiently. Thanks to the detailed empirical work by Alesina and his colleagues, we can see that Keynesian 'demand stimulus' may be exactly the wrong way out of a crisis when governments already spend a large share of GDP. Once citizens and politicians understand how large the benign effects of fiscal retrenchment are, there should be widespread support for the cuts suggested as part of our V concept. The savings in government consumption we consider realistic – about 4 to 6 per cent of GDP – are double the average rate achieved by countries balancing their books in the 1980s and 1990s.

GETTING THE JOB DONE

For Niccolo Machiavelli, who was dismayed by the factitious, weak Italy of his time, reforming government was the highest honour to which one could aspire: 'no man is exalted as much in any of his actions, as are those who have reformed Republics and Kingdoms with (new) Laws and Institutions. These are, after those who have been Gods, the highest praised.'

Today, politicians in many European countries feel rather differently about reforming government and reducing state spending. Try to change unemployment insurance, curtail pensions or deregulate labour contracts, and the eggs will fly at political rallies, the unions will march and students will protest. Your political head may quickly be on the block. No doubt, the process of expenditure cuts and shifts that we propose can be a tough sell. Nonetheless, we are optimistic that the problems can be tackled along the lines we suggest.

The first and most optimistic insight that emerges from our survey is that the job can be done. If consensus-oriented and egalitarian countries like the Scandinavian ones with their huge welfare states can slash government spending, the same should be possible for the rest of Europe. As a matter of fact, 10 of the EU-15 member states have already succeeded in cutting government consumption by the lower limit of the number we propose, 4 per cent. These successes point in the right direction. What is required is a call to 'play it again, state', that is, by continuing reform in the better-performing countries and by copying successful reforms in the laggards.

The Swedish case also shows how reforms can be implemented without much economic harm. A prolonged process of discussing various scenarios and options generates fears and insecurity. Sweden and Finland avoided this problem. If there is a consensus about the right reform process, greater uncertainty and the rise in precautionary savings (which has hurt countries like Germany) can be avoided. If reforms are necessary, they must come swiftly and be implemented decisively.

Also, the willingness of the public to live with and even embrace belt-tightening reforms should not be underestimated. The 2005 survey 'Perspektive Deutschland' suggested that 61 per cent of Germans favoured a more vigorous reform process in their country, and 52 per cent of them wanted society in Germany to change more quickly than it is doing today (McKinsey, 2006). To garner public support, it is important that the cuts are seen as an integral part of a plan to create a brighter future, one in which the welfare state is secure and does its job better, and pensions are once again as 'safe as houses'. If socially progressive Holland has already been able to cut social transfers by more than 6 per cent from their peak, surely Europe as a whole can produce savings of some 2 to 4 per cent overall.

Attitudes are not necessarily static. There are ways of overcoming impediments to reform. Around the world, support for government transfers is higher in countries where most of the population believes that the poor are poor because they are unlucky. Where the population supports the US model of 'tough love', many think that the poor are not making sufficient effort. In Denmark, on the other hand, almost two out of three adults say that luck determines income. Social spending is 15 per cent of GDP. In the United States, fewer than 40 per cent of the population think that chance is the main driver of poverty. Hard work can solve poverty, is the standard answer. Non-health spending on social transfers in the United States, at around 3.5 per cent, is less than a third of Danish levels (Alesina, Glaeser and Sacerdote, 2001).

These two countries are typical in the sense that they show the expected relationship in OECD countries between beliefs in the fairness of economic rewards on the one hand, and welfare spending on the other. The close correlation between beliefs and the size of transfers suggests that there is an obvious way of avoiding this. The more clearly Europeans see that they live in a true meritocracy where hard work and investments in education pay off, and humble origins do not condemn people to a life of hardship and failure, the easier it will be to wean them off the costly and unsustainable social welfare state. That is why reforming the education system is crucial. Europe can become more meritocratic than the United States by offering free, first-rate schools where only talent matters for admission. This will give Europeans trust in the fairness of the societies in which they live, producing a groundswell of support for the leaner, more effective state that the V concept produces.

Economist Mancur Olson argued that it was only possible in the case of major upheaval to push back the influence of special interest groups far enough to make space for more logically designed institutions, with a view to creating the conditions for more robust growth. We know that reforms of European governments are required to increase the quality and efficiency of the state's activities, on the one hand, and to start up new initiatives to achieve category definition in vibrant markets, supported by smart regulation, on the other. Ultimately, only streamlined and intelligent states can provide the powerful leadership necessary to tackle the many vital issues that Europe confronts today.

Managing the reform process itself is a challenge. The potential for improving current procedures is vast. Many ambitious programme founders fail because politicians move on, and administrative units do not drive the process forward themselves. Some countries like the United Kingdom have attempted to tackle it by centralizing control over policy implementation. A special unit in the Prime Minister's Office, the Prime Minister's Delivery Unit, combines detailed monitoring with regular interventions. Even if it is too early to judge all the outcomes of the programme, the basic insight is right: what isn't measured can't be managed. Implementation of change programmes cannot simply be left to administrative units that fear for their own power and influence. Bypassing the standard, old-style procedures offers a chance to hold bureaucrats accountable for what elected politicians have decided to offer the public. Management by objectives, instead of by budget lines, should be part of the European V concept.

If the recommendations presented in this chapter are followed, European welfare states will become more socially just, more efficient in reducing poverty, and cheaper to run. A leaner government, staffed with better people, will get regulations right and help private enterprise, in part by curtailing its own size. This will boost investment and profits. Everybody will have more money in his or her pocket. Europe's efficient, comprehensive health care systems are much better at containing costs than the US model. Worries about the cost of retirement will recede into the distance. All of this will also contribute to a resurgence of economic growth. Europe should turn into a true meritocracy, a modern 'Social Performance Society' showing that the two most fundamental targets of our times are not contradictory. Not 'either–or' but 'both' should be the goal.

9

Epilogue

To maintain a high standard of living for its citizens, to cope with the demographic challenges ahead and to maintain its influence in world affairs, Europe needs to exploit its existing strengths. If it focuses its energies on turning itself into an economic powerhouse in line with its potential, leading the world in innovation and economic dynamism, it will master many of the looming problems with ease. If, on the other hand, it fails, sluggish productivity increases will combine with growing strains on its social welfare systems to produce gradual but irreversible relative decline.

Looking at policy today, it is not easy to be optimistic. The Lisbon agenda's implementation will be long in coming, if it ever does. Europe looks like giving up on the high aspirations it pursued over the past two decades, and without much public discussion. To let this process continue would be, to paraphrase Talleyrand's words, 'worse than a crime – it would be a mistake'. Europe's main project over the next 5 to 10 years should be to turn itself into an economic powerhouse whose momentum matches that of the United States and other leading countries. We add one more reason why this is necessary, and summarize the path that we believe Europe and its people should take.

A VOICE FOR EUROPE IN WORLD AFFAIRS

Nation states used to be the principal actors on the international scene. Today, in many matters at the heart of what citizens care about – from who gets to build airplanes to the price of imported cotton shirts – negotiation takes place at the level of economic blocs. The European Union has been particularly useful in giving a greater voice to member states that would otherwise be too small to matter. Today, in 2007, Europe maintains its standing in world trade negotiations and the like because it combines its fragmented states into one negotiating unit that has more people than the United States. Since their productivity is quite a bit lower, total economic weight – aggregate GDP – is about the same. Looking at the distribution of economic power blocs around the globe today, two giants stand head and shoulders above the rest, the United States and the European Union. China weighs in at barely two-thirds the total output of either one of these areas, India one-third, and Brazil barely achieves half of India's weight.

Over the next 50 years, these relative ratios will shift dramatically. Two factors are key: convergence and demography. As countries that are poor in per capita terms today catch up with Western levels of productivity, their relative economic weight will surge. And the European Union is facing a strong head wind in terms of its unfavourable demographic outlook. This means that two of today's relative dwarfs will become giants by 2050 as well, joining the European Union and United States as centres of (approximately equal) economic power. The United States, which today has 190 million fewer people than the European Union, will catch up in population size as a result of higher fertility and more immigration. This means that in order to stay in the premier league, the European Union's productivity growth has to accelerate as much as possible. The transition from a bipolar world of two economic superpowers to one of multiple, broadly similar 'cores' is inevitable. Europe's plans to turn itself into a viable powerhouse are necessary mainly because the deck of demographic cards that it has been dealt make this the only way to maintain its weight in (economic) world affairs.

China and India will, according to UN population predictions, converge to populations of 1.5 billion each. The United States and

Europe are likely to have populations of 400 million and 470 million respectively. If convergence were complete, China and India would each outstrip the size of the European Union or the United States by a factor of at least three. But convergence will not have run its course by 2050 – yet. China will probably reach about one-third of EU and US productivity levels, making it about 30 per cent larger in total output than either. India will probably only reach 20 per cent of the leading countries' productivity, leaving its GDP trailing by 10 to 15 per cent.

The European Union will have to reach more than 89 per cent of US productivity levels (while working as much per head of population) to remain a peer. We believe that Europe can achieve this aim. If anything, it is not ambitious enough. Nothing should stop the continent from reaching US productivity levels on average (with its leading regions being far ahead) and producing a total GDP that is greater.

We have suggested that in order to do so, Europe should first of all identify its strengths. It should then focus on these by freeing up resources and investing in them. By reallocating funds, Europe can achieve the productivity gains and hence the growth rate necessary to pull level with the United States by 2050 (Figure 9.1).

The aim, while easy enough to write on the back of an envelope, is highly ambitious. Between 1994 and 2004, the old continent's GDP growth rate was a mere 2.2 per cent per annum. Productivity per hour worked increased at 1.7 per cent annually. At the same time, GDP in the United States grew by 3.1 per cent, and output per hour increased by 2.0 per cent a year. Solely to stop the gap from opening up further, EU growth of output per hour worked has to accelerate by 0.3 percentage points. To catch up to US levels of productivity over 46 years would require an additional acceleration by 0.7 percentage points. The required overall acceleration in growth is therefore about 1.0 percentage points, to rates of around 2.7 per cent.

This is a tall order. The last time that the French economy showed such productivity growth over a 10-year period was in 1977–86, and the United Kingdom, in 1970–79. West Germany last reached this figure in the period 1982–91, driven in part by the tail wind of the reunification boom. Yet by releasing resources from wasteful uses and focusing on imaginative strategies to boost its growth rate, the

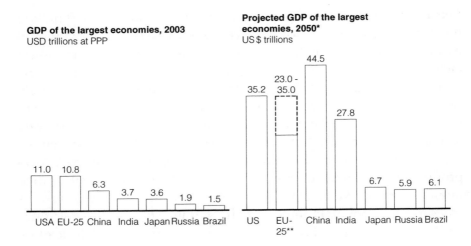

GDP of the largest economies, 2003
USD trillions at PPP

Projected GDP of the largest economies, 2050*
US $ trillions

USA EU-25 China India Japan Russia Brazil

11.0 10.8 6.3 3.7 3.6 1.9 1.5

US EU-25** China India Japan Russia Brazil

35.2 23.0 – 35.0 44.5 27.8 6.7 5.9 6.1

* China will overtake the USA in approximately 2040 according to the Goldman Sachs estimate (estimate highly dependent upon assumptions made about the development of growth rate and exchange rate).
** For 2050, the 4 largest economies (UK 3.8, Germany 3.6, France 3.1, Italy 2.1) in the EU are assumed to grow to USD 12.6 trillion (in Goldman Sachs report). The higher estimate refers to further assumptions: 1.8% growth rate for the other EU-15 countries and 3% for the new 10 in the EU-25.
Sources: Goldman Sachs (2003); Global Insight: World Market Monitor; own calculations

Figure 9.1   Will Europe be a superpower in 2050?

European Union can realistically aim to generate productivity gains in this range.

MAKING IT HAPPEN

Painful reforms are easier to implement when times are tough. Without the 'winter of discontent' in 1979, no Margaret Thatcher; without the defeat at the Battle of Jena and Auerstedt, no abolition of the guilds in Prussia, no reforms under Scharnhorst and Gneisenau. So how can Europe turn itself into an economic powerhouse if conditions are relatively comfortable?

As we look at Europe's political and economic situation in 2006, the chances for radical change appear slim. Things are not going so badly as to make a radical break with the past a foregone conclusion. Europeans are not about to storm the Bastille. Popular protests are largely aimed at defending rigid labour laws (as in France), large pension entitlements (as in Italy) or attempts to raise ecologically inspired fuel taxes (as in the United Kingdom). Politicians who have a natural interest in re-election can be forgiven for preferring not to rock the boat.

If Europe simply waits, its relative decline will accelerate. Economic and social pain will increase to the point that elected officials can gain more from implementing bold initiatives than they lose. Yet to wait for so long would be a very bad decision. Europe can break the deadlock. Not all measures require the kind of leadership that political scientists, journalists and businesspeople like to talk about, and that often amounts to political suicide. The kind of wrenching, 'structural reform' agenda that would make Europe's welfare system lean to the point of emaciation is unnecessary. Focused on its true core and improved in its incentive structures, the welfare state can more than just survive, it can do much to make Europe more competitive.

Globalization is easier to sustain in a world where the poor are well looked after. Increasing trade can also help to spread the cost of the welfare state. The passion for *egalité* can be translated into a genuine advantage on world markets by building a top-flight education system. Europe's health care system is far better at containing costs while maintaining quality than the system in the United States, for example. Yet without a revival of productivity growth, all these latent strengths will amount to very little. Europe can regain economic momentum if it emphasizes its genuine strengths, reaffirms its values and tackles its main areas of weakness.

Governments, Brussels, civil society and businesses all need to play a role here.

EU member states: from smart regulation to intelligent government

Many of the reforms we suggest have to be implemented by national governments. Focusing welfare provision on poverty, freeing up funds for education and the demographic challenge, and stimulating growth require bold initiatives at the national level. Yet the benefits are likely to be large and immediate. Once people stop worrying about their pensions, they can stop saving frantically and start to spend again. Idle capacity will come back on stream, and unemployment can fall. The short-term kick for growth from curtailing waste and reducing government consumption – as documented in the Harvard study by Alesina *et al* (2002a) – will be complemented by long-term investments in education and research and development.

European governments should do many more things than their US equivalent – and should do them very well, too. From reshaping European R&D to providing first-rate universities open to students from all social strata, from implementing smart regulation to running a superior kind of welfare state, the role of governments will certainly not wither in this age of globalization. Europe's government employees will have to wield a lot of power and manage a lot of money in an intelligent fashion.

Only a few countries, such as Singapore, Japan and France, have a tradition of excellence in the provision of public services. However, the more sharply incomes in the private and public sectors diverge and the emptier government coffers become, the less successful the states of Western Europe have become in attracting high-potential candidates to government service. The public sector needs highly qualified and motivated staff, especially for our model of a more intelligent state, which shapes the economic process by means of supervision and smart regulation.

The French École Nationale d'Administration has trained entire generations of well-informed and discerning civil servants (complaints about elitism notwithstanding). Their skills are so valuable that graduates often hold top managerial posts in industry; they also form the majority of the political elite. The UK civil service's Fast Stream programme helps ensure that the best college graduates quickly obtain interesting and important civil service positions. And in the United States, the Kennedy School of Government at Harvard offers future civil servants and diplomats the best-quality education available.

EU member states should create an equally distinguished joint institute and systematically ensure that young talent can take responsibility at an early stage of their careers, and that civil service pay does not lag behind the private sector. A European school of government embedded in a cross-European career path (with stops in the candidate's home country and Brussels) could contribute a great deal more towards creating European unity than all the white and green papers emanating from Brussels.

Brussels

Europe's institutions are in need of a major shake-up. After five rounds of enlargement and expansion from a six-member entity into the world's largest single market with 27 member states and a population of 490 million, the European Union is too big to be run efficiently on the basis of current governance structures as defined by the Nice Treaty. Decisions are easily blocked, and the probability of any initiative succeeding is low. Co-decision procedures with the Parliament slow progress yet further. Time is pressing since more accession candidates are queuing up. In 2005, Bulgaria and Romania signed accession treaties. Negotiations with Croatia and Turkey have already begun.

In order to lead the European Union's change process as laid out in the previous chapters, the Union needs an institutional structure designed for decision making, not gridlock. This requires, for example, qualified majority voting, smaller blocking majorities, clear allocation of responsibilities between the Parliament, the Commission, and the Council, a reduced number of commissioners, and (maybe) an exit clause for member states to leave the Union.

The current stalemate over the European Union's constitution, which attempts to make provision for these things, is an opportunity to revise the text and focus on pragmatic solutions to long-running problems. If the European Union has to contend with even greater complexities in decision making as a result of expansion, Nice needs to be revised and slimmed down significantly. The European Union would also do well to trust itself more, question the sanctity of the 'subsidiarity principle', and delegate some real decision-making powers to Brussels itself. It should also be less shy about defending itself against charges of a 'democratic deficit', which are largely unfounded. As long as the European Union is an association of nation states, sending democratically elected delegates to make the key decisions in Brussels is entirely in keeping with good, representative government.

The European Union's budget should be dominated by expenditure items with a clear pan-European purpose that are crucial for our economic future, such as education, R&D, infrastructure projects and intelligent regulation. Brussels needs to get out of the business of maintaining sectors that can be dealt with by national government, like agriculture. There is no reason for milk quotas and wine subsidies to be at the top of the European agenda. Responsibility for this area should be returned to the member states, who can use the relevant part of their current national contributions to the EU budget to continue current subsidies or turn these funds to new uses.

Civil society

Time was when most school boys learnt ancient Greek and Latin, and knew their Tacitus and Xenophon. One of the most stirring tales ever told in ancient Greek is Xenophon's 'March of the 10,000'. It is a tale of mercenaries in the service of Cyrus, a Persian prince, and it is a tale of defeat. And improbable as it may sound, it may serve as a simile of the kind of spirited civic leadership Europe needs.

Xenophon's mercenaries, almost all Greeks, win all their battles, but their paymaster loses his life through incaution. The army, leaderless, surrounded and thousands of kilometres from home in Mesopotamia, refuses to give up. It elects new leaders, overcomes freezing conditions, high mountains, and survives many a battle, until the survivors finally reach the Black Sea. It is a tale of triumph in defeat, produced by the mettle and allegiance of men who have chosen their own leaders. Cooperation, mutual trust, shared values, a common language and culture drive them forward and make it possible to escape from a seemingly impossible situation.

Europe is not in a predicament that could be compared with that of the 10,000 on the plains by the Euphrates and Tigris. However, another 10,000 ('myriad') could rise up and provide the kind of leadership that could do wonders, with the same characteristically European blend of democracy and respect for what the Greeks called *areté:* excellence, being the best one can be. This myriad of Europeans is a decisive factor. They are the ones who need to carry reforms forward. Their passion for Europe is probably large, and many would like to see it succeed. What is missing is a sense that they can make a difference, and that furthering the cause of Europe is not something that is solely up to the politicians. Europe, in turn, has to actively seek their input, find novel and flexible ways to check the dangers of the 'brain drain', and build a social consensus that is less concerned with limiting high salaries, and more engaged in providing for the poor.

How, in concrete terms, can a 'myriad' support the change process, propelling Europe to the top? First of all, it should become truly European in outlook. European leaders are still largely the products of their national education systems, and broad-based programmes like Erasmus do little to overcome the problem. Highly original career paths often do not fit into structured syllabuses, and funding requirements trip up many ambitious plans. At almost no cost at all, compared with the Union's budget, Europe could commit to fully funding the university education up to PhD level of the best 5 per cent of its secondary school graduates, wherever they choose to go. If Germany then loses most of its highly gifted students to the United Kingdom, for example, the message would be clear: shape up or lose out. And this pool of talented young people could get the education they deserve without being stifled by bureaucracies like academic exchange services, where studying abroad is seen as a temporary detour in the national career path.

Let's take another example. European Nobel laureates and top business managers could be asked to lead a (civilian) 'European DARPA'. DARPA is the Pentagon's agency for advanced technology. It was responsible for funding the original internet, for advanced laser development and for the first multimedia applications. It often uses highly creative, competitive tenders with 'stretch targets' to drive technological change forward. For example, in a bid to accelerate the development of unmanned vehicles, DARPA recently offered the 'Grand Challenge': a US $2 million cash prize for the best robotic vehicle to manoeuvre a difficult desert route. Europe could create a civilian equivalent, and match it with a broad range of seed funds for commercially viable projects that come out of the effort, complete with business parks all over Europe to provide some of the necessary infrastructure.

Two conditions must be fulfilled so that the elite can develop its potential Europe-wide and not only at the level of the individual states. The political world must create incentives that appeal to the myriad, at least in the form of communities in which their members like to work and conduct their private lives, and the members of the elite must have the sense that they can have a real impact on how Europe evolves. We are currently a long way from creating a European myriad of the best and brightest to drive the old continent out of its lethargy. 'Elite' and 'achievement' are words viewed with some suspicion in Europe, in part as a legacy of the 1968 movement. The protests in Paris in May 1968 and the student unrest at German universities and elsewhere created a new focus on social exclusion and a general presumption – especially among the better educated – that egalitarianism was intellectually superior. This consciousness appears to be changing. Where access to the top is governed by ability, not parental income, elites should be celebrated, not condemned. It is hard to imagine how change can occur without this understanding of meritocracy.

Businesses

European businesses need to shape up if the old continent is to get a new lease on economic life. That probably comes as no surprise; to our minds, the real surprise is that profit-maximizing firms are not doing the right thing already. It is in their best interest. Europe's key problem, as our analytical chapters showed, is low productivity. This, in turn, is largely the result of lower competitive intensity. The business community cannot do much about this at the individual company level. Collectively, however, firms can resist the temptation to lobby for anti-dumping duties (on, say, Chinese textiles or shoes), refrain from seeking more subsidies for ever more costly ways of misallocating resources, and work with the Commission and national governments to make smart regulation work.

European businesses should also embrace rather than fight the inclusive social model that is so specific to the old continent. Wages will never be low enough to compete with the developing world. Trade barriers and subsidies will only impoverish us. All too often, business leaders call for a wholesale dismantling of the welfare state and liberalization of labour markets. But many business leaders who have studied and worked abroad have chosen Europe precisely because of the many upsides that Europe enjoys as a result of a more inclusive social model, a more equal distribution of income and a more generous welfare state. In many ways, the continent boasts a superior social model, one that places a great deal of emphasis on the weakest members in society. The model has limits and costs, but it can be a source of competitive advantage. In terms of lower health care costs compared with the United States, the benefits are already tangible today.

In addition, some of the world's most admired products come from Europe, because of the continent's superior ability to mould taste, engineering prowess and creativity into stunningly beautiful, surprisingly useful things that people want to buy. We called this the power to define a category. Whether it is BMW cars, Ducati motorcycles, Zara apparel or Dyson vacuum cleaners, the old continent's ability to take an old and familiar product, add cachet, inspiration and good taste, and thereby turn it into a veritable money spinner, is often breathtaking. And without sophisticated consumers – a broad class of well-educated workers enjoying good wages – and highly skilled employees, none of this would be possible.

We think that the European consciousness is changing. Forty years after 1968, our vision here can stand for the completion of the drive to reform, with the result being a socially progressive and economically strong Europe, self-assured and solidly united, with traditions and a future. This will be a Europe whose people look towards the future optimistically. Their home will be a new European-style social-opportunity and high-performance state.

Notes

CHAPTER 1: EUROPE'S LOST DECADE

1. The external value of a currency is, of course, not a real indication of economic strength, but it is nevertheless regarded as just this by many observers, and participants on the foreign currency markets.

CHAPTER 2: EUROPE'S REAL CRISIS

1. Space does not allow a discussion of the extensive literature on this subject. Barro and Sala-i-Martin (1992), Sala-i-Martin (1996), Dowrick und Nguyen (1989), Pritchett (1997) and Quah (1993, 1996) are some of the most significant contributions.
2. The proportion of people of working age in the total population is almost identical in the United States and EU-15.
3. A 10 percentage-point labour input increase would only take away 10 percentage points of the income-per-capita gap if employed at US labour productivity level.

4. Whereas 17 per cent of European workers work part-time, only 13 per cent of Americans do. We rely on Eurostat figures (based on the EU Labour Force Survey) on full-time equivalents to gauge the impact of these differences. The figures imply that European part-timers work slightly longer than their American peers, at least relative to the rest of the population in their home region.
5. Calculation based on total hours worked per employee (Groningen Total Economy Data Base) and standard work weeks (Alesina, Glaeser and Sacerdote, 2005).
6. Interviewees are shown a list of various professions (doctor, factory worker, judge, etc) and are asked a) to estimate their actual income, and b) to say how much people in such positions should earn. The variation coefficient (standard deviation/average) reflects the degree of perceived and accepted inequality, and is taken as a basis here (see Bøyum, 1997).
7. Exactly the fifth percentile: compare Figure 2.9.
8. Tenth percentile
9. We may assume that health care costs will also continue to rise disproportionately.

CHAPTER 3: WHY THE US MODEL IS NOT SUITED TO EUROPE – AND WHAT WE CAN LEARN ANYWAY

1. OECD, *Society at a Glance 2005*. These are figures for single people and couples without children; the situation for parents is usually significantly better. The OECD does not use the employee's last wage level as a measure for comparison, but instead the net income of a worker who receives two-thirds of the average wage in the manufacturing sector.
2. Taxes cannot be levied until retirement age; payments can be deducted from gross income, and the funds invested can grow free of taxes on capital gains and interest.
3. McKinsey calculation based on Bureau of Labor Statistics, Job Opening and Labor Turnover Survey, and Current Employment Survey, 2001–2004.

4. The Netherlands rate also results from a shift in unemployability.
5. In the survey by Förster and d'Ercole (2005: Appendix Table A4, disposable income after transfers), the figure for the United States is 6.6, higher than any European country. The latest (2004) figure from the Federal Reserve Board's survey of consumer finances is close to 8, but uses a slightly different metric for transfer income.
6. Interestingly, the poorest 20 per cent saw a sharp rise in their assets between 1989 and 1995. They have stagnated since, before jumping up in 2004. The detailed tables in the Survey of Consumer Finances suggests that this is largely the result of house ownership.
7. All national account figures from http://www.bea.gov/bea/ dn/nipaweb/TableView.asp
8. The Bureau of Economic Research calculated that at the end of 2001 the United States had over US $6,891 billion in assets abroad, and that foreigners owned US $9,206 billion (direct investments were calculated at the market price).
9. Many companies have hedged their risk for 2003 with forward transactions. However, problems will arise if the euro continues to be strong.
10. From the point of view of Harvard philosopher Rawls, the poor alone are the deciding factor.

CHAPTER 4. ECONOMIC INDICATORS AND THE RIGHT MEASURES

1. GDP measures domestic production of goods and services after preliminary work has been subtracted. It does not record the income from employment and assets included in GDP that is generated in country and flows to the rest of the world. However, GNP also includes the income from employment and assets that flows to nationals from the rest of the world.
2. The 'inequality adjusted' disposable household income is calculated by weighting per household disposable income in each decile of income distribution with a factor. This factor is computed on the basis of an 'aversion coefficient' representing

the degree of aversion to inequality. For more detailed information about methodology see Boarini, Johansson and Mira d'Ercole
(2006: 24–26).
3. Using panel data on productivity per hour and annual hours
worked from the Groningen Total Economy Database, we ran a
fixed-effects panel for Germany, Italy, France and the United
Kingdom. The estimated elasticity is –0.244.
4. So as not to distort the EU average, the poorest member states –
Greece, Spain and Portugal – are not taken into account. This
seems reasonable because these countries joined the European
Union much later.

CHAPTER 5: THE POWER OF UNITY

1. For the years 1998 to 2001, there is an upward trend for the
European Union as a whole.
2. Securities, banking, insurance and occupational pensions.

CHAPTER 6: WHAT COMES AFTER DEREGULATION? SMART REGULATION!

1. Considering those employees who were integrated in affiliated
companies, total workforce was reduced by about 65.000 people
(Deutsche Telekom, 2005b).
2. About 32,000 posts are planned to be reduced in total, 7,000 of
them through permanent outsourcing. As about 6,000 people are
to be hired, net job reduction is planned to be about 19,000. The
plans are subject to further negotiations (Deutsche Telekom,
2005a).
3. The right level changes over time. From our viewpoint, the entire
European Union would have been the right yardstick for the
issue of 3-G licences.
4. In the smaller European countries there were generally two
network operators, in larger states often four.
5. This avoided the ever recurring 'cashing up' that was designed to
provide information on the reality of the state's finances.

6. Nevertheless, some of the efficiency gains that the OECD believed could be made in the areas of telecommunications and electricity have already been achieved.
7. The particularly high figures result from pessimistic assumptions about the progress and the consequences of the destruction of the ozone layer had the 1990 Clean Air Act not been introduced.

CHAPTER 7: THE CONCEPT OF CATEGORY DEFINITION

1. This figure should be taken with a pinch of salt, as the degree of vertical integration may also have been changed, and there are no figures about the company's profitability. Like many family-owned 'hidden champions' among small and medium-sized companies, Stihl is not listed on the stock exchange and does not publish details of its profits.
2. More often than not, these are particularly labour-intensive goods requiring skilled craftworkers, so it is only natural that prices should develop in parallel to corresponding wage levels. Furthermore, one of the interesting implications is that prices may possibly have been affected by the rapid increases in the incomes of top earners, and are on balance equivalent to significantly lower real wage increases.
3. Related to the sports car company Dr Ing hcF Porsche AG through the founding family, but not through any cross-share-holding.

CHAPTER 8: REINVENTING THE STATE

1. With the important exception of some UK universities, as well as particular strengths in individual subjects, such as international law in Heidelberg, laser physics in Aachen, international economics at the University of Stockholm among numerous others.

2. As some of the new entrants to the European Union are not members of the OECD, consistent data for the EU-25 is not available.

3. A Nobel prize was presented to Georges Charpak in 1992 for his revolutionary design of drift chambers in 1968 that paved the way for electronic particle detectors, and another to Carlo Rubbia and Simon van der Meer in 1984 for the discovery of W and Z bosons in the previous year.

4. More recent data are available for some of the countries, without major modifications. In order to guarantee comparability, we use data from the final report in 2000.

5. Major, detailed surveys of government expenditure like the Gershon Review found potential savings of around 1 per cent of GDP even in a country like the UK, where government spending is already quite low.

6. Transfer payments excluding public insurance schemes like health or pensions.

7. The current system of pay-as-you go, combined with a 'dynamic' pension linked to earnings of current contributors, was introduced under Chancellor Adenauer, and was one of the reasons that his party won an unprecedented absolute majority in 1957.

8. Collado and Iturbe-Ormaetxe (2005). We thank the authors for generously offering summary tables from their database for us.

References

ACNielsen (ed) (2005) New ACNielsen survey points to price convergence in Europe since the introduction of the Euro, September

Aggarwal, N (2004) Outsourcing takes off in Europe in a major way, *Straits Times*, 21 June

Agrawal, V and Farrell, D (2003) Who wins in offshoring, *McKinsey Quarterly Special edition: Global Directions*

Alesina, A (2002) *The Size of Countries: Does it matter?*, unpublished manuscript, August [Online] http://post.economics.harvard.edu/faculty/alesina/papers.html

Alesina, A and Barro, R J (2001) Dollarization, *American Economic Review*, **91** (2), May

Alesina, A, DiTella, R and McCulloch, R (2003) *Inequality and Happiness: Are Europeans and Americans different?*, unpublished, Harvard University

Alesina, A, Glaeser, E and Sacerdote, B (2001) Why doesn't the US have a European-style welfare state? National Bureau for Economic Research (NBER) Working Paper, NBER, Cambridge, Mass

Alesina, A, Glaeser, E and Sacerdote, B (2005) Work and leisure in the US and Europe: Why so different? Centre for Economic Policy Research (CEPR) Discussion Paper no 5140, CEPR, London

Alesina, A and Rodrik, D (1994) Distributive politics and economic growth, *Quarterly Journal of Economics*, **109** (2), May

Alesina, A *et al* (2002a) Fiscal policy, profits, and investment, *American Economic Review*, **92** (3), June, pp 571–89

Apple (2006) Apple reports first quarter results, press release, 18 January [Online] http://www.apple.com/pr/library/(2005)/jan/ 12results. html

Averch, H A and Johnson, L L (1962) Behavior of the firm under regulatory constraint, *American Economic Review*, **52**

Baldwin, R (1989) The growth effects of 1992, *Economic Policy*, **9**

Barro, R J (1999) Inequality, growth and investment, NBER Working Paper no 7038, NBER, Cambridge, Mass, March

Barro, R J and Sala-i-Martin, X (1992) Convergence, *Journal of Political Economy*, **100** (2)

Basu, S and Fernald, J G (1997) Returns to scale in US Production: estimates and implications, *Journal of Political Economy*, **105** (2), April

Beauvoir, S de (1999) *America Day by Day*, trans Carol Cosman, University of California Press, Berkeley

Belzer, M H (2000) *Sweatshops on Wheels: Winners and losers in trucking deregulation*, Oxford University Press, New York

Bentham, J (1966) *Prinzipien der Gesetzgebung*, Topos, Ruggell/ Liechtenstein

Bento, V (2004) *Os estados nacionais e a economia global*, Almedina, Coimbra

Bergmann, M, Gao, P, Mangaleswaran, R *et al* (2005) The global challenge, automotive component sourcing in the globalized world, Perspective from McKinsey's Automotive & Assembly Sector

Berndt, E R and Rappaport, N J (2001) Price and quality of desktop and mobile personal computers: a quarter-century historical overview, *American Economic Review*, **91** (2), May

Bernstein, A (2003) Waking up from the American dream meritocracy and equal opportunity are fading fast, *BusinessWeek*, 1 December

Blanchard, O (2005) European unemployment: the evolution of facts and ideas, NBER Working Paper no 11750, November [Online] www.nber.org/papers/w11750

Blanchard, O and Portugal, P (2001) What hides behind an unemployment rate: comparing Portuguese and US labor markets, *American Economic Review*, **91** (1), March

Blanchard, O and Wolfers, J (2000)The role of shocks and institutions in the rise of european unemployment: the aggregate evidence, *Economic Journal*, March

Boarini, R, Johansson, A and Mira d'Ercole, M (2006) Alternative measures of well-being, Organisation for Economic Cooperation and Development (OECD) Social, Employment and Migration Working Papers no 33 [Online] www.oecd.org/dataoecd/13/38/36165332.pdf

Bonsall, T E (2002) *Disaster in Dearborn: The story of the Edsel*, Stamford University Press, Stamford, Conn

Borghans, L and Loek G (nd) How often do apples fall far from the tree?, University of Maastricht working paper [Online] www2.econ.uu.nl/users/L.Groot/apples.pdf

Börsch-Supan, A *et al* (1998) Pension provision in Germany, Report 98–07, Special research area (Sonderforschungsbereich) 504, University of Mannheim

Boskin, M J *et al* (1996) Toward a more accurate measure of the cost of living, Final Report to the Senate Finance Committee, 4 December [Online] www.ssa.gov/history/reports/boskinrpt.html

Bøyum, B (1997) Attitudes towards social inequality: cross-national data, *NSD Newsletter*, Norsk samfunnsvitenskapelig datatjeneste (Norwegian Social Science Data Services) [Online] www.nsd.uib.no/english/NSD/newsletter/attitudes.shtml

Breuer, P, Klingler, R, Eltze, C *et al* (2005) Where Karstadt goes shopping, global sourcing – perspectives from different industries, McKinsey Working Papers

Broda, C and Weinstein, D (2004) Globalization and the gains from variety, NBER working paper, NBER, Cambridge, Mass

Bryan, L L and Zanini, M (2005) Strategy in an era of global giants, *McKinsey Quarterly*, issue 4, pp 47–59

Burnett, J K and Hahn, R W A (2001) Costly benefit, related publication, AEI-Brookings Joint Center for Regulatory Studies Special Report, November

Carioca, M J, Diniz, R and Pietracci, B (2004) Making Portugal competitive, *McKinsey Quarterly*, issue 3

Cecchini, P and Robinson, J (eds) (1988) *The European Challenge 1992: The benefits of a single market*, Wildwood House, Aldershot

Cipolla, C M and Borchardt, K (eds) (1985) *Europäische Wirtschaftsgeschichte, Vol 3*, Gustav Fischer, Stuttgart

Clark, A E and Oswald, A J (1994) Unhappiness and unemployment, *Economic Journal*, **104** (424), May

Clayton, R and Pontusson, J (1998) Welfare-state retrenchment revisited: entitlement cuts, public sector restructuring, and inegalitarian trends in advanced capitalist societies, *World Politics*, **51** (1), pp 64–98

Coats, D (2004) *Efficiency, Efficiency, Efficiency: The Gershon review, public service efficiency and the management of change*, Work Foundation [Online] www.theworkfoundation.com/pdf/Gershon_response.pdf

Cohen, S S, DeLong, J B and Zysman, J (2000) Tools for thought: what is new and important about the 'e-conomy', Berkeley Roundtable on the International Economy (BRIE) Working Paper no 138, BRIE, Berkeley

Colchester, N (1992) Altered states, *Economist* (survey), 11 July

Collado, M D and Iturbe-Ormaetxe, I (2005) Public transfers to the poor: is Europe really more generous than the United States?, Working Paper, May [Online] www.uib.es/congres/ecopub/ecineq/papers/072collado-iturbe.pdf

Committee of Wise Men (Lamfalussy Committee) (2000) *Initial Report on the Regulation of European Securities Markets*, 9 November

Committee of Wise Men (Lamfalussy Committee) (2001) *Final Report on the Regulation of European Securities Markets*, Brussels, 15 February

Costa, D (2000) Income, leisure and economic well-being, address to the American Enterprise Institute for Public Policy Research (AEI), Washington, DC, 23 March

Court of Auditors (ed) (2003) *Annual Reports Concerning the Financial Year 2003* [Online] www.eca.eu.int/audit_reports/annual_reports/annual_reports_index_en.htm

Covell, J L (1995) Ford Motor Company, in Paula Kepos (ed), *International Directory of Company Histories*, Vol 11, St James Press, New York

Crafts, N F (1985) *British Economic Growth during the Industrial Revolution*, Oxford University Press, Oxford

CSFB (ed) (2005) *European Mobile Quarterly*, issue 4, London, Credit Suisse First Boston

Daly, K (2006) European growth gets better and better (and we're not joking), *European Weekly Analyst*, no 06/02, 12 January

De Grauwe, P and Skudelny, F (2000) The impact of EMU on trade flows, *Review of World Economics*, **136** (3)

Deutsche Bundesbank (2000) *Probleme internationaler Wachstumsvergleiche auf Grund unterschiedlicher Deflationierungsmethoden – dargestellt am Beispiel der EDV-Ausrüstungen in Deutschland and den USA*, monthly report, August [Online] www.bundesbank.de/download/volkswirtschaft/mba/(2000)/(2000)08mba_wirtschaftslage.pdf

Deutsche Telekom (2005a) Deutsche Telekom faces major staff restructuring measures, press release, 2 November [Online]
www.telekom3.de/en-p/medi/2-pr/(2005)/11-n/051102-dtag-
restructuring-ar.html

Deutsche Telekom (ed) (2005b) *Personal- und Nachhaltigkeitsbericht*,
p 12 [Onlline] http://download-dtag.t-online.de/deutsch/nach
haltigkeit/pun_(2005).pdf

Dimson, E, Marsh, P and Staunton, M (2002) *Triumph of the Optimists: 101
years of global investment returns*, Princeton University Press, Princeton,
NJ

DiTella, R, MacCulloch, R J and Oswald, A J (2001) Preferences over
inflation and unemployment: evidence from surveys of happiness,
American Economic Review, **91** (1) , March

Dohrmann, T and Mendonca, L T (2004) Boosting government productivity, *McKinsey Quarterly*, no 4

Dowrick, S and Nguyen, D-T (1989) OECD comparative economic
growth 1950–85: catch-up and convergence, *American Economic
Review*, **79** (5), December

Eco, U (1993) *Über Gott und die Welt, Essays*, Hanser, Munich

Economist (1991) One Europe, one economy, 30 November, p 54

Economist (1992a) Sam, Sam, the paranoid man, 18 January, pp 13–14

Economist (1992b) Altered states (survey), 11 July, p 5

Economist (1999) Call waiting, 7 October

Economist (ed) (2001) *Pocket World in Figures 2002 edition*, Economist
Books, London

Economist (2002a) Starting to work, 16 May

Economist (2002b) Romano Prodi, a desperate integrationist, 23 May

Economist Intelligence Unit (2002) *Worldwide cost of living survey*,
Economist Intelligence Unit, London

Enzensberger, H M (1987) *Ach Europa! Wahrnehmungen aus sieben Ländern
Mit einem Epilog aus dem Jahre 2006*, Frankfurt: Suhrkamp (in English:
Europe, Europe: Forays into a continent, trans Martin Chalmers,
Pantheon Books, New York, 1989)

European Central Bank (ed) (2006) The importance of public expenditure reform for economic growth and stability, *Monthly Bulletin*, April,
pp 61–73

European Commission (ed) (1988) *The cost of non-Europe* (usually
referred to as the Cecchini Report)

European Commission (ed) (2002) *International Market Scoreboard: 10
years internal market without frontiers*, Special edition, November

[Online] http://ec,europa.eu/internal_market/score/ docs/score11/ score11-printed_en.pdf

European Commission (ed) (2004a) *Bulletin Statistique: Le Personnel de la Commission*, October

European Commission (ed) (2004b) The application of the Lamfalussy process to EU securities markets legislation, Commission Staff Working Document SEC (2004) 1459, 15 November

European Commission (2005) *Green Paper on Financial Services Policy (2005–2010)*, Brussels, 3 May

European Commission (ed) (2005a) *Science, Technology and Innovation – key figures 2003–2004*, Brussels

European Commission and Eurostat (ed) (2002) *Die Beteiligung der Europäer an kulturellen Aktivitäten: Eine Eurobarometer-Befragung, Zusammenfassung der Ergebnisse*, April 2002 (*Participation of Europeans in Cultural Activities: A Eurobarometer survey, summary of results, 2002*)

European Commission and Eurostat (ed) (2004) A report on the functioning of public procurement markets in the EU: benefits from the application of EU directives and challenges for the future. [Online] http: ec.europa.eu/eurostat

European Council (2000) Presidency Conclusions, Lisbon European Council, 23–24 March 2000

European Council (2005) Cover note from Presidency to Delegations, 15–16 December

European Opinion Research Group (ed) (2004) *Standard Eurobarometer 61*, Survey carried out between February and March

EU Presidency (2005) Presidency conclusions: Council of the European Union, cover note from Presidency to Delegations, 15–16 December

Eurostat (ed) (2004) Eating, drinking, smoking – comparative price levels in EU, EFTA and Candidate Countries for 2003, *Statistics in Focus, Economy and Finance*, No 30

Eurostat (ed) (2005) *Europe in Figures – Eurostat Yearbook 2005* Eurostat, Luxembourg

Farrell, D (2004) How Germany can win from offshoring, *McKinsey Quarterly*, Issue 4

Federal Reserve (2002) Industrial Production and Capacity Utilization

Federal Reserve (2004) *Survey of Consumer Finances 2004* [Online] www.federalreserve.gov/Pubs/oss/oss2/scfindex.html

Federation of European Securities Exchanges (2006) Member directory [Online] www.fese.be/directory/members/index.htm (accessed 9 May 2006)

Feldstein, M (2002) Milton Friedman and public sector economics, speech on the occasion of Milton Friedman's 90th birthday, NBER, Chicago, 8 November

Fisk, D and Forte, D (1997) The Federal Productivity Measurement Program, *Monthly Labor Review,* **120** (5), May

Folsom, B W, Jr (1998) *Empire Builders: How Michigan entrepreneurs helped make America great,* Rhodes and Easton, Traverse City, Mich

Forbes, K (2000) A reassessment of the relationship between inequality and growth, *American Economic Review,* **90** (4), December

Förster, M (2002) Trends and driving factors in income distribution and poverty in the OECD Area, OECD Labour Market and Social Policy Occasional Papers no 42, OECD, Paris, August

Förster, M and d'Ercole, M (2005) Income distribution and poverty in OECD Countries in the Second Half of the 1990s, OECD Social, Employment and Migration Working Papers no 22, OECD, Paris

Fortune (1992) Repairing our infrastructure, 19 October, p 91

Frankel, J A and Romer, D (1999) Does trade cause growth? *American Economic Review,* **89**, pp 379–99

Fraunhofer Institut Integrierte Schaltungen (2006) MP3: MPEG Audio Layer-3 history [Online] www.iis.fraunhofer.de/amm/projects/mp3/index.html (accessed 10 May 2006)

Frühwald, W (1996) Vor uns die elektronische Sintflut?, *Die Zeit,* no 27, 28 June

Galor, O (1996) Convergence? Inferences from theoretical models, *Economic Journal,* **106** (437), July

Gartner (ed) (2006) *Forecast: Global Telecommunications Market Take,* October, Gartner Inc

Gartner Inc (2005) *IT Services Market Metrics Worldwide Final Market Share,* August, Gartner Inc

Geanakoplos, J, Magill, M and Quinzii, M (2002) Demography and the long run behavior of the stock market, Cowles Foundation Discussion Paper no 1380, Cowles Foundation for Research in Economics, Yale University, New Haven, Conn

German Federal Ministry of Education and Research (BMBF) (eds) (2001) *Projekt Talent: Deutsche Nachwuchswissenschaftler in den USA: Perspektiven der Hochschul- und Wissenschaftspolitik,* BMBF, Bonn

Giersch, H, Paqui, K-H and Schmieding, H (1994) *The Fading Miracle: Four decades of market economy in Germany*, Cambridge University Press, Cambridge, UK

Gladwell, M (2005) The moral hazard myth: the bad idea behind our failed health-care system, *New Yorker*, 29 February [Online] www.newyorker.com/fact/content/articles/050829fa_fact

Glover, I (1998) Ford, Henry, in Malcolm Warner (ed), *The IEBM Handbook of Management Thinking*, International Thomson Business Press, London

Goldman Sachs (2003) *Dreaming with BRICs: The path to 2050*, Global Economics Paper 99

Goldman Sachs (2005) German manufacturing will survive EU enlargement, *Global Economic Survey*, No 135

Groningen Growth and Development Centre and the Conference Board (2006) *Total Economy Database, May 2006* [Online] www.ggdc.net

Gross, D (1996) *Forbes Greatest Business Stories of All Time*, Wiley, New York

Gruber, J and Wise, D (2001) An international perspective on policies for an aging society, NBER Working Paper no 8103, NBER, Cambridge, Mass, January

Guiso, L, Jappelli, T, Padula, M and Pagano, M (2004) Financial market integration and economic growth in the EU, *Economic Policy* 19 (40)

Harvard Business School (2002) Ducati, case study

Harvard Business School (2001) Gucci Group NV (A), case study

Harvard Business School (2003) Zara: fast fashion, case study

Hatton, T (2002) Can productivity growth explain the NAIRU? Long-run evidence from Britain 1871–1999, CEPR Discussion Paper no 3424, June, CEPR, London

Hoch, D, Klimmer, M and Leukert, P (2005) *Erfolgreiches IT-Management im öffentlichen Sektor*, Gabler

Hofmann, W (ed) (2002) *Politik des aufgeklärten Glücks: Jeremy Bentham's philosophisch-politisches Denken*, Akademie Verlag, Berlin

Holden, S and VanDerhei, J (2005) Appendix: additional figures for the EBRI/ICI Participant-Directed Retirement Plan Data Collection Project for Year-End 2004, Perspective web-only edition, Investment Company Institute, Vol 11, no 4A, September

IDC (2006) *Worldwide Software Market Forecaster*, May, Gartner, Framingham

Imperial College (1999) Doing a Dyson: Case A, case study, Imperial College Management School

Informa WCIS database (formerly known as EMC world cellular database)

Inglehart, R (1999) Trust, well-being and democracy, in Mark Warren (ed), *Democracy and Trust*, Cambridge University Press, Cambridge

Institut für Wirtschaft und Gesellschaft (IWG) Bonn eV (not published), as quoted from Meinhard M (1995) *Epochenwende*, Berlin, Propyläen 2005

Institute of International Education (2002) *Open Doors*, report on international educational exchange, Institute of International Education

International Energy Agency (ed) (2003) CO_2 emissions from fossil fuel combustion, International Energy Agency

iSuppli (2006) *Annual 2001 to 2005 Semiconductor Market Share Competitive Landscaping Tool 2006 Database*, iSuppli

Jones, H(2005) RPT-ECB EU tell banks to deliver on single payments, *Reuters online*, 16 November

Kalff, D (2005) *Europas Wirtschaft wird gewinnen: Was wir Amerika voraus haben*, Campus, Frankfurt/Main (English translation,*Unamerican Business*, Kogan Page, London, 2005)

Kamps, C (2004) New estimates of government net capital stocks for 22 OECD countries 1960–2001, International Monetary Fund (IMF) Working Paper 04/67, IMF, Washington, DC, April

Kennedy, P (1987) *The Rise and Fall of the Great Powers: Economic change and military conflict from 1500 to 2000*, Random House, New York

Kluge, J (2003) *Schluss mit der Bildungsmisere: Ein Sanierungskonzept*, Campus, Frankfurt

Kotlikoff, L J and Leibfritz, W (1999) An international comparison of generational accounts, in A J Auerbach, L J Kotlikoff and W Leibfritz (eds), *Generational Accounting around the World*, NBER Project Report, University of Chicago Press, Chicago

Krugman, P (2002) For richer, *New York Times Magazine*, 20 October

Krugman, P (2005) Passing the buck, *New York Times*, 22 April

La Porta, R, Lopez-de-Silanes, F, Schleifer, A *et al* (1997) Legal determinants of external finance, *Journal of Finance*, **52** (3)

La Porta, R, Lopez-de-Silanes, F, Schleifer, A *et al* (1998) Law and finance, *Journal of Political Economy*, **106** (6)

Machiavelli, N (1961) *Arte della guerra e scritti politici minori, a cura di Sergio Bertelli* (Niccoli Machiavelli: Opere II), Feltrinelle, Mailand

Machiavelli, N (1956) *Textauswahl* (Auswahl und Einleitung von Carlo Schmid), Fischer, Frankfurt am Main/Hamburg (English sources for Machiavelli: http://etext.library.adelaide.edu.au/m/m149d/ bk3ch1 .html and http://www.constitution.org/mac/florence.htm)

Maddison, A (2001) *The World Economy: A millennial perspective* (Development Centre Studies), OECD, Paris

Marples, G (2004) The History of Fax Machines – Get the message [Online] www.thehistoryof.net/history-of-fax-machines.html (accessed 11 May 2006)

Mayer, P (ed) (1966) *The Pacifist Conscience*, Henry Holt, New York

McCallum, J (1995) National borders matter: Canada–US regional trade patterns, *American Economic Review*, **85** (3), June

McKinsey & Co (2001) *Survey Perspektive Deutschland 2001 (Perspective Germany 2001)*

McKinsey & Co (2002) *Global Investor Opinion Survey*

McKinsey & Co (2004a) ProNet, Joint research effort with the TU Darmstadt, Frankfurt, December

McKinsey & Co (2004b) Research, Dimensions of offshoring in Germany, Research Center DUS, August

McKinsey & Co (2006) *Vorläufiger Projektbericht Perspektive Deutschland 2005/2006*, April [Online] www.perspektive-deutschland.de/ files/presse_2006/pd5-Projektbericht.pdf

McKinsey Global Institute (ed) (1996) *Capital Productivity*, Washington, DC, June [Online] www.mckinsey.com/knowledge/mgi/ capital_ prod/

McKinsey Global Institute (ed) (2002) *Reaching Higher Productivity Growth in France and Germany*, October [Online] www.mckinsey.com/ mgi/publications/europe/

McKinsey Global Institute (ed) (2003) *Offshoring: Is it a win-win game?*, San Francisco, August [Online] www.mckinsey.com/mgi/publica tions/win_win_game.asp

Merrill Lynch (ed) (2005) *Global Wireless Matrix*, issue 4, Merrill Lynch, London

Miegel, M (2005) *Epochenwende: Gewinnt der Westen die Zukunft?*, Ullstein, Berlin

Mildner, S *Die WTO von 1947–2001 (The World Trade Organization from 1947–2001)*, Deutsche Gesellschaft für Auswärtige Politik (DGAP) eV, Berlin

Mintel (2004) *Luxury goods retailing, retail intelligence*, Mintel, London

Morgenson, G (2004) Explaining (or not) why the boss is paid so much, *New York Times*, 25 January

Muthesius, H (1987) Die Bedeutung des Kunstgewerbes, in Der deutsche Werkbund (ed), *Zwischen Kunst und Industrie*, DVA, Munich

Natali, D (2004) *The Netherlands: The pension system*, research project supported by the Service Public Fédéral Sécurité Sociale [Online] www.ose.be/files/mocpension/NetherlandsOMC.pdf

Nicoletti, G and Scarpetta, S (2003) Regulation, productivity and growth: OECD evidence, OECD Economics Department Working Papers no 347, OECD, Paris, January

Office of Management and Budget (OMB) (ed) *Reports to Congress under the Paperwork Reduction Act of 1995* [Online] www.whitehouse.gov/omb/inforeg/prarep2.html#intro

Organisation for Economic Cooperation and Development (OECD) (ed) (1999a) *OECD Employment Outlook: June 1999*, OECD, Paris

OECD (ed) (1999b) *Regulatory Reform in the United States*, OECD, Paris

OECD (ed) (2000) *Literacy in the Information Age: Final report of the International Adult Literacy Survey*, OECD, Paris

OECD (ed) (2001) *Businesses' Views on Red Tape: Administrative and regulatory burdens on small- and medium-sized enterprises*, OECD, Paris

OECD (ed) (2002) *Society at a Glance: OECD Social Indicators*, OECD, Paris

OECD (ed) (2005a) *Employment Outlook 2005*, OECD, Paris

OECD (ed) (2005b) *Health Data: Statistics and indicators for 30 countries*, OECD, Paris, 8 June

OECD (ed) (2005c) *Labor Force Survey*, OECD, Paris

OECD (ed) (2005d) *Main Science and Technology Indicators, 2005*, OECD, Paris, 15 November

OECD (ed) (2005e) *OECD Economic Outlook*, No 78, OECD, Paris, December

OECD (ed) (2005f) *Society at a Glance: OECD Social Indicators*, OECD, Paris

OECD (ed) (2006a) *Benefits and Wages: gross/net replacement rates, country specific files and tax/benefit models*, March [Online] www.oecd.org/els/social/workincentives

OECD (ed) (2006b) *Economic Policy Reforms: Going for growth 2006*, OECD, Paris

Orwell, G (1936/2001) *The Road to Wigan Pier*, Penguin Classics, London

Persson, T and Tabellini, G (1994) Is inequality harmful to growth? *American Economic Review*, **84** (3), June

Piketty, T and Saez, E (2003) Income inequality in the United States, 1913–1998, *Quarterly Journal of Economics*, **108** (1), February

Porter, M E (1998) *On Competition*, Harvard Business School Press, Boston, Mass

Poterba, J M (2000) Stock market wealth and consumption, *Journal of Economic Perspectives*, **14** (2)

Poterba, J M, Venti, S F and Wise, D A (1998) 401(k) plans and future patterns of retirement saving, *American Economic Review*, **88** (2), May

Pritchett, L (1997) Divergence, big time, *Journal of Economic Perspectives*, **11** (3), Summer

Psacharopoulos, G and Ying Chu Ng (1992) Earnings and education in Latin America: assessing priorities for schooling investments, World Bank Policy Research Working Paper no 1067, World Bank, Washington, DC

Putnam, R D (2000) *Bowling Alone: The collapse and revival of American community*, Simon & Schuster, New York

Quah, D (1993) Galton's fallacy and tests of the convergence hypothesis, *Scandinavian Journal of Economics*, **94** (4), December

Quah, D (1996) Twin peaks: growth and convergence in models of distribution dynamics, *Economic Journal*, **106** (437), July

Rajan, R G and Zingales, L (2001) The great reversals: the politics of financial development in the 20th century, NBER Working Paper no w8178, March

Ratan, S (1992) Repairing our infrastructure, *Fortune*, 19 October

Rawls, J (1998) *Eine Theorie der Gerechtigkeit* (ed Otfried Höffe), Akademie Verlag, Berlin (English version: *A Theory of Justice*, Belknap Press, rev edn September 1999)

Ritschl, A (2002) *Deutschlands Krise and Konjunktur 1924–1934: Binnenkonjunktur, Auslandsverschuldung and Reparationsproblem zwischen Dawes-Plan and Transfersperre*, Akademie Verlag, Berlin

Rose, A and van Wincoop, E (2001) National money as a barrier to international trade: the real case for currency union, *American Economic Review*, **91** (2), May

Sala-i-Martin, X (1996) The classical approach to convergence analysis, *Economic Journal*, **106** (437), July

Samuelson, P A and Nordhaus, W D (1995) *Economics*, 15th edn, McGraw-Hill, New York

Scarpetta, S and Tressel, T (2002) Productivity and convergence in a panel of OECD industries: do regulations and institutions matter?, OECD Economics Department Working Paper no 342, OECD, Paris, September

Schnabel, R (2003) *Verteilung und Zusammensetzung der Rentnereinkommen in Germany: Droht eine neue Altersarmut?*, Essen

Schor, J (1998) *The Overworked American: The unexpected decline of leisure,* Basic Books, New York

Seifert, W G (2001) Europe on the road towards a single capital market, speech on the occasion of Deutsche Börse's annual opening ceremony in Frankfurt am Main, 5 February

Seifert, W G, Achleitner, A-K Mattern, F *et al* (2000) *European Capital Markets,* Macmillan, Basingstoke

Seifert, W G, Mattern, F, Streit, C-C and Voth, H-J (1997) *Aktie, Arbeit, Aufschwung,* Campus, Frankfurt

Sen, A (1997) Inequality, unemployment and contemporary Europe, *International Labour Review,* no 136

Sen, A (1999) *Development as Freedom,* Oxford University Press, Oxford

Servan-Schreiber, Jean-Jacques (1967) *Le Défi Americain,* Denoel, Paris

Shiller, R J (2000) *Irrational Exuberance,* Princeton University Press, Princeton, NJ

Sinha, J, Khanna, T, Woetzel, J *et al* (2004) China and India, the race to growth, *McKinsey Quarterly, Special edition: China Today*

Shefrin, H (2002) *Beyond Greed and Fear: Understanding behavioral finance and the psychology of investing,* Oxford University Press, Oxford

Simms, B (2001) *Unfinest Hour: Britain and the destruction of Bosnia,* Allen Lane/Penguin, London

Smithers, A and Wright, S (2000) *Valuing Wall Street: Protecting wealth in turbulent markets,* McGraw-Hill, New York

Social Security Administration (2002) *Income of the Population 55 or Older*

Späth, L (2005) *Strategie Europa: Ein Zukunftsmodell für die globalisierte Welt,* Rowohlt, Reinbek

Stenzel, S and Voth, H-J (1997) Aktiensparpläne: Förderung ohne Steuerausfälle, *Die Bank,* No 12

Sunden, A and Surette, B (2000) Households' borrowing from 401(k) plans, presentation at the Second Annual Joint for the Retirement Research Consortium, 17–18 May 2000, Washington, DC [Online] www.mrrc.isr.umich.edu/conferences/cp/cp00_sunden.pdf)

Tengs, T O and Graham, J D (1996) The opportunity costs of haphazard social investments in life-saving, in R W Hahn (ed), *Risks, Costs, and Lives Saved: Getting better results from regulation,* Oxford University Press, Oxford

Tocqueville, A de (1835) *Democracy in America* [Online] http://xroads.virginia.edu/ HYPER/DETOC/home.html

Umbach, M (2001) Made in Germany, in H Schulze and E François (eds), *Deutsche Erinnerungsorte, Vol 2*, C H Beck, Munich (English original: E E Williams, *Made in Germany*, Heinemann, 1896)

United Nations (2004) *World Population Prospects: The 2004 revision*, United Nations, New York

United Nations (2005) *World Population Prospects: The 2005 revision*, United Nations, New York

US Department of Labor (2004) *Extended Mass Layoffs Associated with Domestic Overseas Relocation, Q1 2004*, Bureau of Labor Statistics

US Department of Labor *Job Opening and Labor Turnover Survey and Current Employment Survey, 2001–2004*, Bureau of Labor Statistics

Verband deutscher Papierfabriken (2006) *Papier 2006 – ein leistungsbericht*, Bonn, p71

Verheugen, G (2005) *Europa in der Krise: Für eine Neubegründung der europäischen Idee*, Kiepenheuer & Witsch, Cologne

Voth, H-J (2000) *Time and Work in England, 1750–1830*, Oxford University Press, Oxford

Voth, H-J (2003) Living standards and urban disamenities, in R Floud and P Johnson (eds), *Cambridge Economic History of Britain*, Cambridge University Press, Cambridge, UK

Winter, S (2000) *Die Porsche Methode: Die 10 Erfolgsgeheimnisse des unkonventionellen Sportwagenchefs Wendelin Wiedeking*, Ueberreuter Wirtschaft, Frankfurt

Wolff, E N (2002) *Retirement Insecurity: The income shortfalls awaiting the soon-to-retire*, Economic Policy Institute, Washington, DC

World Federation of Exchanges (WFE) (2001) *Annual Report 2001: WFE annual statistics*, WFE, Paris

Wren, D A and Greenwood, R G (1998) *Management Innovators: The people and ideas that have shaped modern business*, Oxford University Press, New York

Zuckerman, M B (1998) Debate: a second American century, *Foreign Affairs*, **77** (3), May / June

Index

italics refer to figures in the text